The Boundaryless Organization

Forewords by
C. K. Prahalad and
Lawrence A. Bossidy

The Boundaryless Organization

Breaking the Chains of Organizational Structure

Ron Ashkenas
Dave Ulrich
Todd Jick
Steve Kerr

JOSSEY-BASS PUBLISHERS / *San Francisco*

FIRST PAPERBACK EDITION PUBLISHED IN 1998.

Jossey-Bass books and products are available through most bookstores. To contact Jossey-Bass directly, call (888) 378-2537, fax to (800) 605-2665, or visit our website at www.josseybass.com.

Substantial discounts on bulk quantities of Jossey-Bass books are available to corporations, professional associations, and other organizations. For details and discount information, contact the special sales department at Jossey-Bass.

 Manufactured in the United States of America on Lyons Falls Turin Book. This paper is acid-free and 100 percent totally chlorine-free.

Library of Congress Cataloging-in-Publication Data

The Boundaryless organization : breaking the chains of organizational structure / Ron Ashkenas . . . [et al.].
    p.   cm.—(the Jossey-Bass management series)
    Includes bibliographical references and index.
    ISBN 0-7879-0113-X
    ISBN 0-7879-4000-3 (paperback)
    1. Organizational change. 2. Industrial organization. 3. Interorganizational relations. 4. Partnership. I. Ashkenas, Ronald N. II. Series.
    HD58.8.B675   1995
    658.4'063—dc20   95-18791

FIRST EDITION

HB Printing   10 9 8 7 6 5 4
PB Printing   10 9 8 7 6 5 4 3 2

The Jossey-Bass Management Series

CONTENTS

PART 2

Free Movement Side to Side: Crossing Horizontal Boundaries

PART 3

Free Movement Along the Value Chain: Crossing External Boundaries

PART 4

Free Global Movement: Crossing Geographic Boundaries

Conclusion

FOREWORD

by C. K. Prahalad

Building a high-performance organization, especially in a volatile business environment, is a worthy, if elusive, goal. With the dramatic changes in the business environment in the last decade—deregulation, disintermediation, new technology and growth of information technology, global competition, shifting customer expectations, and the emergence of new markets in Asia—old ways of doing business are becoming less and less relevant. The new business environment imposes new demands on managers. They have to engage in a fundamental reexamination of strategies, both at the corporate and at the business levels, as well as reassess the capabilities of their organizations to execute the new and often complex strategies. Most managers have little appetite for either fundamentally rethinking strategy or creating radically new organizational capabilities. Both tasks require a capacity to forget as well as a capacity to learn; they require tools for honest assessment of where one is and a capacity to conceive where one ought to be. The process of reexamining and reinventing the company demands a new organizational theory and, at the same time, a critical evaluation of the limits of existing theory. It requires the capacity to think long term and, at the same time, create the financial and the organizational space for change through efficiencies. It is the appetite for this process of reexamining and reinventing that will separate the builders (leaders) from caretakers and the undertakers (managers and cautious administrators).

The Search for High Performance

Under pressure for performance in a changing competitive environment, managers seem to gravitate toward improving the efficiency of existing organizational arrangements and implementing existing strategies. This is "doing what I know" better. Hence, the current managerial preoccupation with "implementation." However, in different companies, a focus on implementation means different things, from downsizing to reengineering to various forms of "cultural change" programs. In the absence of clear guideposts, we see a wide proliferation of tools and fads that promise a simple cure-all. Yet the evidence is that even very popular implementation tools such as reengineering have not been unqualified successes. Moreover, all these initiatives consume an enormous amount of organizational energy.

The need for a comprehensive framework, a theory, to sort out fads from useful initiatives is obvious. Managers building a high-performance firm need a framework that enables them to evaluate initiatives, sequence them, and recognize the risks and time frames they involve. Managers building a high-performance firm must start with a point of view about the building blocks that contribute to the firm.

The Boundaryless Organization provides an excellent start to the process of discovering the essential building blocks of organizations that can cope with the complex strategies needed in the future. Implicit in the message of this book is the strategic imperative of competitive success: traditional notions of efficiency, such as quality of asset management, are not enough. We need to go beyond them and develop a new managerial scorecard.

From Asset Management to Resource Leverage

Beset by the new competitive reality, firms typically start to focus on better asset management (reduction of working capital) as well as on reduction of investment requirements by selective outsourcing. However, vitality in the medium to longer term comes not from asset reduction but from resource leverage. Managers must be able to get a bigger bang for the buck, better commercial results from the infrastructure in which they have invested. The brands, patents and technology, global supply base, physical infrastructure, and competencies that the collective and shared learning of the organization represents—that is, the physical and the invisible, intellectual resources of the firm—need to be leveraged. The reusing of intellectual assets to create new businesses and new sources of competitive advantage is a process of discovering hidden wealth and requires a new management process. *The Boundaryless Organization* implicitly accepts the need for resource leverage. The authors suggest four dominant themes that are critical to such leverage: speed (not size), flexibility (not rigidity, often disguised as role clarity), integration (not specialization), and innovation (not control).

Most often, the reason managers do not move beyond asset management to resource leverage is that the latter requires new ways of managing. The essence of such leverage is learning, sharing knowledge, redeploying knowledge, and bundling physical and intellectual assets in new and creative ways. Therefore, the capacity to transcend current administrative boundaries is a critical precondition for resource leverage. That boundary spanning, or creating of "boundaryless" behavior, is the substance of this book. *The Boundaryless Organization* is about the "how" of strategy.

Creating the Organization of the Future

Basing their findings on their extensive experience in working with senior managers of some of the best-known firms, the authors identify four essential boundaries to be spanned. These include hierarchical levels (breaking the tyranny of the vertical, status-driven boundaries), interunit divisions (breaking functional, business unit, and other horizontal boundaries driven by specialization, expertise, and socialization), barriers between internal and external organizations (breaking the boundary between the customer and the organization), and finally, global differences (breaking the boundaries between geographic markets and cultures). In large, well-established organizations such as GE, General Motors, Sears, IBM, and others, each one of these boundaries was an integral part of the management process. Call them bureaucracy, internal governance, or administrative heritage, these boundaries were real, and implicitly defined the range of competitive options available to each firm. It is no surprise, therefore, that these organizations were unable to adapt speedily to the changing competitive realities. A lack of organizational capacity to reconfigure physical and intellectual resources in new and creative ways—not as resources per se—had become their primary source of competitive weakness. GE was one of the first to realize the suffocating effects of the traditional boundary-based approaches to managing, effects that inhibited the organization's ability to leverage resources. GE initiated a process for systematically creating a "boundaryless" organization. The authors' experience is derived significantly from their work on this process, initially at GE and subsequently at other firms as well.

Boundaryless behavior is not about eliminating all administrative procedures and rules. It is about reducing the threshold of pain when creating new patterns of collaboration, learning, and productive work. It is about removing the restrictions, real and imaginary, imposed on individuals and teams by formal structures. Boundarylessness is about boundary spanning; it is about substituting permeable structures for concrete walls.

The Boundaryless Organization is organized in a user-friendly manner. The authors follow a simple structure to articulate their complex message about each of the four boundaries. They describe:

1. A logical reason for the need to reexamine the effects of a specific kind of organizational boundary (for example, vertical boundaries, or the hierarchy).
2. A method (an instrument) with which you can assess the state of your company along this dimension (for example, how hierarchy-bound your organization is).

3. A brief history of how this kind of boundary evolved. What were the theoretical underpinnings behind the organizing idea?

4. The consequences of the condition. When does an organizational practice become a pathology? (For example, hierarchy-based management was fine in slow-moving businesses, but in businesses that need quick response time and flexibility, hierarchies can become pathologies.)

5. The steps that can be taken to break old patterns and create the new patterns of boundaryless behavior (for example, creating a shared mindset).

6. The benefits to the organization from this approach.

Two themes dominate the book. First, creating a boundaryless organization takes time and perseverance. It takes repetition. It takes small acts, symbols, course corrections, coaching, and celebrations. It is not without pain. It takes training. It should involve all people in the organization. Most often, these simple and, at the same time, profound lessons are not well understood by leaders. Reinventing the company is not about a single initiative; neither is it an off-line activity. It is on-line, involves multiple initiatives, and is cumulative.

The second theme is that success in current business is critical to provide necessary space and confidence to the organization. Focusing on business results is critical as a management group attempts to reinvent itself. Change not anchored in business results is likely to drift. Strategy provides the anchor and the rationale for reinventing the company.

These two underlying themes, so often missing in books on change and transformation, make this a book for line managers as much as a guide for HR professionals. The focus is on general management in a changing marketplace.

The Boundaryless Organization is a very important contribution to the emerging thinking on preparing for competing in the future.

Ann Arbor, Michigan
July 1995

C. K. Prahalad
Coauthor of Competing for the Future
Harvey C. Fruehauf Professor of Business Administration and Professor of Corporate Strategy and International Business Graduate School of Business Administration University of Michigan

FOREWORD

by Lawrence A. Bossidy

Nobody argues anymore with the notion that what it takes to succeed today is radically different from what it took yesterday and that tomorrow's success factors will be different as well. The speed of changes in the global market in an age of accelerating technological innovation means that there are no longer any certainties. New products and competitors emerge almost overnight, and the half-life of market strategies shrinks almost daily. It is the kind of environment in which great companies can be humbled very quickly—but where nimble, creative, and courageous organizations can thrive as never before.

To succeed in this environment, leaders need to rethink the traditional ways that work gets done. Whoever can contribute value— whether he or she is production worker, middle manager, specialist, vendor, customer, or senior executive—needs to be encouraged to collaborate with others and make things happen, without waiting for some central authority to give permission. The old questions of status, role, organizational level, functional affiliation, and geographic location, all the traditional boundaries that we have used for years to define and control the way we work, are much less relevant than getting the best people possible to work together effectively.

For many organizations, this concept of boundaryless behavior sounds threatening and risky. After all, it means transferring decision-making authority away from executives and out to frontline workers; it means listening to customers and changing our products and delivery systems to meet their needs; it means forming partnerships with suppliers rather than just telling them what to do; and it means establishing coalitions with other parts of the company rather than defending turf. And when all this is taken together, it means that the role of manager, executive, and leader changes drastically—from controller and authority figure to stimulator, catalyst, cheerleader, and coach. So it is not an easy shift. However, in the environment of the 1990s and beyond, making such a shift is no longer a choice.

For the past four years at AlliedSignal, we have been working to make this kind of boundaryless transformation, not only in our management team but throughout the company. It has not been painless or easy. Nor is the transformation complete. We still get hung up on titles, status, roles, rules, functions, and geographic differences that divide us rather than bring us together with each other and with our customers. But by becoming more boundaryless, we have been able to establish and achieve new standards of excellence for today. And most importantly, we are far more capable of succeeding in an unpredictable future.

If your organization is ready for this kind of transformation, *The Boundaryless Organization* will provide a simple but provocative framework either for getting started or for accelerating the pace. I will be asking all of our managers to read it, to learn from the rich cases that it contains, and to use the tools that might be helpful to them. But make no mistake, this is not a cookbook or a how-to guide. Too many managers today are looking for the quick-fix elixir that will make them winners overnight. It does not exist, either in this book or elsewhere. The authors of *The Boundaryless Organization* rightly argue that we do not need new buzzwords about organization but new ways of thinking about our organizations. As such a new way of thinking, this book is not a solution but a set of ideas that should cause all managers to rethink how they get work done.

In the final analysis, there is no substitute for your own creativity and leadership, for your creation of your own boundaryless agenda. And that is the uniqueness of *The Boundaryless Organization*. It is not a prescription but a challenge. It is up to you to take advantage of it.

Morristown, New Jersey   Lawrence A. Bossidy
July 1995   *Chairman and Chief Executive Officer*
                                                      AlliedSignal Corporation

PREFACE

This book grew out of our experiences with one of the largest and most ambitious organizational change efforts ever attempted, the GE Work-Out process. Late in 1988, Dave Ulrich was asked by Jack Welch, chairman and CEO of General Electric Company, to pull together a team of academics and consultants who could help GE engineer a major transformation in the way it did business. Among others, Ulrich enlisted Ron Ashkenas, Todd Jick (then at Harvard University) and Steve Kerr (then at the University of Southern California). For the next several years, all of us worked intensively with a variety of GE businesses to reduce bureaucracy, speed cycle times, and create increased capabilities for change. Periodically, we met with others involved in Work-Out to share experiences and learn from each other.

It was at GE that we first heard the term *boundaryless organization,* an integrative theme that Jack Welch began using in 1990. At first, we were not sure what the boundaryless organization meant and feared it might be just another slogan or buzzword. But over and over again, throughout GE, we stumbled on aspects of the boundaryless theme. For example, in the early days of Work-Out, we conducted hundreds of "town meetings," where managers were asked to hold direct dialogues with their employees, and we saw how difficult it was to overcome the vertical boundaries between managers and their people. At the same time, we began to see the disconnections, the horizontal boundaries, between functions and departments.

As Work-Out progressed and the vertical and horizontal boundaries became increasingly more permeable in GE businesses, we began to focus on relationships between GE and its customers and suppliers, the external boundaries. Dave Ulrich already had written extensively on how human resource practices could create greater customer commitment. Building on these ideas, we began helping GE businesses hold town meetings with customers and suppliers. Todd Jick conducted the first one, between GE Appliances and Sears, and it was followed by many more.

By 1991, we also were looking at global linkages, as GE businesses shifted from domestic to truly worldwide concerns. For example, Ron Ashkenas took part in an extended effort to integrate GE Lighting's domestic business with its European acquisitions, including its new Hungarian partner, Tungsram Ltd., the first major acquisition of an Eastern Bloc company by a Western concern.

By 1992, we realized that GE was engaged in a fundamental paradigm shift that encompassed altering multiple organizational boundaries simultaneously. With that shift in mind, Kerr, Jick, and Ulrich began creating a conceptual framework that would shape managers' understanding of the boundaryless organization and what they could do to achieve it. This framework became the GE program known as the Change Acceleration Process (CAP). Since 1992, hundreds of GE managers and many of their customers and suppliers have utilized CAP to break down boundaries of all sorts.

By 1993, we realized that the boundary-breaking issues facing GE were becoming universal. More and more organizations were struggling with new structures and processes meant to increase fluidity across boundaries. Yet most firms lacked a working model for thinking about those issues comprehensively. They were attacking boundaries piecemeal with a variety of strategies. Thus, we decided that the insights we had gained from GE and from dozens of other organizations could form an action framework with general applicability. To make the framework useful, we set out to create not only a conceptual model of the boundaryless organization but also a set of simple tools that managers could tailor to their individual requirements to help them implement boundaryless change. *The Boundaryless Organization* is the result.

We want to emphasize that the framework we have created is not based on GE, nor is *The Boundaryless Organization* a book about GE. Since GE has been a leader in creating a boundaryless organization and has been a formative learning site for all of us, we have drawn on its experience and a number of GE examples. However, we also have drawn on the learnings and insights of numerous other organizations, and GE examples constitute no more than 10 percent of our examples. Further, although Steve Kerr is currently a GE executive, this book was largely written while he was on the faculty of the University of Michigan. Thus, the GE view represented in this book comes solely from the external consulting perspective.

To make the information in *The Boundaryless Organization* easily accessible, we have organized the book as follows. Sections devoted to vertical, horizontal, external, and geographic boundaries describe how these barriers both help and hinder organizations and how managers can permeate them or break them down where necessary. Detailed examples from many organizations show the real difficulties that boundaries cause in today's businesses and the practical solutions that managers and consultants are currently applying. Brief questionnaires assist executives, managers, and their teams to evaluate their own organizational boundaries, need for change, and readiness for change. Finally, our concluding chapter is designed to help executives examine the nature of their personal boundaries and identify the specific leadership challenges they will meet as they take their organizations into the twenty-first century.

Since organizations of all sizes have boundaries that increase costs, slow production, and stifle innovation, our model and related tools for loosening and permeating boundaries can be used by executives and managers in large, midsized, or small businesses of all kinds. And since all levels of management affect how organizational boundaries operate, and since those boundaries in turn affect the work of everyone in an organization, managers at any level can apply appropriate selections of the tools we describe.

We realize that changing the nature of organizational boundaries is a challenging task. *The Boundaryless Organization* was written to make that task a little easier.

Acknowledgments

Many contributors helped us transform this book from an embryonic idea to a finished product. First and foremost are the many clients and management colleagues who asked us to work alongside them in breaking down boundaries and who were willing to share their experiences in this book. It is always easier to give advice from the outside, knowing that others have the ultimate responsibility for implementation and for dealing with the consequences. We have immense respect for the organizational pioneers and leaders noted in this book and for the countless other managers who have trusted our ideas and valued our experiments. We have learned much from them. Credit for results is all theirs. Any inaccuracy regarding their stories is our responsibility.

A number of consultant colleagues also helped to make this book possible. In particular, several members of Robert H. Schaffer & Associates provided cases and read drafts of the manuscript, including Keith Michaelson, Suzanne Francis, Harvey Thomson, Matthew McCreight, Robert Neiman, Nick Craig, Rudi Siddik, Elaine Mandrish, Harlow Cohen, Richard Bobbe, and Nadim Matta. Matta also created much appreciated first drafts of several of the self-diagnostic questionnaires. Robert Schaffer provided not only cases but also general wisdom about the persistence needed to complete a book. Sumantra Ghoshal, now of the London Business School, offered insights and encouragement during Todd Jick's two years of on-site research and teaching at INSEAD about what globalization really means. Wayne Brockbank and Dale Lake, both at the University of Michigan, and Warren Wilhelm of AlliedSignal also provided invaluable feedback.

Jossey-Bass editor Sarah Polster was the first to recognize that the concept of the boundaryless organization could be expanded into a management book. Through many months of rough drafts, she maintained her belief in our ability to create a good book, always reminding us that "there's a book in there somewhere." We hope readers will agree with her assessment.

To produce the final draft, we relied heavily on Rick Benzel, our development editor, surrogate writer, and sometime conscience. More times than we care to remember, Rick took our collective thoughts and structured them, helping us convey them clearly and concisely. We owe him an enormous debt of gratitude.

Emilieanne Koehnlein, administrative assistant at Robert H. Schaffer & Associates, was also critical to our project. She provided word-processing support for the entire manuscript, pulling together multiple documents in different formats, tracking down all of the endnotes, and generally keeping the project together. We could not have completed this book without her. We also wish to acknowledge the contributions of Ginger Bitter, who provides administrative support for Dave Ulrich.

Finally, in any project that requires work beyond the already overstretched boundaries of professional life, families are the real heros. For all their unconditional support, despite our many missed evenings at home and our weekends away, we wish to acknowledge and thank our wives and children: Barbara, Eli, Shira, Ari, Wendy, Carrie, Monika, Michael, Rose, Zoe, and Adina.

We promise not to do it to you again without asking.

July 1995   Ron Ashkenas
                                   Stamford, Connecticut
                               Dave Ulrich
                                   Ann Arbor, Michigan
                               Todd Jick
                                   Cambridge, Massachusetts
                               Steve Kerr
                                   Ossining, New York

THE AUTHORS

Ron Ashkenas is the managing partner of Robert H. Schaffer & Associates, a management consulting firm based in Stamford, Connecticut, and in Toronto. For many years, Ashkenas and his colleagues have pioneered results-driven approaches to organizational change, using many of the methods described in *The Boundaryless Organization*. His clients have included Motorola, General Re, AlliedSignal, General Electric, the World Bank, and many other public and private firms.

Ashkenas also works extensively with corporate staff specialists and internal consultants to help them improve the bottom-line impact of their professional contributions. He has lectured on this subject for the Institute of Management Consultants and has run numerous workshops for corporate staff groups. He has been a member of the New York Human Resource Planners board of directors and currently serves on the editorial board of *Human Resource Management*.

Prior to joining Schaffer & Associates in 1978, Ashkenas received a B.A. degree (1972) from Wesleyan University, an Ed.M. degree (1974) from Harvard University, and a Ph.D. degree (1979) in organizational behavior from Case Western Reserve University, where he also held several research and teaching assignments. He has published dozens of book chapters and articles on organizational change and improvement; his articles have appeared in the *New York Times* and in such journals as the *Harvard Business Review,* the *National Productivity Review,* and *Human Resource Management.*

Dave Ulrich is a professor of business administration at the University of Michigan School of Business. He received his B.A. degree (1979) from Brigham Young University and his Ph.D. degree (1982) from the University of California at Los Angeles. He has taught at Brigham Young University, UCLA, and Pepperdine University. He has taught M.B.A., Ph.D., and executive education courses on how organizations compete through strategic change, organizational design, culture change, human resource practices, and leadership. At the University of Michigan, he is on the core faculty of the Michigan Executive Program and is co-director of the Human Resource Executive Program and the Advanced Human Resource Executive Program.

Ulrich's research assesses how organizations change, formulate strategies for competitive advantage, and integrate human resources into strategic goals. He has generated an award-winning national database on organizations, which assesses how strategies match human resource practices for improved financial performance and HR competencies. He has published over seventy articles and book chapters. His articles have appeared in *Academy of Management Review, Human Resource Management, Human Resource Planning, Organizational Dynamics, Human Relations, Journal of Management, New Management Planning Review,* and *Sloan Management Review.* He is coauthor of *Organizational Capability: Competing from the Inside/Out* (1990) and *Human Resources as a Competitive Advantage: An Empirical Assessment of HR Competencies and Practices in Global Firms* (forthcoming).

Ulrich has served on the board of directors of the Human Resource Planning Society, is the editor of *Human Resource Management,* and serves on the editorial boards of five other journals. He is a fellow in the National Academy of Human Resources. He has been listed by *Business Week* as one of the world's "top ten educators" in management and the top educator in human resources. He has consulted and done research with the Federal Aviation Administration and with over half of the Fortune 200, including Amoco, BAT Industries, Baxter Healthcare, Borg Warner, Caterpillar, Champion International, Digital Equipment Corporation, Eastman Kodak, Exxon, Farm Credit Corporation, General Electric, General Motors, Honeywell, Hughes Tool, Johnson & Johnson, MCI, Marriott, NCR, Pfizer, Ryder, Shell, TRW, USG, Westinghouse, and Whirlpool.

Todd Jick is a managing partner of the Center for Executive Development (CED). He earned a B.A. degree (1971) in social anthropology from Wesleyan University and M.S. (1976) and Ph.D. (1978) degrees in organizational behavior from Cornell University. He was a professor at the Harvard Business School for ten years and a visiting associate professor, organizational behavior–human resource management, at INSEAD. He also taught at the Columbia University Graduate School of Business and York University in Toronto.

He has been actively involved in executive education and consulting in such areas as leadership, organizational change and transformation, new organizational paradigms, service management, customer-supplier partnerships, and human resource management. He has taught in executive programs at Harvard and INSEAD, and worldwide under the auspices of the Asian Institute of Management, Euroform (Spain), Ambrosetti (Italy), the Australian Institute of Management, and the Jerusalem Institute of Management. He has carried out executive education and/or consulting at numerous companies, such as General Electric, AT&T, Price Waterhouse, IBM, Honeywell, General Motors, Chemical Bank, and Merck. His European-based clients have included Unilever, BBV, Philips, SWIRE, Ciba-Geigy, and Alcatel Bell.

Jick has been published widely. His books include *The Challenge of Organizational Change,* with Rosabeth Moss Kanter and Barry Stein (1992); *Managing Change: Cases and Concepts* (1993); and *Management Live!* with Bob Marx and Peter Frost (1991). He has written more than thirty business school cases.

Steve Kerr is vice president, corporate leadership development, for General Electric (including responsibility for Crotonville). During much of the writing of *The Boundaryless Organization,* he was a faculty member at the University of Michigan. He has also taught at Ohio State University and the University of Southern California and was dean of faculty at the USC business school from 1985 to 1989. He was 1989–1990 president of the Academy of Management, the world's largest association of academicians in management, and is a member of six editorial review boards.

Kerr earned his B.A. degree (1961) from Hunter College and his Ph.D. degree (1973) from the City University of New York. He is the author of dozens of articles and book chapters and two textbooks on organizational behavior. His writings on leadership, substitutes for leadership, and "on the folly of rewarding A, while hoping for B" are among the most cited and reprinted in the management sciences.

The Boundaryless Organization

1

A New World Order

Rising to the Challenge of New Success Factors

As the twentieth century comes to a close, a new world order has begun to emerge, replacing familiar patterns of power and privilege that have existed for generations. Leaders have been replaced; centers of governance have been renamed; new patterns for distributing wealth and influence have been created.

But what we are describing is not a political phenomenon caused by the demise of the Soviet Union, the fall of the Berlin Wall, or the end of apartheid in South Africa. Rather, it is a social and economic revolution that is manifest in a new order for organizations as they shift from rigid to permeable organizational structures and processes. We call this shift the dawning of the *boundaryless organization* of the twenty-first century.

Consider these developments, once thought unimaginable and now almost taken for granted:

1

◆ Motorola has taken years out of its new product development cycle by replacing its traditional functional processes with fully accountable cross-functional teams composed of engineers, marketers, manufacturing experts, financial analysts, and others.

◆ General Electric managers routinely have fifteen to twenty direct reports. Often, there are no more than three or four layers of management between the CEO and frontline workers in a company of more than 200,000 people.

◆ General Re, one of the world's largest reinsurance companies, has redirected its marketing force by redefining marketers as "customer advocates" who work closely with customers and represent the customer point of view inside the company.

◆ SmithKline Beecham Pharmaceuticals reorganized its support organization for worldwide clinical trials by involving over one hundred people in a dialogue about how the new organization should work. Thanks to interactive communication technologies, participants engaged in this dialogue over three months and across two continents without having to leave their offices.

Business authors have described hundreds of similar innovations, declaring the rise of a "new organization" to which they have given many names: virtual organization, front/back organization, cluster organization, network organization, chaotic organization, ad hoc organization, horizontal organization, empowered organization, high-performing work team organization, and process reengineered organization, among others.

However, underlying all these descriptions, theories, and experiments, we believe, is a single deeper paradigm shift that we call the emergence of the boundaryless organization. In our view, that shift is the driving force that makes all these new organizations possible, the underpinning that supports their translation from theory to reality. In other words, while the emerging organization may take a number of different forms, the constant will be that it will act differently. Specifically, behavior patterns that are highly conditioned by boundaries between levels, functions, and other constructs will be replaced by patterns of free movement across those same boundaries. No longer will organizations use boundaries to separate people, tasks, processes, and places; instead, they will focus on how to permeate those boundaries—to move ideas, information, decisions, talent, rewards, and actions where they are most needed.

In that context, the purpose of this book is not to herald the rise of another "new organization." Rather, it is to describe the paradigm shift toward boundaryless structures that is at the heart of all the new labels and to lay out the assumptions behind this shift, the changes in behavior it generates, and the results it can yield. To do this, we delineate four types of boundaries that characterize most organizations.

1. *Vertical:* the boundaries between levels and ranks of people
2. *Horizontal:* the boundaries between functions and disciplines
3. *External:* the boundaries between the organization and its suppliers, customers, and regulators
4. *Geographic:* the boundaries between nations, cultures, and markets

We also describe the leadership challenges that managers face in making the shift happen. Most importantly, we provide leaders with a practical set of tools for moving their own organizations forward toward the achievement of a boundaryless organization for the twenty-first century.

Boundaryless Behavior: The Art of the Fluid

Organizations have always had and will continue to have boundaries. People specialize in different tasks, and thus, boundaries exist between functions. Organizational members have differing levels of authority and influence, and so boundaries exist between bosses and subordinates. People inside a firm do different work than suppliers, customers, and others outside; so boundaries exist there as well. And people work in different places, under different conditions and sometimes in different time zones and cultures, thus creating additional boundaries.

The underlying purpose of all these boundaries is to separate people, processes, and production in healthy and necessary ways. Boundaries keep things focused and distinct. Without them, organizations would be *disorganized*. People would not know what to do. There would be no differentiation of tasks, coordination of resources and skills, or clear sense of direction. In essence, the organization would cease to exist.

Given the necessity of boundaries, the boundaryless behavior we describe does not mean a free-for-all removal of all boundaries. That would be silly. Instead, we are talking about making boundaries more permeable, allowing greater fluidity of movement throughout the organization. In essence, we are suggesting that the traditional notion of boundaries as fixed barriers or unyielding separators be replaced by an organic, biological view of boundaries as permeable, flexible, moveable membranes in a living evolving organism.

In living organisms, membranes exist to give the organism shape and definition. They have sufficient structural strength to prevent the organism from devolving into an amorphous mass. Yet they are permeable. Food, blood, oxygen, and chemical transmitters flow through them relatively unimpeded so that each part of the organism can contribute to the other parts.

So it is with the boundaryless organization. Information, resources, ideas, and energy pass throughout the membranes quickly and easily so that the organization as a whole functions far better than each of its separate parts. Yet definition and distinction still exist—there are still leaders who have authority and accountability, there are still people with special functional skills, there are still distinctions between customers and suppliers, and work continues to be done in different places.

Like a living organism, the boundaryless organization also evolves and grows, and the placement of boundaries may shift. Over time, the levels between the top and bottom of the organization may decrease, functions may merge together to combine skills, or partnerships may form between the firm and its customers or suppliers, changing the boundaries of who does what.

Because the boundaryless organization is a living continuum, not a fixed state, the ongoing management challenge is to find the right balance of boundaryless behavior, to determine how permeable to make boundaries and where to place them. But why should organizational leaders make this effort? What is so important about becoming boundaryless?

A Changing Paradigm for Organizational Success

In recent years, almost all organizations have experimented with some type of change process aimed at creating more permeable boundaries. Whether it was called a customer-focus program, total quality, reengineering, reinvention, or business process innovation, organizations have invested untold resources in trying to make change happen.

The impetus behind many of these efforts has been the astounding fall from grace, or actual demise, of some of the most highly regarded and revered organizations in the world: IBM, Philips, Mazda, Sony, Lloyd's of London, Volkswagen, Eastern Airlines, Pan Am, Sears, Aetna, General Motors, Digital Equipment Corporation, Westinghouse, Eastman Kodak, Citicorp, and many others. Each experienced severe financial difficulties, crises in leadership, and major changes in direction. Nor is membership in this fallen-angels club limited to this handful of companies. The phenomenon crosses all industries from retail sales to automotive manufacturing, publishing to airlines, financial services to computers. It crosses geographic boundaries, with troubled giants found not only in North America but also in Europe, Asia, and Latin America.

The difficulties in these companies cannot be explained by lack of long-range strategy or intelligent planning. IBM, Digital, Sears, Philips, and many others had and continue to have world-class planning functions and capabilities. They have not stumbled due to lack of technology or investment. In the past decade, General Motors probably invested more in automation than any other company in the world. IBM's research investment was, for many years, far beyond the business norm.

Naturally, an individual explanation can be provided for each troubled company. IBM was too wedded to mainframe computers; Westinghouse stumbled due to poor judgment over financial services; Eastern Airlines was unable to cope with deregulation; Citicorp misjudged the real-estate cycle. But such microcosmic explanations miss the larger pattern. The stark reality is that each of these organizations slipped from invincible to vincible when it was *faced with a rate of change that exceeded its capability to respond.* When their worlds became highly unstable and turbulent, all these organizations lacked the flexibility and agility to act quickly. Their structures and boundaries had become too rigid and calcified.

It is against this backdrop of highly visible failures and falls that most organizations have launched their change efforts. And while each effort has unique characteristics, conditions, and drivers, in almost every one we have seen a common theme: the attempt to retool the organization so that it meets an entirely new set of criteria for success.

Out with the Old—In with the New

For much of the twentieth century, four critical factors influenced organizational success.

- ◆ *Size.* The larger a company became, the more it was able to attain production or service efficiencies, leverage its capital, and put pressure on customers and suppliers.
- ◆ *Role clarity.* In order to get work done efficiently in larger organizations, tasks were divided and subdivided, clear distinctions were made between manager and worker, and levels of authority were clearly spelled out. In well-functioning organizations, everyone knew his or her place, accepted it, and performed according to specifications.
- ◆ *Specialization.* As tasks were subdivided, specialties were created or encouraged, to provide finely grained levels of expertise. Thus finance, planning, human resources, information technology, manufacturing methods, inventory control, material management, and many other tasks all became disciplines in their own right.
- ◆ *Control.* Given the fine distinctions between roles and specialties, most organizations, especially large ones, needed to create controls to make sure all of the pieces performed as needed, coming together properly to provide whole products or services. Therefore, a major role of management throughout the twentieth century was to control the work of others to ensure that they were doing the right things, in the right order, at the right time.

With these success factors in mind, managers and organizational theorists focused on organizational structure as their primary vehicle for achieving effectiveness. Thus, they invested considerable emotional and financial capital debating such questions as:

◆ How many layers of management do we need?
◆ What signing authority will different levels have?
◆ What is the proper span of control?
◆ What is the best balance between centralization and decentralization?
◆ How do we describe and classify each job and set pay levels?
◆ How do we organize field locations and international operations?

The purpose of these debates was to create the organizational structure, and attendant processes, needed to come as close as possible to the critical success factors listed above. What has happened as the twentieth century comes to its close, however, is that the advent of the microprocessor, the dizzying speed of information processing and communications, and the arrival of the global economy have conspired to radically shift the basis of competitive success. To a large extent, the old success factors have become liabilities, and the new success factors look very different from the old. (The old and the new are summarized in the box below.)

The Shifting Paradigm for Organizational Success

Old Success Factors	*New Success Factors*
• Size	• Speed
• Role clarity	• Flexibility
• Specialization	• Integration
• Control	• Innovation

◆ *Speed.* Successful organizations today are increasingly characterized by speed in everything they do. They respond to customers more quickly, bring new products to market faster, and change strategies more rapidly than ever before. This trend is continuing into the twenty-first century. While size does not preclude speed, large organizations are like tankers. Compared to smaller firms, they need more space and time in which to change direction because they have a greater mass to be mobilized, informed, convinced, and channeled. The challenge for them is to act like a small company while retaining access to the large company's broader resources.

◆ *Flexibility*. Organizations that move quickly are flexible. People do multiple jobs, constantly learn new skills, and willingly shift to different locations and assignments. Similarly, the organization pursues multiple paths, experiments, and makes rapid shifts. Role clarity, the old success factor, often constrains flexibility. When people get locked into specific roles and responsibilities and are rewarded only for those, they become less willing to jump into the breach at a moment's notice and do whatever is needed. Conversely, flexible organizations revel in ambiguity, throw out job descriptions, and thrive on ad hoc teams that form and reform as tasks shift.

◆ *Integration*. Organizations that can shift directions quickly and flexibly have processes that carry concepts of change into the institutional bloodstream, disseminating new initiatives quickly, and mobilizing the right resources to make things happen. In other words, instead of breaking tasks into pieces and assigning specialists to perform those tasks with precision, the organization creates mechanisms to pull together diverse task activities as they are needed. It focuses more on how best to accomplish business or work processes and less on producing specialized pieces of work that management will eventually pull together. Specialists are still needed, but the key to success is often the ability of those same specialists to collaborate with others to create an integrated whole.

◆ *Innovation*. Organizations that succeed in a world of rapid change find innovation essential. Doing today's work in today's way becomes quickly outdated. Boundaryless organizations constantly search for the new, the different, the unthinkable. They create innovative processes and environments that encourage and reward creativity, whereas in organizations that focus on control, the creative spirit and people who innovate are often stifled by systems of approvals, checks, and double-checks, because innovation threatens standard operating procedures.

In short, organizations designed to meet the old set of critical success factors are increasingly incapable of thriving or even surviving in the new world. Their structures are laced with controls that constrain speed, flexibility, integration, and innovation. Consider the contrast between retailers Sears and Wal-Mart.

The Giant and the Upstart

Sears, for many years the world's largest retailer, succeeded with a management process based on structure and control. As the company grew and tremendous critical mass was created, Sears leveraged its buying power through strong centralized functions. Almost all critical decisions were made in its Chicago headquarters. The stores mirrored the control philosophy, allotting different levels of approvals to various managerial levels, with all really important decisions traveling far up the chain of command. This approach succeeded for many years, as long as size, role clarity, specialization, and control were critical to competitiveness.[1]

Then, in the 1980s, the rules of the game changed in the retailing industry. Consumers wanted lower prices, better service, and a constantly changing array of merchandise. In this environment, speed became of the essence. Retailers had to provide the most wanted goods quickly, not ask customers to order them and then wait for them. At the same time, flexibility and integration became more critical as a way of driving out costs. Successful retailers gave people multiple jobs and designed integrated service functions. Innovation became critical to maintaining the edge in merchandise, service, and store layout.

In this new world, Sears began to slip. At first, management asked the same questions it had in the past, looking to structure for answers, and carrying out multiple restructurings, store closings, and leadership changes. Nothing seemed to work. It was not until Sears began a process to become a more "customer-focused company" and asked each store to find ways of identifying and serving customer needs that the firm began to turn around. Once that shift in focus occurred, Sears was able to reduce corporate staff dramatically, moving decision-making responsibility to stores and store managers. The new success factors compelled Sears to redesign itself.

In contrast, upstart Wal-Mart Stores, from the beginning of its existence, focused on the new paradigm success factors. Founder Sam Walton's philosophy was to find out what the customer wanted and to provide it quickly, at lower cost than any competitor. This meant designing fast, flexible processes for gathering consumer and competitive intelligence, and creating innovative responses to that information. One such process and response is a weekly "quick market intelligence" (QMI) exercise that is one factor at the heart of Wal-Mart's success.

QMI works like this: each week, two hundred or more of Wal-Mart's senior executives and managers leave on Monday morning to visit Wal-Mart stores and competitors in different regions of the country. For three and one-half days, they talk to store managers, employees, and customers, learning about what is and is not selling. On Thursday evening, the fleet of Wal-Mart planes returns these executives to the Bentonville, Arkansas, Wal-Mart headquarters. On Friday, in what they call the "huddle," these managers examine the quantitative data (computer-based inventories about what is selling) and match these data with their perceptual data from the field to make decisions about products and promotions. Each Saturday morning, a teleconference is held with over 1,800 stores to share these ideas and give everyone the game plan for the next week. The cycle time for ideas at Wal-Mart is measured in days, not weeks or months. Boundaries that would have led to committee meetings, task forces, and reporting up the chain of command in, for example, the old Sears have been replaced by executives who collect information from the source and act.

Even Wal-Mart store managers can move with speed, flexibility, and creativity. They can set up their own "corners" to market merchandise that they think will sell to their local customers. If an idea works, it is given a larger test and sometimes expanded nationwide. Similarly, they have the authority to make pricing changes on the spot if they think a change is warranted or if a competitor has a lower price. They do not need to call Bentonville for permission.

Similar contrasts can be made between Microsoft and IBM or Digital Equipment, between Southwest and United Airlines, and between

Fidelity Investments and Dreyfus to show that organizations preoccupied with the old success factors and the attendant questions about organizational structure have struggled. Those that focus on the new factors for success and the corresponding boundaryless behaviors are poised to win.

Four Boundaries

In their quest to achieve the success factors of the twenty-first century, organizations must confront and reshape the four types of boundaries we defined briefly earlier: vertical, horizontal, external, and geographic.

Vertical. Vertical boundaries represent layers within a company. They are the floors and ceilings that differentiate status, authority, and power. Traditional elements of vertical boundaries are spans of control, limits of authority, and other manifestations of hierarchy. In a hierarchical organization, roles are clearly defined and more authority resides higher up in the organization than lower down. The degree to which an organization is vertically, or hierarchically, bounded is most evident in the number of levels or reporting relationships that exist between the first-line supervisor and the senior executive. Hierarchical boundaries are defined by title, rank, and privilege. The classic example is the military, where clear symbolic and substantive differences exist by rank: officer clubs differ from enlisted clubs, officers have privileges not available to enlisted personnel, generals have more status and staff than colonels, and so on. When rank has its privilege, it is a clear symbol of vertical boundaries.

In contrast, boundaryless organizations focus less attention on who has authority and rank and more on who has useful ideas. Rank is less relevant than competence. Good ideas from anyone are sought out. And while the total dissolution of all vertical boundaries may be chaos, learning to permeate hierarchies leads organizations to faster and better decisions made by more committed individuals.

Horizontal. Horizontal boundaries exist between organizational functions, product lines, or units. If vertical boundaries are floors and ceilings, horizontal boundaries are walls between rooms. Boundaries between functions exist in the traditional firm when each function has a singular agenda that may compete or conflict with other functional agendas. A common example occurs when engineering wants to create more innovative products and looks for technologically hot ideas, marketing wants more varied and customized products, and manufacturing wants few variations and little innovation because that ensures efficiency in production through long stable runs. Each of these functional areas then maximizes its own goals to the exclusion of overall organizational goals.

Processes that permeate horizontal boundaries carry ideas, resources, information, and competence with them as they move across functions, so that end-user, or customer, needs are well met. Quality, continuous improvement, reengineering, and high-performing work team initiatives often foster such processes. Once managers begin to move work quickly and effectively across functions or product lines, then horizontal boundaries become subservient to the integrated, faster-moving business processes.

External. External boundaries are barriers between firms and the outside world—principally suppliers and customers but also such entities as governmental agencies, special interest groups, and communities. In traditional organizations, clear differentiators exist between insiders and outsiders. Some of these differentiators are legal, but many are psychological, stemming from varied senses of identity, strategic priorities, and cultures. These differences lead most organizations to some form of we-they relationship with external constituents. Business is done through negotiation, haggling, pressure tactics, withholding of information, and the like. When there are multiple customers or suppliers, one may be played off against another.

While external boundaries do provide positive identity for insiders ("I work for Company X!"), they also diffuse effectiveness. Often, customers are the most capable of helping a firm resolve internal problems and the most interested in solutions. They know the output of the firm and are committed to getting high-quality products and services. Similarly, suppliers want to see their customers succeed so that they will be able to sell them more. When boundaries between firms and customers and suppliers are reduced, the resulting confluence of interests can produce much more efficient operations.

Geographic. Geographic, or global, boundaries exist when complexly structured firms operate in different markets and countries. Often stemming from national pride, cultural differences, market peculiarities, or worldwide logistics, these boundaries may isolate innovative practices and good ideas within a single country, keeping the overall company from leveraging the learning from specific countries and markets to increase company success.

With information technology, workforce mobility, and product standardization, global boundaries are quickly disappearing. Traditional work differences in Europe, Asia, and North America are being driven out by the need for more globally integrated products and services. Yet at the same time, successful firms that work across global boundaries respect and value local differences as a source of innovation. Colgate Palmolive, for example, has worked to establish brand equities throughout the world. Their brand of toothpaste and tooth powder, for example, while adapted to local preferences for taste, color, and so on, has become global. They want consumers in Europe, Australia, North America, and Asia to recognize the brand and find value in it. Creating global brand equities requires companies to think across global boundaries.

When vertical, horizontal, external, and geographic boundaries are traversable, the organization of the future begins to take shape. When these four boundaries remain rigid and impenetrable—as they do in many organizations today—they create the slowness to respond and the lack of flexibility and innovation that causes premier companies to fall.

Permeability in Action: Case Study of a Boundaryless Organization

To get an overview of boundaryless behavior, consider the case of GE Capital's credit card business, Retailer Financial Services (RFS)—one of the few organizations that has already made all its boundaries more permeable.

SUCCESSFUL NOW—BUT YOU SHOULD HAVE SEEN US BEFORE

Retailer Financial Services is one of GE Capital's approximately two dozen businesses. Headquartered in Stamford, Connecticut, it provides private label credit card services to various retail chains in the United States and overseas, and through its "bank," it offers its own credit card programs, such as the GE Rewards MasterCard and the GE travel card (for GE employees). RFS customers include such retail chains as Montgomery Ward, Macy's, Caldor, Burton, Filenes' Basement, Exxon, Harrods, Lowes, Home Depot, Disney, IKEA, and hundreds more.

From both a revenue and a human resource standpoint, RFS is one of GE Capital's largest businesses, employing over eight thousand people worldwide in a diverse range of functions and disciplines, including systems, telecommunications, customer service, marketing, finance, and product development. It has twelve state-of-the-art processing centers, including major facilities in Merriam, Kansas, and Macon, Georgia, as well as other processing facilities in the U.K., Austria, Sweden, and Mexico. Regional business centers throughout the United States and Europe provide almost instantaneous customer service to both retailers and cardholders.

Based on 1992 data, RFS is the world's largest provider of private label credit cards, with a 26 percent market share. Overall, it is the ninth largest issuer of bank cards. Assets total over $14 billion, and it generates over $150 million in net income, growing at a double-digit rate each year. In addition, the company is expanding aggressively, looking for major acquisitions in Europe, Mexico, and the Far East, while continuing to bring on major new customers in the United States.

In short, RFS is an enviable, successful business—financially sound, providing attractive rates of return, and satisfying its customers, all while growing aggressively and reinvesting in the infrastructure of the business. More importantly, RFS is a boundaryless organization. For example, in Merriam, Kansas, at the dedicated service center for Montgomery Ward, one leader and a small staff are the only "managers" for nearly five hundred people. Reporting to this management group are eighteen multifunctional customer service teams, each responsible for performing all the credit card, customer service, and accounts receivable functions for a portfolio of stores. Moreover, each frontline associate in these teams has the same authority as the service center leader to resolve customer problems, extend credit, and manage collection issues.

From the standpoint of the credit card holder, these services seem to be provided by the retailer. RFS thus functions as Montgomery Ward's invisible partner, responsible for managing the retailer's financial relationship with all credit card holders. In addition, a small marketing group within RFS also works closely with Montgomery Ward to agree on who should be a cardholder, what rates will be charged, and what marketing programs and promotions should be offered.

Seeing this level of success, few people remember that less than a decade ago, GE was trying desperately to sell Retailer Financial Services, then named Private Label. It had been in business for fifty years, yet its market share was a mere 3 percent. It was perceived to be an old, tired business—a mediocre performer in a declining market. To make matters worse, its own strategic planners did not believe it had much of a future. They were convinced that private label credit cards would go the way of the dinosaurs, displaced by universal cards such as Visa, MasterCard, and American Express. "Why," they reasoned, "would consumers want to carry multiple credit cards when they could carry just one or two? And if that's the case, we don't have a business here!"

Pronounced dead by its own planners, Private Label's outlook in 1982 was bleak. Holding fast to his pledge to sell off businesses that could not become the number one or two performers in their industries, GE Chairman and CEO Jack Welch put the company on the block. Fortunately for GE, potential buyers agreed with GE's assessment that Private Label was a dying business. They stayed away. With little choice other than to make the best of it, GE Capital promoted David A. Ekedahl, who had spent his whole career in Private Label, to run the business. His mission: keep it going as long as you can without losing money. Ekedahl did better than that. He created a successful boundaryless corporation.

REFORMULATING EXTERNAL BOUNDARIES

Private Label's transformation into a high-performance, boundaryless company did not begin with a grand plan. In fact, as Ekedahl describes it, the initial objective was to keep the wolves at bay by aggressively adding new customers. However, Ekedahl and his managers first had to decide who the customers were and how to win their business. That analysis led them to an important insight—the company needed to concentrate not just on the consumer (the end-user of private label cards) but on the retailer as well. The doom-and-gloom planning assumptions were based on the belief that Private Label's customers were consumers, who would not want to carry multiple cards. But if the first customer was the retailer, maybe there were different needs to be met.

By changing the longstanding external boundary that defined the customer, Ekedahl began a transformation that was to take Private Label light-years forward. He realized that fast and flexible processing would be the critical success factor for retailers. If Private Label could get the retailers on-line quickly, manage the volume of business efficiently, provide error-free processing, maintain balances and credit information accurately, and manage customer databases, it would have tremendous leverage with retailers. But at this time, both putting systems in place for a new retailer and keeping them going for an existing one was an incredibly cumbersome process. To achieve fast and flexible processing, another boundary needed to be opened up.

LOOSENING HORIZONTAL BOUNDARIES

Dave Ekedahl's description of what happened next illustrates how key insights open up the path to the boundaryless organization.

> We had just signed up a new company to do their private label credit cards, and I wanted to go through the process of getting that client on board. I found that in order to do that, I had a lot of people in the room, but none of us had any idea what to do by ourselves. We needed dozens of other people. So I figured if this was what it took to get something done, I might as well organize around these kinds of processes. So we began to recreate our own organization around the major processes that needed to get done rather than just do it ad hoc all the time.

Making organizational structure mirror the way work actually got done, Ekedahl gradually transformed Private Label, leveling horizontal boundaries between systems and other business functions. The change was especially difficult because the systems resources were all part of GE Capital's corporate organization, a centralized organization well defended by solid functional walls. No systems people were dedicated to Private Label; different resources were brought to bear whenever there was a particular need. Ekedahl was determined to change this functional dynamic.

But by no means was it a smooth transition. Early in 1989, Ekedahl tried to bridge the functions by sponsoring a joint working conference between his business people and the central systems organization. At a rancorous concluding meeting, the systems people complained that they were not consulted in the early stages of new customer conversions and were given unrealistic requirements and deadlines. On the other side, the marketing people accused the systems professionals of not delivering on their promises. Ekedahl found himself caught in the middle, wanting to create a cross-functional team yet forced to arbitrate between disagreeing sides. The concept of collaboration was right on, but the walls between the functions had not been scaled.

Ekedahl did not give up. First, he influenced the head of GE Capital's systems to dedicate a particular group of systems professionals to his business. Then he insisted that the systems and marketing people find new ways of working together, and he encouraged them to rethink their basic work processes. Although reluctant, the two groups eventually responded to Ekedahl's continuing pressure.

In 1990, Rich Nastasi, head of the group of systems people, began a process of working with the other business functions to radically reduce the time required to bring a new retailer on-line as a customer. A small cross-functional team mapped the typical process, which was taking an average of eight weeks. Nastasi then brought together a group of systems, marketing, finance, and customer service people and challenged them to complete new customer conversions in a matter of days, not weeks. To everyone's amazement, solutions began to emerge: earlier systems involvement in customer negotiations, standardized data collection procedures for getting customers' baselines, ways of training customer personnel to help in the conversion, structured conversion procedures, and technical means of transferring electronic files more quickly.

Over the next few months, as the solutions were implemented, customer conversion times began to drop dramatically, to less than a week for all but the largest new customers. Equally significant, the different functions put the solutions in place together. The walls were coming down. Less than a year later, Nastasi and his people were reporting directly to Dave Ekedahl, as full-fledged members of business team for what was now called Retailer Financial Services (RFS).

FLATTENING VERTICAL BOUNDARIES

As RFS organized around key processes, a different organization gradually took shape. Essentially, the company shifted from a centralized model, in which such functions as systems, credit, marketing, and customer service were all run out of Stamford, to a hybrid model with both centralized and decentralized processes. The guiding idea was that processes to support specific customers should be managed in the field, close to those customers. Processes requiring consistency and control across all customers—financial reporting, credit scoring, systems processing, and telecommunications—should be handled by the head office. Additional head office roles were to facilitate the sharing of best practices, the movement of key personnel, and the allocation of investment resources.

To shift processes to the field, RFS created "regional business centers." The business processes they managed for the retailer customers in their regions included training of retailer staff in systems and procedures, developing mailing and promotional programs with the retailers, providing management information for the retailers, and handling the whole range of customer service for cardholders, both through the mail and on the phone. The centers also managed credit risk—allowing better balance between how much to market and how much risk to allow. The key and single focus of these centers was to help retailer customers become more successful.

Setting up regional centers, however, was expensive. Ekedahl was under pressure to reduce costs by increasing productivity. Although the business was willing to invest in automated dialers and on-line information systems, new technology did not improve productivity enough to pay for the added cost of the centers. So the cost-cutting pressure led to a radically different way of organizing the regional business centers. As Ekedahl explains: "We originally came at it from a productivity point of view. We figured maybe we could save costs by not having so many management levels. So we asked a group of our associates how to do this. The exempt and the nonexempt people got together for a week and went way beyond what we had been expecting. They recommended that we organize around teams, with no managers whatsoever. I said, 'what the heck, let's try it,' So we did, starting with one business center in Danbury."

The dissolution of hierarchical boundaries within the business centers represented a fundamental revolution. And as in any revolution, there were casualties—managers who could not adjust, supervisors who were no longer needed, and in particular, frontline associates who were not willing or able to handle increased accountability. For the first few years, an abiding issue in several centers was a high level of associate turnover. Ekedahl and his team learned it was not easy to find employees who were able to function effectively as team players without supervision and with high degrees of responsibility. Despite careful screening and orientation, many still opted out after less than a year.

Eventually, by involving everyone in the center in a dialogue helped along by a few outside experts in team processes, a pattern for success emerged. Teams were set up to service all the needs of one large or several small retailers and the retailers' customers. All team members were cross-trained in all the skills needed to provide effective service, including handling billing problems and collections, changing credit lines, and changing customer data. The more senior or experienced people (in most cases, former supervisors) became roving trainers, documenters of procedures, and problem solvers.

Gradually, the teams learned to police their own performance against an agreed-upon set of goals, setting up performance improvement programs for team members not performing up to standard. The teams also had the authority to let people go if they did not improve after a certain period of time. The teams even began to hire their own members and provide basic training to get them up to speed. In essence, the teams were given all the same levels of authority as managers had held in the past.

The payoff from the first boundaryless business center was so great that Ekedahl and his team never seriously considered going back to the traditional vertical organization. Even with high levels of turnover, productivity was still many times greater and overall costs far lower. More importantly, the customers loved the service they were now getting from a dedicated team that knew the customers' business, their consumers, their systems, and their issues. They began to see the business teams as extensions of their own companies and not just as service providers. Equally important, over time, a core group of associates settled into each business center and made the centers exciting places to work. For those who could make it in the new organization, there was no way they would ever go back to the old way.

Given the success of the team process in existing business centers, Ekedahl decided that all new business centers should be set up in teams from the beginning. Thus, when RFS bought the Macy's credit card and servicing portfolio in 1991, the entirely new business center established to handle it was organized without managers from the start.

CROSSING GEOGRAPHIC BOUNDARIES

Until 1991, RFS was largely a U.S. business. With the acquisition of the credit card portfolio of Burton—a major U.K. retailer—in 1991, Ekedahl and his team were thrust into the management of a global business. At first, the former Burton organization was kept intact, reporting as one more business center into Stamford. Although there was an exchange of ideas and systems technology, for the most part the U.S. and U.K. centers were kept apart. To people in Stamford, Burton was interesting but not critical. That would soon change.

Two factors propelled RFS into a global role. First, its traditional domestic market for growth was full of uncertainties: retailers struggling and even going out of business, pressure to reduce credit card interest charges, and new credit card strategies, such as co-branded cards, emerging with still unclear results. Second, RFS recognized that the Burton processing capabilities were underused. If RFS took on new portfolios in Europe, they could be run through the Burton operations center with little incremental cost. By applying its world-class technology expertise, RFS could have a significant competitive advantage in Europe.

With these factors in the foreground, RFS began an acquisition binge to grow its European business. In less than two years, dozens of new retail customers were signed up, and whole portfolios were purchased from banks and other financial institutions. Suddenly, RFS had a major presence in Europe.

Now, the question was how to manage that new presence. Given its strategic importance, should it be closely managed from Stamford? Or should it be managed locally, from within Europe? Should its procedures and processes mirror the U.S. organization? Or should RFS Europe be allowed to develop its own way of doing things based on what worked in Europe and each individual country? And how should European and U.S. personnel interact—as representatives of different divisions or as members of a synergistic team?

Early in 1993, Ekedahl appointed Dave Nissen, a seasoned RFS manager who had previously run both the Private Label business and the MasterCard program, to oversee the European expansion. Ekedahl hoped that putting someone who was completely familiar with the U.S. operation in charge of the European acquisitions would result in combining the best thinking from the U.S. side with a deeper understanding of what worked in Europe. By the end of 1993, Ekedahl expanded this approach by appointing Nissen to head RFS International. Essentially, Nissen's charge was to create a European version of the RFS domestic operation—a series of regional business centers to serve specific clients (in their own languages), joined with a central processing facility (Burton) to achieve scale in operations. A small central staff, headquartered in Europe, would provide coordination, technical support, and the sharing of best practices from both Europe and the United States. Nissen also was to search for acquisitions in other parts of the world.

So, that, in broad outline, is the way RFS became a true boundaryless corporation, consciously evolving ways to function across all four boundaries with speed, flexibility, integration, and innovation.

Get Ready for Resistance

RFS journeyed successfully from the traditional structural paradigm to the boundaryless paradigm of the twenty-first century. But that journey took a full decade. At times, it was marked by internal pain, struggle, and doubt. And any organization that intends to become boundaryless must prepare itself for resistance, both from within and without. The trip is not easy, for many reasons.

To start with, for many organizational members and leaders, the mere thought of a boundaryless organization is terrifying. After all, boundaries *are* organizations; they define what's in and what's out; who controls and who has status. To change the nature of boundaries is akin to removing your own skin. So people feel threatened in a very fundamental, almost unconscious way.

Some related threats are more consciously felt. For example, much has been written over the years about middle managers' resistance to various employee empowerment efforts. In our view, such resistance is entirely rational and expected. After all, in most organizations, the core of the middle-management job has been to maintain the barriers between senior management strategy and direction and workers' implementation of that strategy. In this construction, middle managers have a series of vital roles: translating strategy into specific tasks, sequencing work, establishing measures of progress, controlling resources, and assessing performance. Workers generally do not interact directly with senior management and vice versa, except in ceremonial or other circumspect ways.

When senior managers talk about empowerment, middle managers see their roles as boundary controllers vanishing. If employees are given the authority to translate senior management strategy into decisions and to interact directly with senior managers, what is left for middle managers to do? While the reality is that new roles are available for middle managers, the replacement ratio is not one-to-one. Fewer middle managers are needed in the new roles. So the threat they face is not only loss of power but actual loss of their jobs.

Such threatened losses, real or imagined, exist throughout organizations when barriers become more permeable or are moved. For example:

◆ Specialists in functions may fear losing their technical edge if forced to spend much time as generalists in cross-functional team activities.
◆ Individuals from different nationalities or cultures may not want to team with one another or work for one another due to biases and stereotypes and the fears they generate.
◆ Individuals from different cultures may simply have trouble communicating, due not only to different languages but different ways of viewing the world.
◆ People at all levels may fear having to learn new rules of the game if traditional methods of advancement and career tracking change.

◆ Managers may fear embarrassment if information once typically hidden becomes shared with other levels.
◆ Former competitors within an organization or between organizations may find it difficult to learn how to collaborate.

In addition, there are two overriding psychological barriers to people's acceptance of the boundaryless organization. One function of boundaries is to supply protection, a sense of security. Boundaries can be like the solid walls around your house. If those walls became transparent and people could not only see through them but actually pass through them, your sense of security would vanish.

In an organization with permeable boundaries, not only is that kind of security missing but people also have no place to hide. Ineffective performance is highly visible, not just to a few people but to many. This fact can trigger enormous anxiety, especially in someone who feels (as we all do at times) somewhat unsure about his or her ability to do a job or learn new skills.

Given these threats to job, status, and security, it is no wonder that when organizational leaders attempt to make their boundaries more permeable, the organization's immune system is triggered. All kinds of resistance, overt and covert, begin to emerge. The following story is indicative.

Several years ago, a senior manager at what was then the American Can Company decided that the workers in a newly acquired machine-building plant should be reshaped into a "high-performance/high-involvement" workforce. Essentially, he wanted to create an organization with much more permeable vertical and horizontal boundaries. To do so, he brought in a new plant manager who "believed in empowerment," and as a gesture of goodwill to the workforce, he removed the time cards and put all workers on salary. He then instructed his staff to double the size of the plant, in the belief that this newly motivated workforce would become the core of his most productive machine-building site.

Within days of these actions, the forces of resistance went into play. Workers started objecting strenuously to the removal of their time cards, claiming that without punching in hours, they could not use overtime as a vehicle for earning extra money. When the new plant manager tried to convince them that the time clocks were removed because he "trusted them," they came to the conclusion that the new attitude was merely camouflage for cutting their salaries. While this debate was going on, headquarters staff arrived and began a thorough inventory of the machinery and personal tools in preparation for the expansion program. The presence of staff people counting their equipment further fueled the workers' mistrust of management. When the new plant manager tried to stop the inventory until he got things sorted out with the workforce, he found himself in a political power struggle with the corporate head of facilities and engineering. Eventually, the battle escalated to the senior manufacturing executive who had initiated the "model plant" and who was shocked to see his experiment founder so quickly. However, before he could resolve the issues between his staff colleagues and his new plant manager, the International Machinists Union instigated an organizing campaign that the corporate human resource function determined to fight.

Within months, what had started out as a promising, well-intentioned experiment meant to serve as a model for the corporation had gone down in flames. The new plant manager was gone, the workforce was alienated from management, and relations between corporate manufacturing and engineering were strained. The vertical and horizontal boundaries, far from becoming more permeable, had been reinforced. The immune system had done its work, surrounding and engulfing the "foreign body" of change before it could "infect" the rest of the organization.

The shift to permeability is fraught with such threats, barriers, and resistance. Later in this book, we provide specific tools to help leaders better identify and then overcome resistance and make the boundaryless organization a reality.

Making It Happen: Getting the Most from This Book

As the example of RFS illustrated, organizations can transform themselves. They can develop more permeable boundaries despite the immune response. And thanks to such pioneer organizations, such transformation no longer has to take a decade or be based on trial and error. Nor does it have to wait until external or environmental crises force the issue. Our accumulated experience in helping dozens of organizations, of all types, to journey toward boundarylessness has shown us there are effective tools and techniques for change. There are frameworks that can be applied, questions that can be asked, and lessons that can be learned. Using these tools, frameworks, questions, and lessons as they are described in the following chapters, managers become proactive, accelerating their progress toward the boundaryless paradigm for the twenty-first century.

To give readers the easiest access to these frameworks and tools, we have arranged *The Boundaryless Organization* into four major sections, each focused on one of the four types of organizational boundaries: vertical, horizontal, external, and geographic. Each section contains a pair of chapters. The first chapter in each pair explains the boundary in question, its origins, the problems it causes, the benefits of making it more permeable, and some of the immune responses that might kick in to prevent such a change. The second chapter of each pair presents specific action levers. These are tools and techniques organizational leaders can use to implement the shift toward the boundaryless paradigm and to overcome the immune responses resisting it.

Without doubt, much has been written about each of these boundaries individually, and many companies have experienced great success in permeating or loosening one or two of them. But few companies have been able to put together an entire package, to create permeability across all four boundaries. One of our purposes, then, is to show boundaryless transformation from an integrated perspective, one that deals with all four of the boundaries, so that leaders can complete their needed paradigm shift.

At the same time, we have made the practical assumption that different organizations and units within organizations are on different places on the paradigm shift continuum and that different strategies and tactics will be useful to them at different times. Thus, we do not advocate a frontal assault on all four boundaries at once, nor do we advocate a particular sequence of assaults. Each organization must determine how far it has evolved in permeating boundaries and assess where greater permeability will make the most impact most quickly. Organizations just setting out on their journeys may need to employ some very different strategies than organizations that have been traveling for some time. Similarly, organizations in different industries or facing different competitive threats may need to move relatively faster or farther along the continuum than others.

To help you manage these differences, we provide diagnostic instruments that assess where you are and where you want to be on the boundaryless continuum. To start with, your responses to the questionnaire at the end of this introductory chapter will give you an overall picture of where you stand in relation to each boundary and each of the new success factors. More specific questionnaires in each section assess your progress on permeating a particular boundary. In essence, this will allow you to view this book not as a how-to cookbook with a fixed menu, but as a self-paced learning guide. Through the self-assessments, you can set the pace, select the boundaries most in need of change in your organization, and determine which actions might be most useful in fostering that change. Of course, these brief, general instruments cannot provide you with a statistically valid measure of boundaryless behavior. In addition, your ratings themselves will be highly subjective, conditioned by your unique perspectives on your organization. A major purpose of each questionnaire is to stimulate discussion with your colleagues, both within and without your organization, and to help you select the actions that might have the most leverage for you.

A second assumption we make is that creating the boundaryless organization is, at its heart, a leadership challenge. It is more than applying a series of tools and techniques. The transformation of the traditional organization also requires the transformation of the traditional leader. Leaders of a boundaryless organization look and act differently than traditional managers. They spend their time differently; possess a different set of skills, beliefs, and attitudes; judge themselves differently; and view their careers in different ways. Chapter Ten talks about these transformational challenges explicitly, but our assumption throughout is that this paradigm shift requires driving leaders from the CEO to the first-line supervisors, leaders with the fire to make it happen.

A final assumption is that we need to share with you real cases and illustrations of organizations struggling with changes in boundaries. As much as possible, these cases are based on our personal experiences.

Whenever we can, we identify companies by name, with the understanding that we are reporting only parts of the overall company experience and that we are doing so through the filter of our own eyes.

As we described in the Preface, General Electric is the company that we cite most often and the breeding ground for many of our ideas. It is a diverse mixture of twelve separate businesses, each of which is a Fortune 100 company on its own. GE started explicitly on the boundaryless journey in 1988 and is further along than many other organizations, so it is a rich source of learning for others. As Chairman and CEO Jack Welch stated in his 1993 letter to shareholders: "Boundaryless behavior is the soul of today's GE. . . . People seem compelled to build layers and walls between themselves and others. . . . These walls cramp people, inhibit creativity, waste time, restrict vision, smother dreams, and above all, slow things down. . . . The challenge is to chip away at and eventually break down these walls and barriers, both among ourselves and between ourselves and the outside world."[2]

Our intent is to support organizational leaders as they chip away at their own boundaries successfully—so that more organizations can experience the speed, excitement, and energy of the boundaryless world.

The following questionnaire (Questionnaire #1) will gauge approximately how far your organization has evolved toward the boundaryless paradigm. More specifically, it will help you determine where you might most profitably concentrate your change efforts.

Questionnaire #1

Stepping Up to the Line: How Boundaryless Is Your Organization?

Instructions: The following sixteen statements describe the behavior of boundaryless organizations. Assess the extent to which each statement characterizes your current organization, circling a number from 1 (not true at all) to 5 (very true).

	Speed	Flexibility	Integration	Innovation	Total Score
Vertical boundary	Most decisions are made on the spot by those closest to the work, and they are acted on in hours rather than weeks. 1 2 3 4 5	Managers at all levels routinely take on frontline responsibilities as well as broad strategic assignments. 1 2 3 4 5	Key problems are tackled by multilevel teams whose members operate with little regard to formal rank in the organization. 1 2 3 4 5	New ideas are screened and decided on without fancy overheads and multiple rounds of approvals. 1 2 3 4 5	
Horizontal boundary	New products or services are getting to market at an increasingly fast pace. 1 2 3 4 5	Resources quickly, frequently, and effortlessly shift between centers of expertise and operating units. 1 2 3 4 5	Routine work gets done through end-to-end process teams; other work is handled by project teams drawn from shared centers of experience. 1 2 3 4 5	Ad hoc teams representing various stakeholders spontaneously form to explore new ideas. 1 2 3 4 5	

External boundary	Customer requests, complaints, and needs are anticipated and responded to in real time. 1 2 3 4 5	Strategic resources and key managers are often "on loan" to customers and suppliers. 1 2 3 4 5	Supplier and customer reps are key players in teams tackling strategic initiatives. 1 2 3 4 5	Suppliers and customers are regular and prolific contributors of new product and process ideas. 1 2 3 4 5
Geographic boundary	Best practices are disseminated and leveraged quickly across country operations. 1 2 3 4 5	Business leaders rotate regularly between country operations. 1 2 3 4 5	There are standard product platforms, common practices, and shared centers of experience across countries. 1 2 3 4 5	New product ideas are evaluated for viability beyond the country where they emerged. 1 2 3 4 5
Total Score				

Questionnaire Scoring

After you have rated each statement, total your scores across the rows and down the columns. Each row and column score should be a number between 4 and 20.

Column scores represent your organization's relative achievement of the new success factors. A score of 12 or less on any one factor suggests significant work may be needed, especially if the factor will be critical in your industry or type of organization. A score of 16 or higher suggests your organization already has achieved significant strength in the factor. It will be important to build on that strength. Overall, your scores can help you and your colleagues begin to think about the overall urgency for change facing your organization.

Row scores represent your organization's relative success at achieving permeability of the four boundaries. Again, a score of 12 or less on any one boundary suggests an opportunity for significant improvement, and a score of 16 or higher probably indicates an area of strength.

Questionnaire Follow-Up

With these scores in hand, you may want to begin your reading with the section on the boundary where you find most urgency or opportunity for change. Or you may want begin with a section that covers your area of strength to find ways of building out from that success.

While you certainly can complete the questionnaire by yourself, you might find it valuable to ask others in your organization to complete it as well. It can then be the basis of a group discussion that will help you and your team develop a shared view of your organization and a more common understanding of changes that might be needed. Developing this common understanding is, in itself, one step toward becoming a boundaryless organization.

PART 1

Free Movement Up and Down

Crossing Vertical Boundaries

2

Toward a Healthy Hierarchy

Like Napoleon's troops who whiled away their time in Egypt by shooting at the Sphinx, organizational critics have always found the concept of hierarchy an easy target. Whether for economic, social, ideological, or political reasons, hierarchies have been blamed for all manner of organizational ills—slow decision making, isolation from customers, inequality in compensation, and more. Yet despite the barrage of criticism, hierarchies, like the Sphinx, have endured.

The purpose of this chapter is not to add to the chorus of critics who have proclaimed that hierarchical organizations are outmoded or dangerous or ineffective. In fact, our view is just the opposite—that hierarchies are necessary, inevitable, and desired fixtures for organizational life. As long as organizations have limited resources and contain multiple perspectives, there will be a need for some people to be leaders and make decisions for others.

33

Given that assumption, this chapter is not about how to eliminate hierarchies, but to make sure they function healthily in a boundaryless world. Therefore, we first explore briefly why hierarchies have continued to survive and thrive despite decades of criticism. Second, we identify the warning signs of unhealthy vertical boundaries, that is, boundaries not aligned with the new success factors discussed in Chapter One. Third, we describe four specific leverage points on which you can create permeable and healthy hierarchies. And finally, we warn you against seven myths about changing vertical boundaries. In Chapter Three, we provide a set of specific tools you can use to create a more healthy hierarchy for a boundaryless world.

The Persistent Vertical Organization

Like buildings with multiple floors, organizations are commonly thought of first and foremost as vertical structures. Managers are at the top and workers are at the bottom. Orders flow down the chain of command, and production takes place below. At the top is the head, and at the bottom are the hands. In between are multiple layers that translate orders, provide materials, measure output, make corrections, and report to the top on the final results.

Naturally, this is a simplistic and largely inaccurate picture of organizational life. Yet it is what most people imagine when they hear the word "organization," and it is reinforced by the language all of us in business use daily to describe organizations and their dynamics. We talk of "*headquarters*"—implying that it houses the brains of the organization; "managers" versus "workers"—suggesting that management and work are different things; "exempt" versus "nonexempt"—suggesting that workers fall into scaled categories; "rolling up the numbers"—indicating our belief that results need to be aggregated to be useful for those at the "top"; "superiors" and "subordinates"—suggesting that some people are of "higher" status or "better" than others; and "career ladders"—showing that we see successful careers as moving upward from rung to rung.

Our language reflects that we think of organizations largely in vertical terms. We do so because the concept of hierarchy (of an up-down arrangement) is an archetype for us, a first principle that underlies the way we think about the world. It is an almost primeval and unconscious sense of how things should be, perhaps stemming from the fact that we are born into families, which are, at least temporarily, hierarchies. We begin life helpless and dependent, and our parents have total authority and responsibility for our welfare. They control information, make decisions, and direct our actions. It is a natural order that makes our survival and growth possible. As our families grow, our experience with hierarchies is expanded. Older siblings are given authority over younger ones; in some extended families, grandparents or older relatives provide another layer of deference and are given the status of patriarch or matriarch.

A STRUCTURE THAT WORKS

Given the almost biological underpinning of hierarchy, it is no wonder that vertical organizations are so prevalent. It is difficult to find any organization that does not have some form of up-down structure in which some people have more authority than others to make decisions and set direction, some people direct others in how to do work, and rewards are based not only on contribution but also on vertical position.

Hierarchical organization is not only natural to us, it is also an effective tool for getting things done. The Bible informs us that one of the earliest instances of management consulting recommended it: Jethro, Moses' father-in-law, suggested that Moses set up a hierarchy of judges in order to govern the children of Israel in the wilderness.[1] In most societies, both Eastern and Western, religions are based on some form of vertical structure, with high priest, acolytes, attendants, and followers. The Catholic Church is the classic example. The Pope is the chief executive, representing the highest authority. Power flows down from him through multiple organizational levels (cardinals, bishops, priests, and lay people), each with a different name and degree of authority. Military organizations have long structured themselves with levels of power cascading down from generals to colonels to lieutenants to sergeants to privates. And almost all governments have relied on elected, appointed, or self-appointed "rulers" to provide leadership and direction through layers of officials and followers.

Our basic work units have been hierarchically organized for thousands of years, often using slave or conscripted labor supervised by taskmasters and "owners." Skilled workers organized themselves into hierarchical structures of apprentices, tradesmen, and master craftsmen.

Given this long history, the industrialists of the early twentieth century certainly did not invent the concept of hierarchy. They did, however, raise it to a new level of power and sophistication. The time and motion studies of Frederick Taylor and his development of the field of industrial engineering provided tools for harnessing newfound technologies and organizing work to maximize that technology. By breaking work into small components and creating vertically based controls to integrate the components "up the line," scientific management of work led to amazing gains in efficiency. In many cases, it did not just double or triple production but obtained tens or hundreds of times greater output.

The implementation of these concepts by industrialists such as Henry Ford, Andrew Carnegie, and John D. Rockefeller created what is commonly called the industrial revolution. Their ability to manage mass production and distribution of goods and services by building massive hierarchical organizations fueled an unprecedented period of worldwide economic growth and a rise in standards of living far beyond what had ever been achieved before.

Equally important, the application of scientific thinking to hierarchical organization led to the evolution of a management morality and the gradual reduction of personal abuse, nepotism, and corruption that was all too common in earlier incarnations of vertical organizations. The development of rules of behavior, legal mechanisms for the protection of workers, and workers' unions to counter the power of senior management all became commonplace. In short, the modern hierarchy was an unqualified success.

BUT CONTINUING CRITICISM, TOO

Despite hierarchies' proven effectiveness, they have always been subjects of criticism and intense debate. Frederick Taylor himself appeared before congressional committees in the early part of the twentieth century to explain scientific management to skeptical lawmakers who were concerned that too much power would be concentrated in the hands of industrial barons. In 1905, a prominent industrial engineer named H. Fitz John Porter wrote passionately that for organizations to be effective, managers and workers had to collaborate and workers' ideas had to be incorporated into managerial direction. Porter's view was the opposite of Taylor's. Taylor's studies led him to believe that workers should not take any initiative but just do their jobs the scientifically proven one best way. Porter's observations were markedly different:

> I have never failed to see a marked change come over the entire organization . . . as soon as the members felt they were accorded recognition as rational beings and to be consulted on matters of common interest. Generally, the rank and file of the working organization is considered in the same category as privates in an army; they are not supposed to think, but to do as someone above them has planned. The usual result, as might be expected, is that they do not use their brains for the benefit of the concern. . . . The operative, if encouraged to think, will soon effect great savings in the work at which he is more of an expert than anyone else who is not constantly engaged at it.[2]

The "industrial democracy" movement of the 1920s called for the creation of worker committees and councils and even worker representation on boards of directors. In a 1923 government report, eighty specific firms were cited as having formal mechanisms for management and employees to participate jointly in decisions.[3] Even President Woodrow Wilson supported the concept, saying: "the genuine democratization of industry [is] based upon a full recognition of the right of those who work, in whatever rank, to participate in some organic way in every decision which directly affects their welfare or the part they are to play in industry."[4]

In the 1930s, the now famous Hawthorne experiments, led by Harvard professor Elton Mayo at the Chicago Hawthorne Plant of Western Electric, proved that workers' productivity increased dramatically when management paid attention to them and did not treat them like cogs in a machine.[5] But the Depression of the thirties and the subsequent world war prevented most mainstream Western management from paying much attention to Mayo's findings. Instead, the strict vertical hierarchy prevailed as organizations focused on maximizing production through massive assembly lines and top-down direction.

After World War II, criticism of vertical hierarchies resurfaced as people began to look beyond production to quality of work life and the ability of workers to feel greater personal fulfillment on the job. The clearest expression of this movement was voiced by Douglas McGregor, an MIT professor who made the now classic differentiation between Theory X and Theory Y management. Theory X, of course, was management through the traditional vertical hierarchy with power concentrated at the top. It was based on the assumption that average people worked as little as possible and were mostly concerned with their own well-being. Therefore, the job of management was to counter these worker tendencies with clear organizational direction and firm control. Theory Y was a much more benign system in which managers consulted workers and took their views and needs into consideration. It was based on the assumption that people want to do a good job both for themselves and for the larger organization. In other words, Theory Y offered a much more permeable structure than Theory X. Ideas, information, and even rewards flowed more freely up and down the organization. In McGregor's view, the more permeable organization was far more conducive both to productivity and to employee satisfaction, and he declared that "the essential task of management is to arrange organizational conditions and methods of operation so that people can achieve their own goals best by directing their own efforts toward organizational objectives. This is a process primarily of creating opportunities, releasing potential, removing obstacles, encouraging growth, providing guidance."[6]

But while McGregor and other human relations theorists received a great deal of attention, the basic vertical structure of most organizations remained unchanged—largely because it continued to work.

Since McGregor, an almost unrelenting chorus of critics has continued to rail against the evils of hierarchy: the pecking order of positions, titles, and reporting relationships based on rank rather than on competence; the internal competition for power, influence, and rewards; the slow pace of decision making; the senior management that is out of touch with day-to-day happenings in the field; and the focus on internal issues and requirements rather than customer needs.

In response to these criticisms, a steady stream of organizational change programs has taken aim at breaking down vertical boundaries and hierarchical distinctions in organizations. Every generation trumpets anew the discovery that a magical alternative is just around the corner. Compare these two declarations, for example:

> There are at lease four relevant threats to bureaucracy: (1) rapid and unexpected change; (2) growth in size; and (3) complexity of modern technology. . . . A fourth factor is a new concept of power, based on collaboration and reason, which replaces a model of power based on coercion and threat.

> As the power of position continues to erode, corporate leaders are going to resemble not so much captains of ships as candidates running for office. . . . Call it whatever you like: Post-heroic leadership, servant leadership, distributed leadership or, to suggest a tag, virtual leadership. . . . It's real, it's radical, and it's challenging the very definition of corporate leadership for the 21st Century.

The first statement was written in the mid sixties by the well-known professor of organizational development Warren Bennis.[7] The second statement, predicting the very same demise of hierarchical leadership, appeared in *Fortune* magazine in 1994[8]—almost thirty years later.

Yet hierarchical organizations persist. All the dire predictions about their coming death have not come close to being realized. And as long as hierarchies have their roots in family life, form the basis of most human social structures, and continue to work, they will have immense staying power. We suggest it is time to stop trying to eliminate them or pretending they will somehow go away. Instead, we propose asking a new question about them.

Reframing the Debate

In our view, the question that should concern companies today is not how to eliminate hierarchies but how to have healthy hierarchies, structures that meet the success requirements of organizations for the twenty-first century: speed, flexibility, innovation, and integration.

Most organizations today have hierarchies designed around the old success factors of size, role clarity, specialization, and control. It is these hierarchies that have become dysfunctional in a world of exponentially accelerating rates of change. For example, few people realize that the first developers of the personal computer were not Apple's Steve Jobs and Steve Wozniak but researchers from Xerox Corporation's Palo Alto Research Center who developed their PC, the Alto, in 1973, a full three years before Apple's first product. They were unable, however, to sell their idea up the chain of command. Since their idea was not about copiers, the company's mainstream product, it received little attention and funding from the hierarchical powers that be. Frustrated by the vertical barriers to going forward, many of the key developers left Xerox, taking their technology with them. Some joined the less hierarchical start-up company that became Apple.[9]

A rigid hierarchical structure also worked against Chase Manhattan Bank in the late 1980s. At a time when profits from commercial real-estate loans were booming, a small team of lower-level finance people was analyzing bank profits from commercial real estate over the previous forty years. Team members concluded that Chase had actually made very little money in real-estate lending because profits were almost always canceled out by subsequent loss cycles. Their recommendation was to cut back lending and focus the business more on investment banking. The team tried to present its findings and recommendations up the chain of command, both in finance and in real-estate lending but to no avail. In reality, the findings threatened the profits and bonuses of the senior managers and thus were never seriously considered. Yet within two years, the bank was reeling from the downturn in the commercial real-estate market, and the responsible senior managers all either left the bank or were reassigned.

Warning Signs in Unhealthy Hierarchies

Almost all organizations, large and small, have similar stories of innovation or change slowed down by too many approvals, of wrong decisions made because data from lower levels were not considered, of otherwise well-meaning and motivated employees disheartened by lack of response from superiors, or of people's personal incentives not matching what made sense for the organization. All these situations are warning signs, red flags signaling dysfunctional hierarchies. Here are other warning signs:

Slow response time. When an organization takes too long to make decisions, respond to customer requests, or react effectively to changes in market conditions, it is signaling its dysfunctional hierarchy. For example, when redesigning the core lending process of a quasi-governmental development bank, a team discovered dozens of review points in the process, each one generating a multitude of paperwork. The result was a process so cumbersome that the bank could not lend all of the money it had available for certain country development projects.

Rigidity toward change. When organizations continue to do things because "we've always done it this way," or spend more effort finding ways not to change than they spend on changing, it usually means that their vertical boundaries have become calcified. This was the case in a large pharmaceutical company unaccustomed to facing competitive and regulatory threats. In this new environment, senior management decided that research funding needed to be focused on a limited number of targeted disease categories where chances of success were greatest—a radical shift for a company where research funding had previously been almost unlimited. For months after that decision was made, however, more research energy went into justifying research than actually pursuing it.

Underground activity. Another sure sign of a dysfunctional hierarchy is that creativity and innovation are driven underground because people know that new ideas will receive adverse reactions. For example, although one large financial organization stressed innovation, very few requests for funding of new projects came to the senior management group. When asked why, a number of middle managers said the way to get things done was to keep new ideas "under the radar screen" until they were fully formed.

Internal frustration. Another sure sign of a dysfunctional hierarchy is that employees and managers feel dissatisfied with the organization, the way it works, and the way it treats them. They may feel that their contributions go unacknowledged or unrewarded or that managers in their chain of command do not care about them. Often, this indicates that people are not being listened to. In severe cases, it also can suggest that people do not feel a sense of equity in such areas as pay, promotions, and recognition. Such was the case in a large insurance company that was experiencing an unexpectedly high turnover of talented women middle managers. In interviews, it came out that a number of the middle-management women perceived that men in comparable jobs were paid more and had greater opportunities for promotion. When the human resource manager ran the numbers, he found this perception was borne out, to the great surprise of the male-dominated management team.

Customer alienation. A final warning sign is that customers feel frustrated and angry. The warning is especially acute when customers feel they are not listened to. Often, it is sales and service people who catch the brunt of this dissatisfaction, and when they are not able to respond immediately or must kick customer complaints up through the chain of command, they, too, get frustrated. For example, a specialty chemicals manufacturer shared the customer service people of a sister commodity chemicals group. The service people had strict instructions to respond only to requests for information about orders or to accept routine sales information, a system that was perfectly appropriate for a cost-driven commodity business. For the specialty business, however, the system was a disaster. Anything out of the ordinary—and in specialty chemicals almost everything is out of the ordinary—required a second, third, or fourth call to a more senior person who could expedite an order or put in a special request. Naturally, the customer response time was poor, morale among the customer service people was low, and the overall growth of the business was severely constrained.

Acting on the Warning Signs: Four Leverage Points for Loosening Vertical Boundaries

The presence of red flags like those described above usually indicates that an organization's vertical boundaries need some degree of loosening. The extent to which this should occur is a judgment call that depends on what is needed to meet the success requirements of a particular organization or situation. In other words, permeability of vertical boundaries must be thought of as a continuum, not an either/or duality. Gary Wendt, the CEO of GE Capital, drove home this point during a group discussion of how to speed up the approval cycle for a certain type of deal. He said: "We can speed up the cycle by not having an approval process—just let each person approve his or her own deals. But that would give us an unacceptable degree of risk. What we need to do is find the right balance so that we can approve deals quickly, but still feel confident that we've looked at all the different angles."

Finding the right balance of hierarchical looseness versus control is a central task of leadership in the boundaryless organization. Moreover, the balance must be struck on multiple dimensions. Think of adjusting the various component switches on a digital graphic equalizer, selecting the right levels of bass and treble for each kind of music you play. Similarly, in adjusting vertical boundaries, leaders will move "switches" from controlled to loose on four critical dimensions.[10]

◆ *Information* moves from information closely held or integrated at the top to open information sharing throughout the organization.
◆ *Competence* moves from leadership skills exercised at senior levels and technical skills exercised at lower levels to competencies distributed through all levels.
◆ *Authority* moves from decisions made only at the top to decisions made all along the line, at whatever points are appropriate.
◆ *Rewards* moves from rewards based on position to rewards and incentives based on accomplishment.

The following sections examine how each dimension can be adjusted for greater or lesser permeability.

INFORMATION: HOW MUCH SHOULD BE SHARED?

In a traditional hierarchy, information is funneled up the organization to those in power. Only at the top of the organizational pyramid is that information from lower levels collated, analyzed, and interpreted. Senior managers stay senior because they are the only ones with complete information, and that information gives them power. In the extreme case, this information is gathered through a system akin to a spy network in that no one but the very senior manager knows all the sources of information and can put all the pieces together. As in top secret government projects, each lower-level person works in his or her own area, unaware of others' areas or the end product.

The traditional tightly held information process is most effective for extremely confidential or sensitive issues. For example, planning for a major acquisition, merger, or stock offering or determining a significant personnel or organizational change often requires a closed, centralized, and highly controlled flow of information if the result is to be effective or harmful speculation prevented.

In a hierarchy with more permeable vertical boundaries, data and ideas are shared widely throughout the organization. Owing to this shared information, all employees have a common sense of purpose and an understanding of organizational goals. They are therefore more accepting of organizational directives. Understanding the *why*, they are more likely to accept the *what*. Shared information makes the boundaryless hierarchy like a hologram in that every part of it has all the attributes of the whole. Each employee or team of employees can set goals consistent with the overall organizational goals.

COMPETENCIES: WHO HAS SKILLS AND ABILITY?

In traditional hierarchies, the leadership competencies of knowledge, skill, and ability reside at the top of the organizational pyramid, and it is assumed that the leaders have the know-how to create a competitive corporation. At lower levels, people have more narrow technical skills, mostly directed to producing products or services. The implicit boundary assumption is that every player in the hierarchy has a clearly defined role and that senior managers are orchestrators of the multiple roles.

In hierarchies with loose boundaries, competencies reside throughout the organization. Regardless of title or position, when an individual has the skill to do a job, he or she is encouraged to pitch in and do it. The excuse that "it's not my job" does not exist. Thus, ability to act comes from skill, not just position, and actions are taken by trained and talented individuals wherever they are in the organization. People's competencies are also reinforced through training at all levels. Contrast this with the findings of Lee Dyer and his colleagues at Cornell that 80 percent of training budgets in traditional organizations was allocated for middle and senior managers and just 20 percent was spent on lower-level employees.[11]

In boundaryless hierarchies, not only is training given across all levels of the organization but its focus is more equivalent across levels. Traditional organizations give lower-level employees skills training while senior employees receive strategic education, but boundaryless organizations offer all employees similar strategic education. For example, training courses for new professional hires at General Electric examine career development and what it takes to succeed at GE. However, in the same course, senior managers are invited to talk about business conditions and business strategies. The reasoning is that all employees, even new ones, need to have a shared view of what it takes for the company to succeed.

Gaining competent employees throughout an organization results from more than training; it also comes from changes in staffing and recruiting philosophy. Rather than viewing employees as cogs that can be repaired or replaced, the organization with loosened vertical boundaries sees employees as the engine that drives the firm—perhaps the single most significant asset the company holds. Thinking about employees as long-term investments or capital assets forces firms to think about hiring practices, job rotation programs, developmental assignments, performance management, and a host of other human resource practices in a new light. In essence, the aim is to establish higher performance standards and then do everything possible to build capability, commitment, and retention among those who meet those standards.

This does not mean that traditional organizations do not have competent people. They do, but they deploy them differently. The contrast between a symphony orchestra and a jazz band illustrates the point. In the orchestra, the more traditional organization, all the musicians are talented. Each is an individual expert in his or her instrument. The conductor, then, has the responsibility to make sure all the musicians in the orchestra interpret the music in the same way. The orchestra succeeds when competencies are integrated and coordinated. The jazz band, the more contemporary organization, comprises talented individuals as well. Each plays his or her instrument with competence. But coordination does not occur through a central authority, rather it is shared among the band members. A jazz band is a boundaryless organization, with the musicians individually internalizing the feeling and mood of the music and then harmonizing their instruments with the others.

In the current world, the issue is not whether one prefers jazz or classical music. The issue is that a classical orchestra requires a fixed score, defined in advance. Only in prearranged solos is there room for improvisation or change. But for most organizations, the world in which fixed scores are needed scarcely exists anymore. Constant improvisation is the rule, not the exception, in today's rapidly changing environment.

Improvisation requires both the ability to act independently and a range of competencies. That is another reason why diffusing all kinds of competency throughout an organization is important. With the demand for increased speed in decision making, decisions typically need to be made on-site rather than through a hierarchy. Customers, in particular, are rarely willing to wait for a problem to be resolved, a price to be quoted, an inquiry to be answered. They expect to deal with competent, empowered employees on the front line.

AUTHORITY: WHO DECIDES WHAT?

In traditional hierarchies, decisions are made at the top, and lines of authority are clearly drawn to prescribe limits of signing authority and approvals. Decisions are made at senior levels because the information and certain competencies needed to make successful choices of action have been restricted to these levels.

In boundaryless hierarchies, decisions are made by the person who is closest to the issue and who has to live with the consequences of the decision. Authority is less a function of position or title and more a function of information and competence. As decision making moves down the organization, the distance between decision and implementation is shortened.

The traditional rationale for centralized decision-making processes was that the more individuals who reviewed a decision, the higher the quality of that decision. It was this logic that led to one case we found in which sixteen signatures were required for approval of a project. (The most senior manager even complained that there was no room left on the paper for his name.) The reality is that when numerous signatures are required for a project, the quality of decisions actually goes down. The first few who sign and approve the project may do so without investigating the details, assuming that later signers, having more authority and insight, will do the requisite serious analysis. However, if the project is approved by many lower-level managers, the senior managers assume that those closer to the work have done the serious analysis. So they sign perfunctorily, too. In the end, the project may never receive thorough analysis because no one "owns" the project decision. All the sign-off process has produced is wasted time. In one small study, we found that each approval signature took an average of five working days. So a sixteen-signature approval might take four months, and the quality of the decision might be less than if only three or four approvals were required.

Moving decision-making authority down the organization requires trust that employees at lower levels will make accurate, well-informed decisions. This trust is directly linked to the loosening of boundaries surrounding competence and information. Employees are more trustworthy when they have accurate information and are competent to make decisions.

Sometimes decision making creeps upward in an organization unintentionally. A senior executive will talk about a program or policy, and because the executive has power in the organization, others assume that such talk equals a decision.

A costly example of this occurred once at Cummins Engine. In the late 1960s, J. Irwin Miller was chairman of the company and also known to be a shareholder in a truck company that bought engines from Cummins. Once, Miller was shown a mock-up of an advertisement with pictures of trucks that had Cummins engines but were made by a different truck company. He approved the campaign but wrote in the margin, "Why this truck?" At considerable cost, all the ads were rephotographed using politically correct trucks. Miller later ruefully remarked, "I was just asking."

REWARDS: DO INCENTIVES MATCH GOALS?

In traditional hierarchies, rewards to people are carefully based on their vertical positions. In essence, such organizations pay jobs rather than people, typically using some sort of evaluation plan to assign points to jobs and giving positive weight to such factors as span of control, budgetary authority, and scope of responsibility. The result is huge discrepancies in compensation between senior managers and entry-level employees. In recent years, a number of studies have sought to compare the compensation of CEOs to that of new hires or to median pay rates within a firm. Most of these studies found huge differences between the compensation of American CEOs and that of low-level workers, with ratios of 50:1 not uncommon. A few critics of these studies have pointed out that attention has been over-focused on a relatively small number of highly visible corporate giants and that the situation is much less severe in firms with sales between one-half and one billion dollars.[12] Nevertheless, nearly all studies have concluded that the ratio of CEO to low-level employee compensation is much greater in the United States than in either Europe or Japan.

But that is only the perceived tip of the actual iceberg. In addition, high-level people receive other benefits: first-class or company plane travel, deferred compensation and stock options, use of company cars and preferred parking spaces, meetings in five-star resorts, larger offices, better furniture, personal secretaries, and more. So there is no real incentive for the lower-level employee to become the best programmer, financial analyst, or production worker. The incentive is to get the next job "up." When rewards are based on position, they send the message that what counts is vertical advancement up the hierarchy.

When rewards exist to recognize and encourage superior performance regardless of level, boundaries become more permeable and the hierarchy becomes healthier. People in healthy hierarchies are still motivated by money and/or power, but they can earn those rewards by being high performers and by managing important processes effectively. They can benefit from staying in one job and doing it well. They do not feel compelled to get promoted or moved, often to something they may do less competently.

People's desire to move up in traditional hierarchies often gets in the way of healthy organizational functioning. For example, in a large insurance company, one of the best claims examiners was promoted to supervisor. Basically an introvert who enjoyed detailed paperwork and could competently talk to people on the phone, this person did not relish dealing with people face to face. But the claims supervisor role required direct, competent interaction with other claims examiners, extensive discussions with irate customers, and presentations to more senior managers. These were areas where no amount of training would make this person comfortable. As a result, the person ignored training and coaching of the claims staff and gave customers short shrift, and the overall performance of the claims processing area suffered. The company had lost one of its best claims examiners and gained a terrible supervisor.

To an outsider, this kind of Peter principle promotion makes little sense. But if the logic of the corporation requires that rewards be based on vertical position, then the promotion of people ill-suited to their new jobs is almost inevitable. In a traditional organization, how else could this person have been rewarded for excellent performance other than by moving him up? If the company had not promoted him, showing recognition of his fine work as a claims examiner, the likelihood was that he would have become embittered, have started to perform poorly, or have left, requiring the company to spend money recruiting and training another examiner who might not be as capable. To further the dilemma, if the company had promoted someone who would do a very good job as a supervisor but who had not "earned" the promotion by being a high-performing examiner, the resulting perception of inequity would probably affect morale and job performance.

Moreover, most traditional hierarchies do not promote just production people to supervisors. The phenomenon of inappropriate promotion occurs at all levels, up to and including that of CEO.

Organizations' need for an alternative is growing exponentially. Delayered and downsized organizations have far fewer promotion opportunities than their predecessors. At the same time, the maturing of the post–World War II baby boomers has produced a sizable number of middle-aged employees, many of whom feel frustrated in their careers as they compete for ever-smaller numbers of executive positions.

To create healthy hierarchies, organizations must change the logic behind their rewards. In the boundaryless organization, rewards have two organizational objectives: to equitably recognize past performance (that is, to say thank you) and to stimulate and motivate people to perform competently or differently in the future. These objectives change the logic. Rather than paying jobs, so that people will be motivated to get the next job up, boundaryless organizations pay people for expanding their capabilities so as to make the maximum contribution to the organization. When people make a good contribution and add to their skills, they are rewarded; when they do not make a sufficient contribution and do not advance in competence, they are either not rewarded or rewarded to a much lesser degree than others.

With their pay systems that reward people for adding to their skills base and tie pay closely to performance, healthy hierarchies have more than superficial distinctions between high- and low-performing individuals. In addition, healthy hierarchies continue to reward people who remain in certain job categories as long as they continue to grow and contribute. They do not need to become supervisors or managers or to take on any other role for which they may have little inclination or ability simply for more pay.

The classic example of an organization in which employees succeed by being high performers rather than upwardly mobile ladder-climbers is the university. Educators come into the university as assistant professors and may receive one or two promotions during an entire career. Their rewards are tied to instructional quality as indicated by student evaluations or teaching awards, quality and quantity of research and publications, and election to professional associations, not primarily to moving along to more senior positions. Nor is title or rank singularly important. At most universities, every instructor, whether a junior or senior faculty member, is referred to as "professor."

Sticky Switches: Myths About Creating a Healthy Hierarchy

Even though there are only four principle switches that can be moved to shift an organization toward a healthy hierarchy, calibrating these switches is complex—especially when the "music" in the environment is constantly changing. Not only does each dimension need to be aligned properly with varying business and competitive needs but dimensions must also be coordinated with one another.

Yet many organizations ignore the complexity and attack hierarchical dysfunctions unsuccessfully through overly simplistic or unidimensional means. An examination of these attempts reveals seven common myths about how to permeate vertical boundaries and create healthy hierarchies.

Myth 1: Delayering creates healthy hierarchies. Many firms have downsized and claimed that they have vanquished vertical boundaries. This is like limiting scholarships for college football and then claiming you have changed the game. The number of scholarships limits the number of players, but it does not ensure that the game is played differently. Similarly, removing layers does not mean that vertical boundaries are loosened and that information, competence, decision making, and rewards are now spread through lower levels of the organization.

During the past decade, we have seen many prominent companies fall prey to this myth, thinking flattening their hierarchies would automatically change their organizational dynamics. It just isn't so. One of the most dramatic examples of acting on this myth occurred when GE Lighting acquired Hungary's Tungsram Ltd., Eastern Europe's largest lighting company, in 1989. Due to forty years of control by a government that guaranteed full employment, Tungsram was heavily overstaffed. When GE began removing layers of management, laying off thousands of people, it found that the old habits of hierarchical management engendered under communist rule remained. Tungsram had fewer layers, but much more was needed to make its hierarchy healthy.

Myth 2: Training creates healthy hierarchies. Some organizations spend enormous amounts of money training all employees. As a result, employees are more competent, but if they cannot apply that competence, they are not operating in a more effective hierarchy. Acquiring competence and using it are two separate matters. If employees want to act and are trained to act but then are not allowed to act—to make decisions with good information—they are highly likely to become frustrated.

This was the case at Chase Manhattan Bank in the mid 1980s. The bank's vice chairman had realized that traditional corporate lending was becoming less profitable and that the bank would need to shift from standard commercial bank products, such as loans, to more sophisticated investment banking products, such as trading, advisory services, and financial engineering. To accelerate this change, he insisted that every corporate lending professional go through a required curriculum of courses on various investment banking subjects. After spending millions of dollars on this training, the bank had many more relationship managers who understood investment banking products but who also had no information system to support the new products, had a measurement and reward system still geared to corporate lending, and had a decision-making process that required deals to be evaluated on the same credit-risk parameters as previously. In short, Chase bankers were all dressed up but with nowhere to go. It was not for another five years that changes on many of the other dimensions needed for Chase to succeed in the investment banking markets were put in place.

Myth 3: Shared decision making creates healthy hierarchies. One of the most widely used levers for organizational change is moving decision making to lower levels on the assumption that employees will automatically become more satisfied and empowered and overall decision making will speed up. The reality is that lowering decision-making levels, as a change by itself, may be more entrapment than empowerment.

Entrapment occurs when employees have responsibility to make decisions but no ability to make good ones. Think of a sixteen-year-old who receives a driver's license with her parents' permission. She has the authority to drive a car. If she gets into an accident, she will lose her driving privileges. Her parents neglect to train her adequately in how to drive, and she does have an accident. She is then blamed for the bad driving and her license is suspended. However, the problem here is not the new driver, but the parents. When her parents gave her permission but did not train her, they entrapped not empowered her.

  Likewise, in many organizations, managers are given authority to reach decisions, but they are not adequately trained to reach them. When empowered but untrained managers make poor decisions, it may not be their fault but the fault of those who gave them authority without ability. This was probably one of the underlying reasons that a number of commercial banks ended up with disastrous real-estate portfolios in the early 1990s. For example, at Ameritrust, an Ohio-based regional bank (since merged with Society Bank), lending officers had the authority to make deals but were given very little central guidance and few standards for acceptable deals. As a result, each lending officer used his or her own judgment and put the numbers together in ways that would make the deal look attractive. Later, when trying to clean up the portfolio, management realized that each lending officer was using different evaluation standards, which meant that the bank had *no* standards. Decision making was dispersed, but tools for making good decisions were not in place.

  In a similar vein, decision making and authority may be moved down into the organization without shared rewards and risks. Managers assume that employees will make effective decisions for the greater good alone, but simply desiring altruism and a sense of organizational interest among employees does not make it so. The invisible hand of self-interest is also at work. For example, if the Ameritrust bankers had been given their share of the real-estate lending profits over time, they would have had an incentive to reduce the medium and long-term lending risks. But because they were paid up front on the basis of production (volume of loans), their focus was almost exclusively on this short-term result.

  Myth 4: Sharing information creates healthy hierarchies. Giving employees more information without opportunity to act on the information is like telling someone he won the lottery but not telling him where to collect the money. Expectations rise, but when people cannot act on their expectations, they come to see information as a liability, not an asset. Similarly, without competence to act and authority to make decisions, employees are informed but not able to deliver.

  A classic example comes from analysis of the Challenger space shuttle disaster. In this case, employees of the key subcontractor, Morton Thiokol, as well as many NASA engineers, had extensive reports about potential O-ring failures in the shuttle engine assembly. But top management of the space agency had a deadline to meet and did not want to hear probable causes of delays. So the information was laundered as it went up the chain of command, being made to appear less threatening than it was. In short, having subordinates with information but no authority to act or competence to create decisions led to a disaster.

Myth 5: Broad sharing of rewards creates healthy hierarchies. A common organizational myth is that the way to employees' hearts is through their pocketbooks. If you give people enough money and recognition, the myth goes, then they will perform effectively and create a healthy hierarchy. The reality, however, is that rewards alone often encourage random or even counterproductive behavior. People also require competence, information, and appropriate authority to act.

There are two reasons why rewards alone are not enough. First, incentive structures are never crystal clear. They always have gray areas that require subjective judgment when performance is evaluated, no matter how many measures and standards and formulas are employed. In addition, employees usually have multiple paths for achieving the rewards. That is why commissioned sales representatives spend endless amounts of time studying their compensation plans. They are looking for new income-adding angles—perhaps they can push one product over another or trade off margin for volume or focus on after-sales services. If salespeople make these decisions without a thorough understanding of company strategy and the ability to execute in line with that strategy, their sales efforts may miss the mark. Often, each salesperson will aim at a different mark, which explains the huge variance in performance within most salesforces.

The second reason why rewards alone do not create healthy hierarchies is that individuals' satisfaction with rewards is a function of their subjective expectations, while the rewards reflect objective measures of success. Without widely shared information about company performance, people will often judge the appropriateness of their compensation against fantasies or incomplete pictures of how the company is really doing. Their judgment may then lead to dissatisfaction and low morale, no matter how much they get paid. For example, following the

Time Warner merger, the combined companies' operating performance continued to be very healthy. However, a series of events flowing from the merger forced Time Warner to cut back on its stock options grant practice for a couple of years. This move left many executives and managers feeling they would have been better off without a merger.

Myth 6: All employees want to be empowered in the healthy hierarchy. A sixth myth that constrains the development of healthy hierarchies is that all employees want to be uniformly empowered, unleashed, and liberated. Under this scenario, management simply needs to pass out information, authority, training, and rewards to everyone; let people loose; and good things will happen. It is not so simple.

People work in organizations for many reasons: to earn a paycheck, to get away from home, to contribute to society, to make friends, to master particular skills, to get recognition, and the like. Some people even come to work because they enjoy being told what to do, or they feel most secure in a structured, well-ordered environment, or they get satisfaction out of doing one thing well, over and over. In other words, not all people want to be empowered to make their own decisions, and assuming they do can create dysfunction.

The American Can Company plant mentioned in Chapter One is a classic example of managers acting on the empowerment myth. In that case, senior management pulled out time clocks unilaterally, assuming that the workers would want the freedom to come in late or leave early as long as they accomplished their work for the day. Many workers, however, did not want that freedom—they wanted the structure inherent in clocking in and out, and they wanted to know that if they spontaneously took a day off to go hunting, they would be docked for it instead of having to make up the work the next day.

In a world with either unlimited resources or unlimited cooperation, vertical hierarchies would not be needed. Everyone would agree on how to use machines, apply skills, sell products, and allocate rewards. But in the real world, people need leaders to break ties, resolve conflicts, allot resources, and make decisions about how to proceed. At every level, people need to know who is in charge, who represents them, who speaks for them to the rest of the organization and to the outside world. Although much of that leadership can be shared and distributed, and everyone can contribute to it, it still must exist. The assumption that it is not needed produces either anarchy (everyone decides what to do on his or her own) or a sense of resentment ("Why doesn't someone make decisions around here?"). Anarchy and resentment do not reflect a healthy hierarchy. The assumption that leadership is not needed is akin to what Randall Tobias, the CEO of Eli Lilly & Company, calls "anarchic empowerment"—an abnegation of leadership rather than a mobilization of organizational resources.

Myth 7: Middle managers resist healthy hierarchies because they will lose power. The final myth is a misdiagnosis of middle managers' resistance to loosening vertical boundaries. The common wisdom is that middle managers do not want to strengthen competence and share information, decisions, and rewards because they will then lose power and status. To a degree, this is true—if power and rewards are still being distributed according to hierarchical position. But if the power and reward structure is aligned with performance and skills, as suggested above, why do middle managers still resist?

In this situation, the issue for middle managers is less what they have to give up (power and authority) and more what they have to learn how to do differently. A healthy hierarchy, with shared information and authority, requires a completely new role of the middle manager. Instead of controlling, directing, evaluating, and ordering, the middle manager must facilitate, coach and counsel, mentor, translate strategies into goals, and design processes for joint assessment. The resistance comes from the fear—often well-founded—of not being able to make the role transition.

A prime example of this dynamic occurred a number of years ago at a small university in Los Angeles where a senior university officer wanted help in making his team "more innovative." After observing a meeting between this officer and his people, one of the authors suggested to the manager that he learn some new behaviors and skills in order to stimulate his people to come up with creative answers. Currently, he was just tossing out a problem and waiting for a solution, and that was not working, especially since his people assumed that he knew the answer already. The officer replied, "That's the same thing the last consultant told me—and I fired him too, just like I'm firing you." This middle manager was intellectually willing to share power, to hear other people's creative inputs, but he was unwilling to retool himself to make that sharing possible.

Getting Started: How Healthy Is Your Hierarchy?

When organizations avoid the seven myths and calibrate the four dimensions of vertical boundaries correctly, matching the calibration to the external requirements for success, they can create powerful, effective, and healthy boundaryless hierarchies. As we have discussed in this chapter, the boundaryless hierarchy is not an oxymoron—an inherently contradictory condition. Hierarchies are necessary because leaders are necessary to resolve conflicts, allocate resources, set direction, and represent the organization to the outside world. But today's healthy hierarchies have an appropriate two-way flow of information, widely distributed competencies, authority to act settled close to where decisions need to be made, and rewards that reinforce performance. When these conditions are met, to the appropriate degrees, organizations can realize significant gains in speed, flexibility, integration, and innovation.

An example of an organization that met these conditions effectively is the St. Louis branch of the Farm Credit Bank. When Farm Credit got into trouble because its loan portfolio was greater than the value of the farmland on which the loans were based, the St. Louis branch did not blame the loan agents but instead gave them what they needed to work in the best interests of both the bank and their customers. They were given detailed information about the status of each farmer's loan, so that they could stay in constant contact with their customers and work with them to meet the obligations. They were also trained to work with the customers in a cooperative way in crises, to get both the bank and the farmer out of the difficult situation. In addition, agents were given the authority to devise individual plans to help each farmer work his or her way out of financial trouble. If they felt that foreclosure was the only option, they also had the authority to do that. Finally, agents were rewarded not only by how quickly they resolved property loan issues but also by their relationships with the farmers. As a measure of agent performance, customers completed surveys rating loan agent fairness and attitude. After taking these steps, the bank discovered that farmer morale around St. Louis was much better than in the bank's other markets. Through the move to a healthy hierarchy, the St. Louis branch had not only managed the short-term crisis but had also built relationships for future business.[13]

Similarly, at Merrill Lynch, financial "consultants" are given the autonomy and the tools to work in their clients' best interests. The tools include information about all the investing instruments they can use and data about each client's various investments and investing priorities. The consultants also have the authority to make investments on behalf of clients wherever they deem appropriate given clients' financial goals; they are not restricted to investing in Merrill Lynch funds. Training and certification programs ensure that the consultants are skilled. And their rewards are tied to client satisfaction as measured by frequent mail surveys. Previously, Merrill Lynch clients had to meet with several experts, specialists in insurance, bonds, mutual funds, pensions, and stocks. No one person was responsible for integrating financial information and helping each client make decisions. By giving financial consultants all four elements of the healthy hierarchy, Merrill Lynch better serves its clients and the organization functions more effectively.

Your organization, too, may have opportunities to strengthen performance, making its vertical boundaries more permeable through recalibrating the four dimensions of a healthy hierarchy. In the next chapter, we will outline a number of specific action steps you can use to move in this direction. We also define some overall principles for creating an action strategy for the healthy hierarchy. Before you begin that chapter, however, we recommend that you assess the health of your hierarchy today and where it needs to change if you are to better meet the success criteria most important to you.

The following diagnostic instrument (Questionnaire #2) will give you a baseline snapshot of your organization and its hierarchy. Use the first two sections to assess the extent to which your company needs to be driven by the new paradigm success factors and to consider how often the warning signs of dysfunctional hierarchy appear in your organization or unit. The third section allows you to assess your current vertical boundaries against the four dimensions of the healthy hierarchy in order to produce an organizational profile.

Questionnaire #2

Stepping Up to the Line: How Healthy Is Your Organization's Hierarchy?

Part 1: Success Factors

Instructions: Determine how critical the four new paradigm success factors are in your organization, circling High, Medium, or Low for each factor.

1. Speed	High	Medium	Low
2. Flexibility	High	Medium	Low
3. Integration	High	Medium	Low
4. Innovation	High	Medium	Low

Part 2: Red Flags

Instructions: Evaluate how often the following five danger signs appear in your organization, circling a number from 1 (too often) to 10 (seldom).

	Too often				Sometimes				Seldom	
1. Slow response time	1	2	3	4	5	6	7	8	9	10
2. Rigidity to change	1	2	3	4	5	6	7	8	9	10
3. Underground activity	1	2	3	4	5	6	7	8	9	10
4. Internal employee frustration	1	2	3	4	5	6	7	8	9	10
5. Customer alienation	1	2	3	4	5	6	7	8	9	10

Part 3: Profile of Vertical Boundaries

Instructions: Assess where your company stands today on the four dimensions of information, authority, competence, and rewards, circling a number from 1 (traditional) to 10 (healthy).

	Traditional Hierarchy										Healthy Hierarchy
Information closely held at top.	1	2	3	4	5	6	7	8	9	10	Information widely shared.
Authority to make decisions centralized at top.	1	2	3	4	5	6	7	8	9	10	Authority to make decisions distributed to wherever appropriate.
Competence specialized and focused—people do one job.	1	2	3	4	5	6	7	8	9	10	Competence widespread— people do multiple tasks as needed.
Rewards based on position.	1	2	3	4	5	6	7	8	9	10	Rewards based on skills and accomplishments.

Questionnaire Follow-Up

We suggest that you complete the questionnaire by yourself first. Then ask a group of colleagues to complete it. In a group forum, compare your answers and discuss the following questions:

- How important is it to our organization's success that we loosen our vertical boundaries? In other words, do we really need to operate faster and more flexibly?
- Are the red flags serious and recurrent? Which ones are most worrisome?
- To what extent is our current vertical profile dragging us down and causing us problems?
- In the current profile of our hierarchy, which dimensions are strongest? Where do we most need to change in order to be more successful?
- What is our desired profile of vertical boundaries? Where would we like to be on each of the four dimensions in the next year or two—that is, what profile do we need to compete successfully now and into the future?

3
Rewiring and Retuning the Hierarchy

In Chapter Two, we described how the loosening of vertical boundaries on four dimensions can create a more healthy hierarchy, that is, a process of authority and decision making that better meets the new success criteria of speed, flexibility, integration, and innovation. Our goal in this chapter is to provide practical guidance for those who want to loosen their own vertical boundaries while avoiding the myths we reviewed in the previous chapter.

One of our underlying premises is that creating a healthy hierarchy is an organic process—the organizational equivalent to a personal fitness plan. As in the fitness plan, success does not come from a succession of fad diets and exercise-of-the-month programs. Rather, leaders must implement a systemic process, sustained over time, that puts the various change activities together properly. We will describe two sets of actions for creating a healthy hierarchy through a systemic process: these action sets are wiring the system and tuning the system.

Wiring the system involves putting in place components such as management commitment and alignment between organizational structure and business strategy that are prerequisites for permeable vertical boundaries. A fine music system requires speakers, a receiver, a tuner, a CD player, a tape deck, an equalizer, and an antenna all wired together in the right way—otherwise, no amount of electricity or digital input will produce audio output, that is, music. In just the same way, an organization requires key components to be wired together and integrated—otherwise, no amount of delayering, empowering, profit sharing, or training will produce a truly healthy hierarchy.

Wiring the system, however, is only half the job. In a music system, music is not an inevitable outcome of stringing the electronic components together properly. The sound produced may still be discordant, too loud, full of static, or inappropriately configured for the size of the room. Only a system tuned and calibrated to the needs of the moment produces wonderful music. In organizations, too, once the components are in place, they need constant tuning—especially along the four dimensions described in Chapter Two: information, competence, authority, and rewards. Without such tuning, organizations are likely to succumb to one or more of the seven myths, resulting in further calcification of the vertical boundaries.

Although this wiring and tuning sound straightforward, we have seen all too many instances in which organizations failed because they did not concentrate on *both*. For example, we have seen many managers focus effectively on wiring by writing mission and vision statements that extol the virtues of employee involvement, participative management, empowerment, and other healthy hierarchy initiatives. They put a key component in place—conceptual alignment between business strategy and organizational structure. But these mission statements become fodder for cynicism when employees do not see any tuning, any actions that bring the practices to life.

Conversely, we also have seen managers grasp at current fads and so-called cutting-edge management practices, such as quality circles or delayering, because they learned about them from "best-practice" companies. They start out with the tuning and give little thought to the wiring, the choice of components to be tuned. Their actions are parachuted into the organization, and the effect is short lived at best. Again, the result may be greater rigidity in the vertical boundaries than before.

We believe that to loosen vertical boundaries, managers need to engage both in wiring, to provide the framework for the long term, and tuning, to generate momentum for the short term. Thus, we describe first a set of wiring steps on which healthy hierarchies are built. Then we review the four dimensions of information, competence, authority, and rewards in order to suggest specific activities managers can use as digital switches to tune these dimensions to their situations. Our goal is to give you enough information so that you can put together your own plan for loosening your organization's vertical boundaries.

Wiring the Components for Vertical Boundary Change

Much has been written about the fact that many organizations invest considerable resources in seemingly powerful organizational change programs and are then disappointed in the meager or even counterproductive results.[1] One major reason for these failures is that managers often skip the process of wiring the system.

All four of the components shown in the box below need to be wired together to loosen vertical boundaries within an organization.

System Components for Loosening Vertical Boundaries

- Align healthy hierarchy concepts with business strategy.
- Develop a sustained and visible management commitment through constant actions, big and small.
- Take a cumulative approach.
- Develop a shared mindset.

ALIGN HEALTHY HIERARCHY CONCEPTS WITH BUSINESS STRATEGY

For concepts like empowerment, involvement, participation, and joint problem solving to be more than slogans, there must be alignment between business strategy and change efforts to implement these concepts. In particular, organizational members must view change efforts as critical means of reaching business ends—not just "nice to have" principles that make everyone feel good.

This alignment means that the actual practices for creating and maintaining healthy hierarchies must be critical to the day-to-day accomplishment of the business's goals, that managers must connect activities that dismantle rigid hierarchies to business results, and that such initiatives as employee involvement, participative management, empowerment, or reengineering must affect strategy and not be just ends in themselves.

Without such alignment, executives may talk about reengineering, reinventing, or redesigning their organizations, but coordinated actions do not follow. Instead, managers see a bifurcation between organizational change activities and working on business goals. Faced with a choice, they almost always will focus on the business goals (appropriately so) and forgo the "softer" issues of loosening vertical boundaries.

For example, a large firm in a changing industry went through an elaborate strategic planning process using this framework:

Vision:	The future
Mission:	The focus
Goals and measures:	The goals
Companywide strategies and competitive advantages:	The foundation
Portfolio strategies:	The business mix
Strategic plans:	The actions

After spending enormous effort completing this six-step planning process, senior management put together a few quick thoughts about "organizational effectiveness" but made no changes in the organization to align these thoughts with the strategy. To some extent, they assumed that the organization would align itself. The organization ended up with a well-conceived strategy but no organizational infrastructure to sustain it.

Contrast to that situation the following vision and mission statements that do show an awareness of the issues critical to making vision happen: "To become a dynamic learning organization where people are enthusiastic partners in attaining organizational objectives" (Delco Chassis); "We are dedicated to being the world's best at bringing people together and giving them easy access to each other and to the information and services they want and need anytime, anywhere" (AT&T). These visions acknowledge that business results occur through healthy hierarchies.

A simple test of the alignment between strategy and vertical structure in your organization is to read your organization's mission statement and ask: Does it mention how the organization must act/behave in order to meet business objectives? If it does not, organizational practices may not be aligned to business goals.

To further discover the logic of alignment, answer these three simple questions:

1. *What are the future goals of our business?* Whatever framework you choose for articulating where your business is headed (vision, mission, strategic intent, aspiration, or foresight), the challenge is to paint an exciting picture of what the business needs to look like in the future in order to succeed—not only today but two or more years out. This picture should include markets served, financial objectives, products delivered, and technology required as well as the unique competitive advantages you might exploit.

2. *What capabilities will be required to meet our goals?*[2] Capability will be needed in both the processes and the people skills needed to accomplish the goals. For example, to reach financial goals, a firm must be capable not only in financial processes that cut across the entire organization—such as monitoring and controlling costs, squeezing inventories, and managing receivables—but also in its people—skilled financial analysts, cost accountants, auditors, and systems designers. And all these skilled people must have such general capabilities as dependability, predictability, speed, responsiveness, and ability to learn.

3. *What organizational initiatives will ensure that the capabilities are in place?* By viewing organizational initiatives in the context of building capability for the achievement of business strategies, organizations can avoid disconnected initiatives and management fads. They can connect the wires. Then, as new initiatives inevitably emerge in management's thinking, the ability to assess and implement them in an ongoing, integrated stream woven around capabilities ensures that the organization will change more effectively over time.

These three questions are tools for drawing an intellectual circuit blueprint of the way activities and business strategies and goals can be wired together.

DEVELOP A SUSTAINED AND VISIBLE MANAGEMENT COMMITMENT

In creating a healthy life-style, the critical challenge is to translate intention into action. Likewise, firms succeed in creating healthy hierarchies because they translate the concepts of vertical boundarylessness into specific behavior on the part of employees in each and every nook and cranny of the firm. When employees go home at the end of the day, they can articulate and specify how their work that day differed because of the healthy hierarchy initiatives. This should be particularly true for senior executives, since it is with them that commitment to action needs to start.

Consider the case of motorcycle manufacturer Harley-Davidson. If you were to ask any Harley employee what Chairman Richard Teerlink believes in, you would likely receive this answer: "Creating a competitive organization through people and processes centered on learning." This agenda is not new to Teerlink. It has been a theme of his professional career. But as chairman, he has sustained this message for over ten years while dealing with a multitude of diverse business issues such as building the Harley Owners Group, diversifying into Holiday Rambler, increasing manufacturing quality, and transplanting the U.S. bike philosophy to Europe and Asia. He has kept to his agenda by consistently (like a "scratched record") challenging his management team to answer the same set of questions no matter what the specific issue: "What have we learned?" "What will be the impact on our people?" "How can we get everyone involved and excited?" By holding to his underlying theme in the face of every business initiative, he has built a long-term commitment to healthy hierarchy activities.

Another example comes from the first few years of the GE cultural transformation, started in late 1988, which met with initial skepticism among many employees. In one workshop, a twenty-year employee privately remarked, "This culture change effort will be another of a long stream of corporate initiatives that go away over time." The employee questioned Chairman and CEO Jack Welch's commitment to recrafting the GE organization. Welch, however, carried out his commitment, not just through words but through actions. Right from the beginning, he devoted a significant portion of the agenda at every Corporate Executive Council meeting to the transformation. In essence, he insisted that each of his business leaders report regularly, both to him and to the leader's peers, about change activities and accomplishments. In addition, Welch devoted significant portions of his own time to talking with groups of employees, particularly those in training, about the change and how it was going. He constantly passed on the employees' responses to his business leaders, often through handwritten notes. Finally, three years into the effort, Welch made it clear that he expected his senior team to not only produce business results but also to "demonstrate the values" of the new GE. And he dramatically removed several leaders who were getting results but in the old GE style. Now, more than five years later, few employees question Jack Welch's commitment to sustained cultural change.

Senior managers, however, are not the only ones who need to act. Wiring the right components together requires many actions, many of them mini-steps, at every level. In the final analysis, it is the encouragement of the mini-steps by managers throughout the organization that perhaps makes the most difference. For example:

◆ Every supervisor can spend a portion of his or her staff meeting asking for employee advice on how to do work more effectively. While this may sound trite, it works—the resulting dialogue gives employees a powerful signal that it is all right to voice opinions and suggestions.

◆ Managers can make frequent and informal visits to plants and operations where they can encourage employees to come forward with ideas for improving work. Managers' walk-arounds can bring them face to face with employees and their problems.

◆ Managers can hold all-plant, all-department, or all-employee meetings to share information and lead to action.

◆ Organizations can form process improvement teams to work in areas that affect team members. Executives can personally commit to dedicate significant time each month to hear and respond to team reports and recommendations.

◆ Managers can get quick results in work improvement with simple but realistic suggestion systems. Employees must be assured that management will respond to ideas within seven days. When a cost-cutting idea is implemented, the employee gets a share of the savings.

◆ Managers can pull together quarterly summaries of new ideas and practices implemented within their groups and use these documents to build awareness among employees and to share ideas with other managers.

William S. Stavropoulos, president and COO of Dow Chemical, is one executive who has acted on the premise that multiple actions at multiple levels demonstrate management commitment. When Stavropoulos ended his November 1993 meeting with the top two hundred managers of Dow, he knew that he had conveyed the essence of Dow's needed business imperatives. He also knew that he had articulated as best he could the set of new managerial behaviors required to change the firm's culture and achieve its business goals. But he also knew that unless the two hundred managers could translate his ideas into their actions, he would be unsuccessful. As a result, he made "achieving the new culture" a priority by requiring every manager to take a series of specific actions: to present the Dow blueprint to his or her employees; to engage in a problem identification process to remove barriers to change in each work unit; and to do a multilevel feedback exercise in which all managers would receive feedback not only from their superiors but also from peers and subordinates. These actions made the creation of a healthy hierarchy as much a management priority as the business imperatives. As Stavropoulos put it: "If managers don't invest the people time, it is unlikely they will succeed. Leaders at all levels of the company must devote 20 to 30 percent of their time to people. . . . What will employees think if we don't spend enough time defining accountability and coaching—so they end up needing to constantly double-check things with us before taking action? In short, hell will freeze over before employees believe that we want to change this company."

TAKE A CUMULATIVE APPROACH

A corollary key to shifting healthy hierarchy initiatives from marginal to mainstream requires that managers see organizational initiatives as evolutionary not revolutionary. Management practices are *revolutionary* when each new management technique such as quality circles, continuous improvement, TQM, or reengineering is regarded as a redeemer of the previous practice, now regarded as antiquated and inept. Revolutionary management practices easily become fads to be tasted and tested, then rejected and renounced. Moreover, champions of different initiatives may end up competing against each other for management attention.

Management practices are *evolutionary* when new management initiatives are intended to add value to previous initiatives. From this point of view, quality circles helped employees learn to explore the importance of quality and teamwork, continuous improvement added a disciplined process to examine quality, TQM showed the importance of customer focus for quality, and reengineering showed the importance of improving work processes to ensure quality. Evolutionary practices encourage managers to sustain commitment to change over long periods.

No one practice makes a healthy hierarchy; rather, it is the cumulation of many practices that makes the impact. For example, Tony Larussa, manager for the Oakland A's baseball team, has devised a "law of accumulation."[3] Basically, it says that little things add up. So focus on them. In baseball, four base hits equal a run, three walks equal a run, three stolen bases equal a run, and three runs can equal a win. The more Larussa can dissect his goal of scoring more runs than the other team into subgoals and focus attention on each of those subgoals, the more little things he can add up, putting them together for success.

Likewise, no one practice will guarantee a healthy hierarchy, but the cumulation of lots of the right subgoals will make a healthy hierarchy happen.

DEVELOP A SHARED MINDSET

Nordstrom, a specialty retailer, has received enormously good marks for building a new form of management and governance in a dynamic and aggressive industry. At a time when many retailers were struggling, Nordstrom tripled its number of stores, raised its sales tenfold, and grew from a small regional firm in the Northwest to a national presence.

No one factor explains Nordstrom's success. The stores are easy for customers to access. Live piano music sets the tone. And the stores have exceptional inventory, particularly in shoes—some stores have over 100,000 pairs. However, if you ask any customer why he or she shops at Nordstrom, the answer will not refer merely to merchandise, inventory, or price. Generally, customer loyalty comes from the commitment shoppers feel from dedicated employees. Often called Nordies, Nordstrom employees are devoted to customer service and proud of service stories that have become legends: for example, the time when an employee graciously gave a customer credit for a returned set of automobile tires even though Nordstrom does not sell tires. Employees routinely accompany customers throughout a store to find accessories for outfits, locate desired merchandise in other Nordstrom stores, and accept return items unquestioningly.[4]

To make this level of service a reality, Nordstrom created a new form of governance. Store executives ensure employees' commitment to exceptional customer service not by inspecting employee behavior with many supervisors or phantom customers wandering the floor but by supporting a culture in which employee expectations of being able to deliver outstanding service are inviolate.

Traditional firms govern employees through direct observation. Their employees tend to do the right thing in the right way mostly because managers are available to visibly check on how employees behave. Healthy hierarchy firms govern employee behavior through shared mindsets. Layers of supervision can be removed when employees share the values and beliefs of the firm and choose to do the right thing in the right way.

Nordstrom has achieved its shared mindset through carefully screening applicants and hiring vivacious people who enjoy interacting with customers, through an incentive system that rewards customer loyalty, and through symbols of and constant communication about the company heros who command customer loyalty. Disney is another example of an organization in which employees are hired, trained, and constantly reinforced through communication and rewards in accordance with the aim of giving guests in the Disney park an exceptional experience.

You can test the degree to which a shared mindset is present in your organization with the following relatively simple but highly revealing six-step exercise:

1. Identify your organization's top team. (It may be the top managers' direct reports or their direct reports. It will generally consist of from ten to twenty people.)
2. Give each team member three 3 x 5 cards.
3. Ask each person to write one "top thing" per card in answer to the question: What are the top three things we want to be known for by our customers? (This information is critical to a shared mindset. It tells employees what customers should automatically think about the organization.)
4. Collect the 3 x 5 cards and sort them into clusters of common answers. (We have found it important to be strict in the sorting process and to put cards into different piles when their wording differs, even if some of the underlying meaning is similar.)
5. Determine the extent to which there is a shared mindset by counting the percentage of cards that fall in the top three clusters. (Our rule of thumb is that a shared mindset exists when 75 percent of the answers are in the top three clusters.)
6. Discuss the exercise results and what you want customers to know you for.

The mindset exercise may be done with an entire corporation or a business or function within the corporation. We predict that if Nordstrom executives did this exercise, the unity measure would probably be well into the 90 percent range. However, after running about thirty groups through the exercise, we have learned that (1) most management teams lack a shared mindset about what they want to be known for by customers; (2) a focus on a shared mindset for the outside (customers) helps unify the mindset inside (among the team); and (3) once the clusters found are shared with the group, the process of creating a shared mindset is relatively straightforward.

For example, in one company, we did this exercise with twenty-two of the top human resource executives. Only 45 percent of the cards ended up in the top three piles. However, after putting all the responses on the table and discussing the customer implications of each response, the team create a shared mindset for the HR function during a one-day workshop.

Tuning the System: Calibrating Four Dimensions to Permeate Vertical Boundaries

Wiring together the components of alignment, commitment through action, cumulation, and shared mindset results in the overall system needed to build a healthy hierarchy. Getting the system to produce music and not just noise, however, requires a great deal of tuning among the four dimensions of information, competence, authority, and rewards.

First, each dimension must be carefully tuned to meet specific operational and business requirements. Tuning any one dimension too much in one direction may cause only a minor distortion in results for a short time, while tuning the same dimension too far or too fast the other way may cause a major blowout. For example, driving more authority for complex customer decisions out to the field may increase speed, customer satisfaction, and short-term revenues; but if the field commits to products that manufacturing or distribution cannot deliver, then any gains will quickly sink in a sea of contention.

Second, the tuning of each dimension needs to be integrated with the tuning of the others; otherwise this can be like trying to work on a table with uneven legs: there is little stability. However, the notion that managers can create a healthy hierarchy by tuning single dimensions is, as we discussed earlier, a myth.

In the following sections, a number of tuning actions are suggested. However, they should not be considered as set recipes. Businesses are living organisms, and as such, they are moving targets. Managers may implement an action only to have the organization throw up its immune defense and prevent the action from working. Alternatively, people may understand an action's purpose, assimilate the action, and be ready to move on to the next action practically in the same breath. Therefore, these actions represent a menu of possibilities to be selected and integrated to fit your unique situation. Also, there are many good resources that can provide more detail on implementing the actions we suggest. Our purpose here is to define the parameters of the actions and goals that will loosen vertical boundaries, rather than to discuss details of day-to-day execution.

SHARING INFORMATION

In nearly every employee attitude survey, communication is listed as a problem. Employees generally feel they are not informed enough or are actually misinformed about organizational goals and initiatives. Without information, they know they cannot keep customers in the loop of product changes and development, service procedures, or pricing. They find it difficult to take empowered actions on their own or to feel they have a voice in the firm.

The five specific actions listed below are the ones we have found useful for sharing information effectively.

Actions for Effectively Sharing Information

- Align channel and message.
- Share good and bad news.
- Use both cognitive and emotive news.
- Make messages both complex and simple.
- Use information to encourage change.

Align Channel and Message

Many means, or channels, for sharing information exist. When the channel matches the message, communication is improved. For example, memos, videos, and policy statements are all important channels for factual information. However, one-on-one or small-group meetings are much more useful channels for information meant to help employees change behavior. Aligning the purpose and the medium allows managers to share information effectively, while misalignment produces communication failures. In one firm, managers held weekly staff "communication meetings" where each person described what he or she had done and would do that week. Although the information was useful, most staff members resented the time required when the same information could have been shared more efficiently through static media.

Figure 3.1 is an visual guide to alignment of purpose and channel. The shadowed section indicates whether a channel is most appropriate for sharing factual information or shaping behavior. For example, if the purpose of communication is primarily to share factual information, then bulletins, flyers, and videos can be used successfully. Federal Express, for example, produces daily videos of the previous day's performance to pass along information to all employees about work flow. Conversely, if a change in employee behavior is desired (for example, employees might need to be informed about a new performance assessment process), a memo is *not* the right way to communicate. Such changes require some personal contact that makes employees part of the change process.

Each organization needs to decide what formats are best for it—reflecting its own resources and information collection systems, and the level of frequency that makes sense for its people. For example, Honda distributes printed copies of its strategic plan to all employees. The Marriott Hotel chain's newsletters have a question-and-answer section from customers about excellent service. Microsoft created a "best-practice" database to share ideas across units about innovative work practices. Baxter Healthcare shares weekly information about cash flow to keep employee attention focused on financial results. Federal Express reports daily activity statistics to all employees to keep attention on customer commitment targets. The World Bank has an information "kiosk"

Figure 3.1. Aligning Communication.

How to Communicate	Purposes of Communication	
Channel	*Share Information*	*Shape Behavior*
Face-to-face (one-on-one)		
Symbolic (meeting, rally)		
Interactive media (telephone, voice mail, fax, e-mail)		
Personal static media (letter, memo, report)		
Impersonal static media (bulletin, flyer, newsletter, video)		

Aligned

on its shared electronic mail system so that critical information can be quickly distributed. Of course, whatever format is used, the distribution of information should be open and honest and more than lip-service.

Given the amount of information that may need to be shared, it is often worthwhile to consider creating a *communication plan* that identifies a year's worth of activities and shows your commitment to share information. If it identifies what information is to be shared, who it is to be shared with, when it is to be shared, and how it is to be shared, the plan can be a strong support for a healthy hierarchy.

For example, in a company making significant changes in its financial reporting system, managers employed the following four steps to build a communication plan.

First, they identified the message they wanted to share about the new system, concluding that the message had four parts: general background information, benefits of the new system, culture change required by the new system, and personal concerns and implications.

Second, they identified five audiences for the message: site leaders and project managers, senior managers, all system users, all employees affected by the system, and all external customers affected by the system.

Third, they planned to share the message over a twenty-month period broken into seven quarters. And fourth, they designated multiple tools for communicating the message.

The sum of their efforts was the chart in Figure 3.2. At first, this chart may seem overwhelming, an overspecification of the communication effort. However, using this plan, the company found that the new financial system received much less resistance than other changes had, that consistent messages about the new system pervaded all parts of the organization, and that the new system was implemented more quickly than had been thought possible.

Share Good and Bad News

Some managers focus on either good or bad news. Cheerleaders tell the good news, then employees are surprised by the bad. Pessimists harp on problems, and employees never hear the good news. Successful sharing of information has both ingredients. For example, Stephen Frangos, manager of the Kodak Black & White Film Division, has a practice of sharing all news with employees, realistically and without embellishment. When the division was struggling in the early 1990s, he told employees of the

Figure 3.2. Sample Communication and Training Plan.

Schedule for System-Roll-Out

Audience	4Q	1Q	2Q	3Q	4Q	1Q	2Q
	Design		Load & Test		Implement	Parallel Run/Test	
	(8 Months)		(5 Months)		(3 Months)	(4 Months)	
	All Groups (Fixed Schedule)				Implementation Group 1 (Shifts by Implementation Group)		
Group 1 Site leaders, project teams, developers							
Group 2 Senior management		D 1	A D 1/2/32	G A B M D L 2 1/2/3 4 4 4 4	G 2		
Group 3 All users					A	B M D L 1/2/34 4 4 4	
Group 4 All employees		P 1	C D P PN 1 1 1 1	P1 IP1 I/P 1122 3	HOKQKE 323343	OFH 233	J 4
Group 5 External customers	As required C D →	D 1			G 2		A BMD 1/2/3 444

Media Type:

A. Videotape

B. Interactive video

C. Talking points

D. Personal approach

E. Voicemail

F. Broadcast

G. Prototype

H. Brochure handed out with paychecks

I. Posters

J. Message printed on paycheck

K. Local (site) news

L. Promotional handouts

M. Documentation/manuals

N. Personal letter from executive

O. All-hands meetings, quarterly results

P. Newsletter

Q. Letter from local GMs

Message to Communicate:

1. General background information

2. Benefits

3. Culture change explanation

4. Personal concerns

declining market for black and white film. He taught them about profit margins, showed the sad story in their division, and did not hide the business challenges they faced. His theory was that every one of the division employees should know enough about the business aspects of the organization that he or she could talk knowledgeably to customers, people at corporate, or family about the business.

Frangos, however, also shared good news. He knew how to create celebrations—division dinners, reward programs, and other forums where employees who did great work were recognized.[5] As we show later, Frangos's efforts paid off.

Use Both Cognitive and Emotive News

When Tony Rucci was senior vice president of human resources at Baxter Healthcare,[6] he was respected for his cognitive abilities. Rucci, who has a Ph.D. in organizational psychology, could creatively realign and restructure the organization. He knew how to create models and frameworks. In many ways, he was the intellectual architect of the Baxter and American Hospital Supply merger in the 1980s and the Baxter global strategy in the 1990s. However, much of his success came when he shared with employees his personal experiences of having a father who worked in the coal mines, whose company abused him and other employees with bad policies, and who brought some of his organizational suffering into his home. When Rucci talked about policies and values, everyone knew not only his intellectual prowess but his emotional commitment to these policies. This combination gave him enormous credibility.

Many managers hesitate to share the emotional impacts of information with their people, perhaps assuming that mature adults handle everything rationally and logically. It is more realistic to assume that everyone in the workplace has emotions and that information, particularly about change, triggers those emotions. Sharing emotional as well as rational messages is important to increasing the permeability of vertical hierarchies.

Make Messages Both Complex and Simple

Information can be shared in both complex and simple ways. When Lawrence A. Bossidy became chief executive officer of AlliedSignal in 1991, he talked about "three P's": performance (meeting the numbers), portfolio (getting the right product mix), and people (attracting and motivating the employees). This simple message could be and was communicated to all employees. Since 1991, each year has brought another simple message from Bossidy about key priorities. For example, in 1994, the three priorities were performance, international operations (particularly Asia), and quality.

No one at AlliedSignal believes these simple messages are simple to implement. They require complex initiatives and actions. But in the midst of that complexity, AlliedSignal executives derive an exceedingly clear focus from the basic messages. That focus anchors their work and makes it easy to relate change to all levels of employees.

Other senior executives also have employed this simple-complex information strategy, with powerful results. GE's Jack Welch is well known for the simplicity of his transformational theme in the early 1990s: speed, simplicity, and self-confidence. In the midst of major organizational, strategic, process, and cultural changes, this theme gave thousands of employees a common framework for understanding the kind of organization GE aimed to be. Similarly, during the Chase Manhattan Bank turnaround in 1992 to 1993, then-President Arthur F. Ryan emphasized the theme of "One Chase" as a rallying cry for complex strategies of cross-selling, common systems, customer integration, and greater strategic focus.

Use Information to Encourage Change

In times of rapid change, sharing information widely is even more important than it is in less stressful situations to counter people's natural anxieties and fears of the unknown. Without extensive information, employees will grasp at rumors about what is or is not happening and may become preoccupied with them.

For example, in an insurance firm undergoing a change to account management from geographic management, rumors were rampant that the company would divest some businesses, fire many managers, and completely transform itself. Because management did not use comprehensive strategies for sharing factual information, the rumors created employee anxiety beyond reason, and employees did not accept and effectively implement the new direction, thinking erroneously that more changes were to come.

In contrast, when one of drugmaker SmithKline Beecham's R&D management teams set out to change clinical data operations from a functional to a team organization in the United States and the U.K., it included a number of creative communication mechanisms in its plan. First, in both countries, the management team held a series of all-hands meetings to explain the team concept and what it would involve. The human resource manager then conducted a number of "systematic meetings" with employees (without other managers present) to get employee views. Simultaneously, the management team created an interactive database, using Lotus Notes technology, so that any data operations employee could raise questions, make comments, or voice concerns. That database was then used to stimulate an ongoing "virtual dialogue" among hundreds of affected employees. In addition, management set up a formal "discussion group" of representatives from the key functional groups to think through all ramifications of the change in such areas as staffing, job rotation, skill mix, training, and compensation, posting the notes from their meetings on the database. The result of this open communication "blitz" was fascinating: employees started pressing management to "get on with the change," to stop talking about it and actually make it happen. Management responded by accelerating its original schedule and completing the transition in less than nine months instead of the planned year and a half.

In general, then, employees are willing to change and to act in the best interests of the firm, but they often are not given the information they need to do so effectively. The broad dissemination of information is one dimension that can be tuned—that is, legitimated—to various degrees to make vertical boundaries more permeable.

DEVELOPING COMPETENCIES

As we described in Chapter Two, competencies are the critical skills needed to do jobs effectively. In healthy hierarchies, these competencies are developed wherever they are needed, without regard to rank, position, or status. When competencies are not developed at all levels, companies often get into trouble.

The five ways we propose for building competence across vertical boundaries are listed in the following box.

Actions for Building Competencies

- Conduct a competence audit.
- Improve staffing.
- Train and develop.
- Establish career banding.
- Establish a 360-degree feedback process.

Conduct a Competence Audit

Creating healthy hierarchies often requires the development of new skills at many different levels. For example, managers may need to strengthen their ability to stand before employees, discuss ideas openly and candidly, and respond to questions without the crutches of staff and subordinates; salespeople may need to learn how to do their own credit checks without relying on the head office; and shop workers may need to learn how to inspect their own work or make their own rework decisions. To identify these changing competency requirements, managers can conduct a competence audit.

Competence audits revolve around two questions:

◆ *Given the goal of creating a healthy hierarchy, what technical competencies will be required of employees at all levels of the organization?* Technical competencies are the know-how required to do a job. For example, employees in manufacturing might need to know more about marketing and vice versa.

◆ *Given the goal of creating a healthy hierarchy, what cultural competencies will be required of employees at all levels of the organization?* Cultural competencies guide how employees operate at each level of the organization.

Figure 3.3 is a model for determining a company's *competence gap,* the difference between current technical and cultural competencies and competencies that will be needed in the future, given the changes the company faces. Today, such changes often include such issues as globalization, technological innovation, customer demand, competitive pressure, or government regulation.

Figure 3.3. Model for Competence Audit.

Type of Competence	Skills We Have Currently	Changes Facing Our Business	Skills We Will Need in the Future
Technical			
Cultural			

└────── Competence Gap ──────┘

When we perform the analysis suggested in Figure 3.3, we generally find that the largest gap is in cultural competencies. For example, while employees in the newly formed Saturn division of General Motors required new technical skills (for example, computer skills and abilities to use new materials), the largest competence gap at Saturn was in how employees would work together (for example, in cross-functional teams and shared decision making).

Because the real value of the competence audit comes less from the information and more from the dialogue that it generates (as is true for many change tools), we recommend using an iterative, interactive method both for collecting and assessing the data. A small, cross-hierarchy team might start the process by putting together a first-cut list of current competencies, both technical and cultural. That list can then be turned into a questionnaire and either sent to employees or used in discussions with them at various levels. Next, the team can work with senior management to agree on key changes facing the organization and speculate about new competencies that will be needed to succeed. This information can be further enriched through focus group discussions with multiple levels of employees and through discussions with customers. Finally, cross-organizational groups can identify and discuss some of the gaps between current competency levels and what will be needed in the future.

Stan Schrager, senior vice president for human resources at Chase Manhattan Bank, conducted a variation on this process for Chase's wholesale bank in 1993 and 1994. He focused on identifying the key competencies that Chase's wholesale customers would be demanding from the bank's relationship officers in the coming years and the extent to which the bank's current professional complement would be able to respond. He found that customers would be (and are) seeking a much more tailored set of skills from their bankers, expecting them to be experienced in a customer's particular industry, have in-depth knowledge of financial instruments and markets unique to customer needs, and know the customer company in some detail. As a result, Schrager worked with the managers of the wholesale bank to create a database for matching relationship managers with particular and changing needs of corporate customers. The database also identified across-the-board competency gaps to be filled either through recruiting or training.

Improve Staffing

Once a competence gap has been identified, two choices exist for reducing it: buying (hiring) or building (training and developing) talent. Therefore, staffing decisions must focus on who comes into the organization, who moves up, and who moves out.

Sourcing the right talent into the organization is the first and perhaps most critical staffing decision because it determines a firm's long-term skill base. Three lessons in particular on hiring have been learned from successful companies.

Spend time screening applicants. In their St. Louis brewery, Miller Brewing Company managers spent over one hundred hours per hire reviewing applications, testing and interviewing applicants, and making sure that the two hundred employees hired into the plant were the right match. Miller executives believe their St. Louis facility is now staffed with one of the most talented workforces in the brewing industry.

Involve customers in screening. Southwest Airlines asks frequent fliers to interview flight attendant finalists after they have passed the Southwest screen for technical skills. Passengers look for attitude, personality, and energy. Anyone traveling on Southwest can probably perceive a service difference.

Bring in new talent. When Stan Gault became the chairman of Rubbermaid in 1982, he replaced 160 out of the top 161 senior people. This influx of talent enabled Rubbermaid to redefine its culture and become more innovative. To increase workforce competence, Lawrence Bossidy at AlliedSignal similarly replaced 90 out of the top 120 positions in his first fifteen months in office. In contrast, we have worked with a number of senior executives who came into new positions and tried to engineer major transformations without bringing in any new people. In almost all cases, they eventually changed their stance.

Sourcing new talent from the outside, however, is not without a price. Clearly, when too many individuals come into an organization from outside, the firm loses its continuity.[7] At firms like Rubbermaid, such transformation was probably appropriate. At other firms, continuity may be more important.

In addition to hiring new talent, managers should concentrate on succession planning, making sure backup talent is fully developed within the firm. At Baxter Healthcare, executives spend a significant amount of time reviewing talent. They identify business needs, then prepare suggested career moves for critical employees. As a result of this attention, Baxter executives believe they have created management depth to lead the company into the future.

Finally, organizations also need to move people out in a constructive way, as part of the firm's natural evolution. If the process is painful, managers may compromise on competence rather than let people go, contributing to a build-up of incompetence, or mismatched competence, which usually leads to a knee-jerk downsizing later. For example, as part of an effort to create a more flexible and responsive organization, the World Bank has constructed a number of mechanisms to help managers and employees separate. They include a "performance advisory service," where trained specialists advise managers in various ways of dealing with staffing situations; a "job search center" to help employees at all levels find alternative employment; a "career advisory service" to help employees match their skills with career options; and a number of financial alternatives for employees to make exiting the bank an easier process.

Train and Develop

When organizations build competence through training and development, the key to success is providing experience that focuses directly on closing identified competence gaps.

Lawrence Bossidy, for example, while bringing new talent into AlliedSignal, also required thousands of managers and employees to go through a series of training courses and projects to learn customer-focused quality skills—competencies he and his team had determined were critical for future success. At the World Bank, also, senior managers have identified a set of competencies they believe are critical for their technical development specialists, creating a required core curriculum and a series of tailored seminars to develop those competencies.

Several effective strategies for building competence through training and development are worth noting.

Define programs around competencies that align with strategy.   At Boeing and PPG, training programs are clearly linked to business strategies and the core values of the company. Training programs are not in a catalogue of courses merely because they have been offered in the past, but because they are linked to the business goals.

Train in teams.   Increasingly, we see companies using teams for training experiences. Teams have the ability to apply what is learned more directly to real job issues. Teams lead to action learning. For example, at TRINOVA, an Ohio manufacturing firm, teams of managers each identify a business problem that needs to be solved. Then they attend a one-week seminar and apply the lessons from the training modules to that problem. Over twenty teams attend the seminar, and TRINOVA finds the training leads directly to action for the majority of the teams.

Find alternatives to training.   The Center for Creative Leadership has identified twenty-two "development in place" activities, that is, ways to develop talent without formal training.[8] Essentially, companies should look for opportunities to use task force assignments, job rotation, and other means to deliver experiences employees would not otherwise receive.

Include customers.   Increasingly, we see firms opening their training activities to customers and suppliers. At Motorola University, 45 percent of participants are *not* Motorola employees but supplier employees and customers who have been invited to attend as a way to build their loyalty while building their competencies.

Leverage technology.   Technology today allows firms to train many employees at one time and at multiple sites. For example, Coopers & Lybrand trains managers around the world through video conferences.

Increase Competence Through Career Banding

Many traditional companies "grade" both jobs and people to give employees fair pay for work performed, resulting in a point system by which jobs can be compared and a pay system devised to ensure internal and external equity. In other words, a person is identified as a "level 10" or "level 25" no matter whether he or she works in production, sales, or finance, and a similar pay schedule is employed across these different units. Similar classification systems can be used to determine who can appropriately fill a job. At one time, classification systems like this were exceedingly useful, fostering pay equity across complex functional organizations and providing a rational system for filling jobs that was less prone than previously to nepotism or subjectivity and that resulted in an understood pathway for career advancement.

Today, however, job-grading systems are often dysfunctional, serving only to reinforce hierarchical inflexibility. In particular, they lead to narrow, rigid definitions of jobs that need to change along with fast-changing environments. They also limit an organization's ability to match competence with job requirements, since the only pool to draw from is the one with the "right" grade, even though the needed skills may reside at higher or lower grades. In fact, in most jobs today, the employee needs to shape the job more than the job needs to be unalterably tied to certain responsibilities. Moreover, job-grading systems tend not to allow for team-based work, where the essence of the task is to orchestrate and mobilize skills drawn from many sources. Finally, job grading reinforces the problem discussed earlier of career advancement that has more to do with vertical position than with competence and contribution.

An alternative to job grading is *career banding,* the process of organizing jobs around broad, flexible career categories. Within each category, employees can receive a wide range of salaries, based largely on competence and performance. For example, one bank that had at least seven levels of vice presidents, so many that no one really cared and the title lost meaning, has shifted to four career bands: executive, manager, contributor, and member. Executives are those who direct bank operations. Managers supervise groups of employees. Contributors perform individual specialty jobs, such as loan officer. Members perform jobs such as teller that interface with customers. Having careers options within these broad bands replaces employees' need to move up a single career ladder. If, however, a person does want to shift career focus, he or she can apply to move into another career band. Such a move, however, is based as much on a desire to do different work as on a desire to receive more pay or advancement.

It is hard to get people to work together when they are constantly competing for the next grade up. Career banding leads to groups of employees focused more on what needs to get done than on how to advance. Banded hierarchies are healthier because the organization becomes more flexible when employees can be rewarded and reinforced through lateral moves. Banding is particularly useful in downsized firms where there are not enough openings to move high performers up the hierarchy anyway. People can focus on becoming the best in their career band instead of aiming for vertical advancement up that single ladder.

Of course, when organizations violate the spirit of career bands by establishing many subcategories of plus and minus within a band, the concept is effectively neutralized. The power of the career band lies in simplicity, having a limited number of career categories within which managers and employees have a wide and flexible range of salaries.

Establish a 360-Degree Feedback Process

The final means of building competence is through what we call *360-degree feedback*. In this process, a manager's supervisor, peers, employees, and even customers answer questions about the extent to which the manager demonstrates certain desired competencies, giving the manager a 360-degree view of the perceptions of all those he or she affects. With this kind of rich feedback, managers can easily identify the key competence-building areas they need to address for both personal and organizational success. Contrast this with the traditional practice of giving managers formal feedback only from their bosses, feedback that focuses managers on personal compensation and advancement.

Here is a first-step, low-risk version of 360-degree feedback: a week before a subordinate's scheduled appraisal, suggest this to him or her: "Come in prepared to tell me one thing I could do differently that would help you do your job better." No hard copy of this feedback goes into a formal HR file, and the feedback is not passed on to the manager's boss. But the action does begin to tap the potential of 360-degree feedback. Also, it is appropriate for the manager who wants employees to start getting their own 360-degree feedback to go through the process first.

A number of organizations have incorporated 360-degree feedback processes into their competence-building activities with great success[9] and have produced some rules-of-thumb from their experiences.

◆ *Make sure everyone knows how the data will be used.* It is important that everyone involved knows that confidentiality will be preserved in the ways data are collected, stored, and used.
◆ *Define behaviors to be appraised.* Generic requests for feedback ("How is Sally doing as your supervisor?") will elicit generic responses ("Fine"). Specify the behaviors that supervisors, peers, and subordinates are to assess.
◆ *Involve customers.* At Marriott, the satisfaction forms left on the pillows at night become part of the feedback given employees who serviced the customer. Customer feedback completes the picture of employee performance.
◆ *Specify the purpose.* In many firms, 360-degree feedback is used exclusively for development, and the information is primarily shared with the person who is the object of the feedback. Increasingly, however, firms like General Electric, Boeing, AT&T, and Hewlett-Packard are using 360-degree feedback as a form of performance appraisal. It is crucial to specify how the feedback will be used before it is collected.
◆ *Use the data.* To get the most from 360-degree feedback, do more than prepare a computer-generated report for the individual being scored. Discuss implications, review results for development, and possibly tie results to rewards.
◆ *Track data over time.* To get the full developmental benefit of the 360-degree feedback process, track the data over time. For example, at GE Appliances, 360-degree feedback data are tracked annually. Success is measured by trends, not any one point in time.

One major outcome of 360-degree feedback is that boundaries are permeated as employees learn to look in all directions for learning, not just to the boss. More importantly, the competence-building process is vastly accelerated and enriched through multiple sources of input.

SHIFTING AUTHORITY TO THE POINT OF IMPACT: WHO DECIDES WHAT

Authority is the third dimension that requires digital tuning in a healthy hierarchy. Often, this means shifting some degree of responsibility and accountability from the top to the bottom of the organization. The goal is to place decisions as close to the action as possible—so that people who have the most current "read" on the situation are able to act immediately.

The classic example of shifting authority is the now well-accepted but previously revolutionary concept of allowing assembly line workers to stop the line to solve the problems they see, rather than catching problems later through inspection and quality checks. It is now well accepted that, with shifted authority, the overall production of perfect units is much higher and the overall costs (without armies of inspectors) much lower.

Other examples of driving authority closer to the action can be seen when salespeople can close deals and negotiate prices without checking in with the home office, when telephone customer service representatives can resolve problems and complete transactions on-line, and when employees can purchase their own materials without getting approvals. In all of these cases, not only are decisions speeded up but employee commitment to doing a good job is much increased.

There are four specific actions, summarized below, that leaders can take to tune the authority dimension to a level that produces fast but effective decisions.

Actions for Shifting Authority

- Challenge current decision-making assumptions.
- Use town meetings to shift authority.
- Shift management roles from controller to coach.
- Remove layers if necessary.

Challenge Current Decision-Making Assumptions

Most organizations are infused with assumptions about who can and cannot make various types of decisions. Some are based on rational analysis, but many of them are historical artifacts ("Remember the sales person who promised delivery of a product we didn't make!") or long-standing images of role and competence ("That's a senior management decision!"). Yet often, when these assumptions are changed, the previous way of doing things looks ridiculous in retrospect. Today, few people raise an eyebrow when they hear that Saturn employees can stop the assembly line at any time if they experience problems, that Nordstrom employees can make special arrangements to meet customer needs without going to management for approval, that the Boeing team that created the 777 aircraft was given nearly total control over design and delivery, and that Electronic Data Systems (EDS) client managers have the authority to meet client needs even if it means contracting services for the client outside EDS.

To move decisions to the right level, managers need to challenge their hidden assumptions. They can start by asking themselves a series of simple questions.

◆ Who has the information and skills necessary to make sure that this is a high-quality decision? Have these people been involved in the decision?

◆ If you had to trust one person in the organization to make this decision, who would it be? Has this person been involved in the decision?

◆ Who will be required to implement and carry out this decision? Have these people been involved in making the decision?

A shift in authority at GE Medical Systems, manufacturers of CAT scans and other large medical imaging devices, illustrates the necessary thought process. In the early 1990s, company executives realized their markets were increasingly global. In this global environment, their approval process for orchestrating major sales, requiring a head office committee decision, was unacceptably slow, particularly when the different time zones were factored in. In response, they gave increased latitude to field sales personnel to make pricing and delivery decisions on their own, allowing them to utilize available information regarding inventories, manufacturing costs and schedules, competitor prices, and more. The only caveat included was that the salesperson who made commitments had to ensure that the organization could meet them and understand that he or she would be held accountable for the customer's satisfaction.

Driving decisions downward requires continual reexamination and letting go. When a subordinate comes to a manager for a decision or approval, the manager needs to ask, "What keeps me from letting my subordinate make that decision?" If the answer is that the manager has information the subordinate lacks, the next question must be, "What keeps me from making that information available to my subordinate?" Managers also need to ask themselves constantly, "How often have I reversed, or declined to approve, a decision of this kind?" If the answer is never, then the next question should be, "What value am I adding by signing off on every decision of this kind [travel request, supplies reorder, tuition reimbursement, or whatever]?" And again, "What keeps me from letting my subordinate make this decision?"

The oil service firm B.J. Hughes illustrates how things can look quite different when decisions are moved closer to the point of action. At Hughes, senior managers had realized that the price of centralized decision making was lack of speed (decisions centrally made were slower to implement), questionable accuracy (each new layer of management involved in a decision took that decision further away from the point of impact), and lowered commitment (employees were able to pass the buck on decisions, removing themselves from responsibility). To shift the locus of decision making, the entire salesforce underwent enormous amounts of training in how to make decisions on product mix, meeting customer requirements, and even pricing so that salespeople could be asked to make customer-focused decisions at the point of impact.

After sales personnel became frontline decision makers and cycle time for meeting customer needs dropped significantly, senior managers assumed new roles. No longer responsible for command and control activities centered around making decisions, they focused attention on coaching and on ensuring that employees had the information and competence to do their work. Essentially, the organization was turned upside down.

Use Town Meetings to Shift Authority

The *town meeting* is a vehicle first used by General Electric as part of its transformational Work-Out. The metaphor comes from the original governance system of colonial New England, where town residents would meet as a total community, in marathon sessions, to debate issues and make decisions about town laws, procedures, and policies.

In a typical GE town meeting, employees come together for dialogue and debate about organizational and business issues, often off-site and away from the pressures of work. Participants are in some way connected, either by reporting to the same boss, working with a similar customer, or working on a common business process, but they always represent multiple levels of the hierarchy. Prior to the town meeting, participants work in small groups for one to two days to generate ideas for changing or improving the business. These ideas may include relatively simple actions, such as removing reports, canceling or focusing meetings, eliminating or streamlining approval processes, or changing policies. Or they may involve more profound and complex changes, such as redesigning a manufacturing process, setting up a new business venture, or changing a customer service routine.

Once participants have generated ideas, the actual town meeting begins. It is a boundaryless decision-making forum where the entire community reviews and debates the ideas and comes to a decision. A senior business leader chairs the session, which can include anywhere from 15 to 150 people. The leader's responsibility is to make sure that every idea is either approved or killed (or occasionally sent back to the drawing board) and that everyone understands the decision.

Town meetings drive change in authority patterns by making the decision-making process visible in a public forum. In effective town meetings, business leaders do not just make decisions in front of an audience; rather, they work through the decision thought process with the group. For example, here is an actual dialogue from a GE town meeting focused on reducing cycle times in a leasing business:

GROUP MEMBER [*Presenting a recommendation*]: Let's eliminate the regional manager's signature on all the paperwork when we have to liquidate an asset coming off lease. . . . We can let the branch manager sign off. It takes an extra thirty minutes for the regional manager to sign all the papers for each unit. It's at least forty hours per month for each regional manager—not to mention the slow down of our processing, particularly when the regional manager is not immediately available.

BUSINESS LEADER: What value does the regional manager's signature add?

FIRST REGIONAL MANAGER [*Uncomfortable about letting go of the signing authority*]: There are some cost considerations here regarding the price for liquidation. It's got to be a management-controlled decision.

BUSINESS LEADER: Do the regional managers pay any real attention to what they are signing? In other words, do they ever not sign, or change the price, or change anything on the paper?

SECOND REGIONAL MANAGER: It's basically a rubber stamp. We never look at the numbers. We just sign.

FINANCE MANAGER: None of these papers are ever kicked back. The salesperson knows what the numbers are, and our computer systems provide a final check anyway.

BUSINESS LEADER: So there doesn't seem to be any reason for the regional manager to get involved. Let's make the change!

GROUP: [*Loud cheers*].

Note that the dialogue included a safe way for people to challenge the regional manager who did not want to shift authority downward. In many town meetings, the senior business leader also is challenged. This kind of challenging would rarely, if ever, happen in the normal course of organizational events.

Town meetings also help to shift authority by educating people in their real degrees of freedom. Often, decisions move up the hierarchical line not because senior people want to make all the decisions but because people close to the work lack the self-confidence to decide things on their own. So they pass the buck up—and up and up. Or even more often, they make no decision, assuming that someone higher up will take care of things.

In town meetings, organizational leaders have an opportunity to challenge employees to grab control of decisions that they can more appropriately make. An extreme example of this took place during a town meeting at Tungsram, GE's Hungarian lighting acquisition. After years of state ownership, employees were unused to making any decisions on their own and, in fact, were afraid to do so. At a town meeting chaired by George Varga, the Hungarian-born manager who was GE's first chairman of Tungsram, dozens of ideas were presented for improving product quality and speeding development of a particular lamp. After each and every idea was presented, Varga responded by saying, "You don't need me to decide whether or not to do that. Make your own decision!" After two hours of dialogue in this pattern, an engineer began the presentation of his idea by saying, "I know I don't need you to make this decision, . . . so here's what we're going to do, whether you like it or not." At that point, Varga stood up and applauded—and the authority process of Tungsram made an almost palpable shift.

At General Electric, New York Life, Aetna, Southern California Edison, Digital Equipment Corporation, Philips, Ameritech, Baxter Healthcare, Exxon, PPG, Dow, SmithKline Beecham, the World Bank, and dozens of other organizations, managers have used town meetings as a means of removing vertical boundaries and engaging employees in the creation of a more healthy hierarchy. Lessons from these companies suggest that "magic" seems to happen when:

◆ Participants work on issues important both to them and to the company. There needs to be a passion about the issues that helps to promote real change.

◆ Leaders have no staff to insulate them from their employees. Leaders' staff members can participate but not serve as filters.

◆ Decisions are made in real time. The leader does not defer decisions for further thought but works with the group to make decisions on the spot.

◆ An atmosphere is created (by a facilitator, warm-up exercises, and so on) in which private concerns can be openly shared and solved. People need to feel safe enough to challenge their bosses, without fear of later consequences.

◆ Champions are assigned who follow up to make sure that the decisions made actually happen. This helps ensure that the town meeting truly becomes part of a process for shifting authority and not just a one-time event.

◆ Senior managers demonstrate commitment to change by spending significant time at the town meeting. Often, good town meetings last for many hours, with both grueling and exciting debate. The willingness of senior people to devote this kind of time is itself a powerful symbol of change.

Shift Management Roles from Controller to Coach

Most managers are proud to be managers. They feel that the managerial title and rank is an honor. It gives them privilege, respect, and status. And part of that status is the manager's traditional role of being in control and making tough decisions for others. Therefore, as we have discussed, many managers resist the shift to a healthy hierarchy because they fear they may be made redundant or will not know how to play the new role of coach.

To fine-tune the authority dimension, an organization needs to shift this mentality. First of all, managers need to be educated about what it means to be a coach instead of a controller. In presentations and workshops, managers can be asked to inductively derive the characteristics of good coaches and then to apply those attributes to their work. Such characteristics will include helping employees discover how to perform, not telling them what needs to be done; facilitating and leading by example more than edict and earning respect from action more than title; working with and for employees; laying out game plans then letting the employees execute the plans; and disciplining as teachers, to help employees learn and improve, rather than as auditors, to catch and punish inadequate behavior.

Second, executives can provide opportunities for managers to learn how to coach. Training modules on facilitation, team building, and group problem solving can teach managers the tools of coaching. Managers can be encouraged to work in pairs in a *buddy-feedback* system through which they learn from observing and giving feedback to peers.

Third, executives can treat as heros managers who make their goals through team and individual coaching, recognizing and rewarding those known as good coaches and developers of talent. For example, executives can develop a "coach of the month" award for managers nominated by employees.

The controller-to-coach shift has been a critical element in the ongoing transformation of Consolidated Edison's East River power plant for New York City. For fifty years, East River had been strongly hierarchical with several layers of decision makers. The system worked well when Con Edison, as a public utility, had a virtual monopoly on the generation of electricity and steam in New York City and the main focus of management was to ensure stable, reliable power at rates agreed upon by the regulatory commission. In the new environment of the 1990s, however, as power generation became a competitive commodity, the plant had to become much more flexible, able to increase or decrease output quickly and reliably and with significantly lower operating costs than in the past.

One of the critical ingredients in this change was to get equipment repair prioritized, planned, and implemented without close supervision from higher-ups. To do so, plant management experimented with having a number of fully autonomous mini-units run sections of the plant, with each unit containing its own operations, maintenance, and technical staff. However, faced with the loss of their familiar and comfortable roles in the chain of command and without a consolidated understanding of their new roles, the supervisors of maintenance, operations, and technical services tended to fall back into their old patterns, continuing to supervise the details of a task, and even doing the work themselves, instead of orchestrating the new units. Eventually, the plant manager realized that he needed to more clearly articulate an alternative role for these supervisors as coaches, trainers, and on-the-spot problem solvers. To instill an understanding of the new role, he involved the supervisors in task teams and projects. They also attended various seminars with a consultant. After a number of months, it started to become clear which supervisors would be able to avoid the traditional trap of doing the detail work and make the transition to the new role. And the plant manager began to consider the personnel changes that would be required to move forward with the new organization.

Remove Layers If Necessary

The fourth part of tuning the authority dimension and creating more healthy hierarchies is removing excess layers of decision makers. GE's Jack Welch once noted that layers of management are like sweaters—when you wear a lot of them, you cannot tell if it is cold outside. Removing layers of managers gets the organization closer to reality and helps management decision making move faster, tie in with customer needs, and be more responsive to immediately changing situations. Also, removing layers of management and increasing span of control ensures that the remaining managers cannot get too engrossed in details. Unable to watch all their employees closely, they are forced to ensure that employees have the skills to do the work and then let those employees decide how to get things done on their own. Increasing span of control leaves managers almost no choice but to liberate employees to act responsibly.

Removing layers of managers in a way that loosens vertical boundaries, however, is not as easy as taking off sweaters. There are three distinct challenges to be addressed.

Structure.   The basic structural design of the organization must be examined. If management layers provide integration between diverse work tasks or processes, this integration may not happen naturally or easily without the layers. For example, taking out layers of engineering management may require new mechanisms for coordinating product designs with manufacturing and marketing.

People movement.   A mechanism for dealing with the resulting personnel issues must be in place. In the short-term, the former managers themselves will need to be retrained, replaced, or possibly outplaced or retired. Long-term, with fewer managerial positions available for promotion, different career paths and compensation and incentive systems also need to be considered.

Governance.   A new process of governance needs to be created. At the minimum, management must determine forums for decision making (for example, who will come to staff meetings), create means of performance appraisal, and develop new communication channels.

This kind of thinking is exemplified by Sally Richardson's approach when she set about to change the manager-to-employee ratio in the Medicaid Bureau of the Federal Health Care Administration (HCFA) from 1:5 to 1:12. Before beginning the process, HCFA agreed to create a technical career path that would allow former managers to move into policy and project roles without losing compensation or promotional opportunities. Richardson, the director of the Medicaid Bureau, then commissioned a "streamlining team" of employees and managers to design a new organization that would meet the delayering criteria and also be more flexible, be more responsive to changing policies, and provide better service to the states and other constituents. The team was asked to consider the possibilities for organizing around processes, around customers, or around strategic goals, and to create an open dialogue about team thinking with the whole organization. In this way, Richardson avoided making delayering a painful organizational event. Instead, she used it as an opportunity to encourage empowerment and stimulate innovative thinking throughout the Medicaid Bureau.

MATCHING REWARDS WITH GOALS

Since people generally behave according to the incentives available, reward systems are a significant dimension for loosening vertical boundaries. However, reward systems generally are not well tuned. Managers often unintentionally mismanage reward systems because they *hope* employees will be motivated toward a particular goal, but they *reward* something else. In a university, deans hope faculty are excellent teachers but often reward research. It should not be a surprise, then, that faculty spend more time on research than teaching. Similarly, in many commercial firms, executives hope managers will exhibit collaboration, teamwork, and other organizational values but base rewards on meeting individual targets, causing most managers to concentrate their efforts in their own functions. Reward systems are also often out of tune because organizations reward what is easy to measure. One reason deans measure research is that it is easy to quantify. The number of articles a faculty member publishes is indisputable. In contrast, quality of teaching is a fuzzy quantity, and end-of-the-semester student evaluations may not be true indicators of quality teaching (a teacher may receive student adulation by being an easy grader). Similarly, companies often measure objective, or hard, outcomes like profitability, performance against plan, and other financial goals. Teamwork and collaboration goals may be what are desired, but they are soft and difficult to measure.

We have found three practices (summarized in the box below) particularly useful in tuning the rewards dimension.

Practices for Shifting Rewards

- Base rewards on performance and skill.
- Share rewards up and down the organization.
- Use nonfinancial rewards.

Base Rewards on Performance and Skill

We have discussed how, in most organizations, people are rewarded for their position in the hierarchy as much, if not more, than for their performance. In essence, their compensation and perquisites are rewards for past achievement and are not necessarily linked to current job performance. As organizations flatten their hierarchies and more people vie for fewer vertical positions, this reward system becomes dysfunctional. Realizing they cannot advance, more people limit their contributions by "retiring in place" or becoming cynical.

One powerful way of shifting a reward system is to base compensation less on position and much more on performance and skills, using these three components:

◆ A fixed base salary determined by past contributions, and adjusted yearly for cost-of-living and market equity.
◆ Skills pay based on demonstrated competence or proficiency in certain skills valued by the organization and relevant to the job category (for example, language skills, technical skills, negotiation skills, analytical abilities, and so on).
◆ Performance pay based on a combination of firm performance, unit performance, and individual performance.

The percentages of these three components will vary depending on the organization, the market, and the position. But the general principle is that the base salary should be no more than 60 percent of the total. This forces people to focus on achievements and competency development as means of increasing compensation.

Naturally, to put such a system in place, organizations must have appropriate measurement systems that can track performance and proficiency, and they must have a process for allocation. For example, Canadian mounted police who are members of the border patrol are tested for language skills, and those who are bilingual in French and English receive larger salaries than those who speak only one language. The bilingual officers are also given annual proficiency exams to encourage the upkeep and continued usage of their skill. Similarly, companies like Sun Oil and General Electric have formalized technical career options to encourage scientists, engineers, and others who want to make their contributions through technical rather than managerial means to remain in their professional specialties. They can advance in pay and status without having to worry about hierarchical position.

Wall Street firms have had these kinds of systems for many years, with compensation tied directly to deal or trading performance. This has allowed many traders to make far more money than senior managers, giving the best performers an incentive to remain "in the game." However, the Wall Street bonus system has also all-too-often been abused, usually when traders or deal makers focus on achieving the results at any cost. A solution to such abuses of a reward system is often to design the measurement systems to also assess long-term performance, team contribution, customer relationships, and ethical/legal behavior.

Share Rewards Up and Down the Organization

In the 1980s, a number of firms underwent management buy-outs. The theory was that if the incentives were right, managers would work harder and smarter, and their private firms would be more competitive than public ones. After the Borg Warner management buy-out, managers who stayed on were required to invest from $50,000 to $1 million of their personal worth in the new firm. The intent was to make each manager's financial investment in the new firm significant and challenging, enough to change behavior in the firm. And indeed, unpublished data collected by the Sibson Consulting Firm in Princeton, New Jersey, showed that buy-out firms were three times as productive as public firms in the same industry.

Incentives work. When managers and employees have much of their net worth committed to their firm, they make different decisions. Rather than fly business class, they fly coach; rather than fly three people to a meeting, they fly one; rather than hold needless face-to-face meetings, they use teleconferencing.

Other corporatewide initiatives can invest employees in the firm. PepsiCo's Sharepower program gives all employees shares in the company as part of their compensation. At United Parcel Service, employees are also paid in part in ownership. In both cases, the implicit contract is that if you stay with the company, perform well, and the company succeeds, you also will be successful. Sara Lee and Eastman Kodak have instituted programs that encourage (and at times require) managers at different levels to own significant shares of company stock. The rationale is that even without the firm's going private through a buy-out, managers can have financial commitments to the performance of the firm. Nordstrom's high commission based on sales has been seen as an important part of employee commitment to customer service. Nordies know that when they form long-term relationships with customers, those customers will buy numerous products from them over time, and they will be rewarded.

Some firms find stock options helpful for management commitment, but it is important to verify how far across the board they go. While bragging about an "extended" stock option program, one executive was surprised to learn that only 8 percent of the total company payroll would be affected. In contrast, part of Wal-Mart's success over the years has been a systematic stock option program for all employees, from check-out associates to senior managers. It has encouraged employees to satisfy the customer and achieve store performance targets and has helped create a relatively stable workforce in an industry characterized by extensive turnover.

Targeted financial bonuses have been helpful at TRINOVA, where Chairman Awards have been allocated to employees who have made exceptional contributions to firm performance. First of America has instituted a "gotcha" rewards program: managers can give immediate rewards (money, stock, prizes) to employees who are caught doing something above and beyond.

Use Nonfinancial Rewards

Nonfinancial rewards can be incredibly varied, limited only by an organization's creativity. Such rewards can include a parking space allocated to the employee of the month, congratulatory letters from executives to employees (or their families), special dinners and recognition for exceptional performance, press releases in the local media to praise employees, valued temporary assignments, learning visits to best-practice companies, attendance at professional seminars, or the opportunity for advanced training. Again, however, these rewards only break through vertical boundaries when they are given for performance, not position.

One of the more creative applications of nonfinancial rewards comes from the professional development committee chaired by Jeana Wirtenberg in AT&T's human resource division. For three years, this committee has accepted self- and other nominations for "role models of HR excellence" anywhere throughout AT&T. Judged by a panel using criteria based on the HR vision at AT&T, winning employees are given individual and/or team awards and honored at an awards dinner. Their recognition receives wide publicizing throughout the company and in local newspapers. They also have an opportunity to present their best practices at an annual AT&T-wide HR symposium.

Putting It All Together: How Do You Know It's Working?

This chapter has laid out four components that need to be wired together and four dimensions that can be tuned to create more permeable vertical boundaries (summarized in Figure 3.4). To help yourself begin putting these ideas together in a change strategy for your organization, we suggest that you make some notes on the following questions and then review them with your colleagues.

Figure 3.4. Wiring and Tuning Dimensions for Creating Healthy Hierarchies.

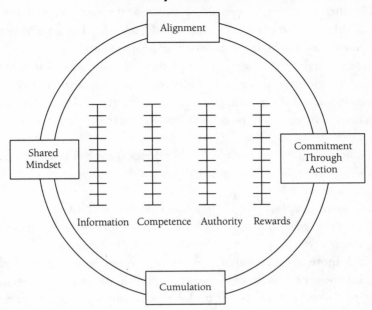

1. *To what extent are the four components (alignment, commitment, cumulation, and shared mindset) in place in our organization?* Are they wired together properly? What specific steps should we take to tighten the wiring?

2. *Which of the four dimensions is most out of tune and could use the most work?* What specific steps can we take to tune this dimension in the proper direction?

3. *If we tune one dimension, are there adjustments we need to make in the other three dimensions to keep our vertical boundaries in tune?*

Your answers to these three questions will give you the basis for an action-based work program aimed at loosening vertical boundaries and creating a healthy hierarchy. As you proceed to implement, however, you also need to consider how you will know if the actions are working.

AT&T has adopted three measures to assess progress toward a more healthy hierarchy. Economic Value Added (EVA) is a measure of financial results. A healthy hierarchy reduces costs through increased productivity. Customer Value Added (CVA) is a measure of customer service scores. A healthy hierarchy increases speed of service and responsiveness. Finally, People Value Added (PVA) is a measure of leadership behavior, diversity, and values. Healthy hierarchies empower people to act.

Here are five broad categories in which you can examine whether actions to increase the permeability of your organization's vertical boundaries are making your organization different. The evidence that you should consider will be both direct and indirect.

1. *Check the ratio of managers to employees.* This is a crude indicator of the span of control and will indicate whether layers are being removed.

2. *Examine employees' commitment to the business.* Employees' commitment may be measured with attitude surveys, but it may also be apparent in how employees behave. Employees should begin to ask more questions about meeting customer goals and improving business performance. Employees should begin to take personal initiative to fix customer problems without waiting for approval. Customers should be sending more unsolicited letters of commendation about employees and their acts of service.

3. *Check whether cycle times are reduced.* Increased speed can be evidenced in a number of areas: time to respond to customer questions about price; time in the order-remittance cycle; time to implement a new training program; time to change a manufacturing process; time to design a new plant; time to implement a new information system; time to replace employees; and time to complete financial reports.

4. *Examine employees' "self-leadership" behaviors.* When employees are treated as leaders, they likely act as such. Healthy hierarchies substitute for personal leadership. Therefore, when employees act as leaders for themselves, executives should find they have been freed up to spend more time on strategic and customer issues.

5. *Check whether a new mindset is in evidence.* When asking employees, suppliers, and customers what the business is known for, managers should begin to get different and more consistent answers.

In Part One, we have focused on the theory and practice of creating the permeable vertical boundaries that lead to a more healthy hierarchy. But vertical boundaries are just one of the four boundary types to be recalibrated in the boundaryless world of speed, flexibility, integration, and innovation. In Part Two, we turn our attention to the boundaries between functions, specialties, and other job categories—the horizontal boundaries that divide a company from itself.

PART 2

Free Movement Side to Side

Crossing Horizontal Boundaries

4

Beyond Turf and Territory

We have compared vertical boundaries to the floors and ceilings of an organization's house and horizontal boundaries to the room walls. As such, horizontal boundaries are the dividing lines between divisions, departments, groups, units, and functions. While vertical boundaries shape definitions of status, rank, and career progression, horizontal boundaries define functional specialties, such as marketing, sales, or engineering. The boundaries that distinguish people within a function—for example, hourly from salaried employees, union from nonunion, bonus eligible from noneligible, permanent from temporary—are also horizontal dividers, with each group having its own rules and regulations, ways of tracking work time, access to buildings or files, and so on. In short, horizontal boundaries are the lines of demarcation that organizations use to divide up the territory within the firm.

Just as we affirmed the organization's need to maintain some vertical boundaries, our position in this chapter is that some degree of horizontal task delineation is equally necessary. A house with no load-bearing walls has no structure and will collapse. However, we still can build our houses with more open space than formerly, more modular walls, more light flowing from room to room, and much more traffic throughout. In other words, this chapter examines how you can make your horizontal boundaries more adjustable and permeable so that your entire organization can operate with greater speed, flexibility, integration, and innovation.

Boxes, Boxes, Boxes

Horizontal boundaries are almost as ingrained in our minds as are the vertical, particularly since they, too, arise from the natural order of social life. While vertical boundaries derived from parent-child authority relationships, horizontal boundaries emerged from task differentiations in primitive societies, as leaders divided work between categories of clan and family members, sometimes based on skills and sometimes based on social definitions. Thus, for example, young children would be assigned to gather herbs or berries; older boys and men would specialize in hunting; women would provide medical treatments and manage the food preparation. These were the original specialties that helped to make social organization possible by splitting up diverse tasks among groups of people.

Just as our prehistoric ancestors made specialties of tasks, today's organizations arrange themselves around such specialties as engineering, manufacturing, marketing and sales, human resources, administration, and so on. Some organizations may have upward of twenty such departments, each forming a mini-organization with its own agenda, resources, and vertical leadership structure. Organizations with such multiple, hierarchical specialty units are often called silo, stovepipe, or chimney organizations, because they appear as series of stacks on the organization chart.

The modern history of the silo structure can be traced to two developments. First, as Adam Smith described in 1776, in his classic treatise *The Wealth of Nations,* economists recognized that organizations gained tremendous productivity when each worker focused on performing a single task then passed the product to another worker.[1] Smith described a number of settings where this system was more efficient than having each person handle the full range of tasks required to produce a product. He saw that fragmenting a large process into individual jobs allowed employees to learn to do a single task well and also avoided the lost time that occurred when individual workers had to change tools, locations, and frame of mind to move from task to task.

The second development that spurred horizontal task specialization, particularly in manufacturing industries such as steel, railroads, and automobiles, was technology. One of the first manifestations of technology's power was the assembly line, created in large scale by Henry Ford as a key to increasing productivity. In essence, the moving assembly line allowed the work to be brought to the workers rather than the other way around. Combined with task specialization, it meant that huge efficiencies could be gained by dividing the workforce into welders, polishers, inspectors, and so on.

Eventually the mentality of task specialization was extended beyond the manufacturing floor. As technology spurred large-scale mass production, a whole series of support functions such as purchasing, engineering, equipment maintenance, quality control, inventory management, and training were needed to keep the production machine going. Then the product needed to be shipped, held in warehouses, distributed, marketed, and sold, and each of these tasks was given over to specialists who could provide focus and expertise. Finally, as these separate functions proliferated, additional functions were needed at the corporate level to tie tasks together, ensure cross-functional equity, and provide overall control. This need led to the rise of further specialties such as finance, personnel, legal, audit, tax, and more.

To further complicate this already massive proliferation of specialties, leaders such as Alfred Sloan, Jr., of GM grouped the multitude of functions into decentralized and parallel divisions, each producing a different product or category of products (for example, the Chevrolet Division or the Cadillac Division). Thus was born the modern vertical/horizontal corporation with handfuls of divisions, each with its own multiple functions, all reporting upward to a centralized executive group.

This horizontal organizational model proliferated wildly after World War II. Manufacturing organizations expanded by leaps and bounds, adding workers and departments to the horizontal spread, and management to the vertical layers. Like out-of-control cell division, each new surge in growth added a new field office, a new product division, or a new department. The 1950s and 1960s saw the rise of gigantic corporations employing tens of thousands of people with hundreds of departments and divisions.

In the 1970s and 1980s, knowledge specialization added fuel to this horizontal growth furnace. Companies no longer had departments of chemists, for example, but departments of biochemists, geochemists, thermonuclear chemists, and so on. Engineers split between process engineers, electrical engineers, chemical engineers, and more, each specialty with its own knowledge base. Even manufacturing jobs became more segmented, as workers had to learn to use new highly complex machines or computers to perform their jobs. Thus, for example, tool and die makers, who once were able to run assorted lathes, grinding machines, drills, and presses, now had to specialize in particular computer-controlled machine tools that required months of rigorous training. Similarly, corporate finance people began to divide themselves into cost accountants, budget analysts, tax experts, and more.

Today, there are more horizontal lines and degrees of specialization in our educational systems and work structures than ever before. The cell division appears never ending, and the rapid pace of change makes the proliferation geometrically harder to stop.

Further fueling the process is the fact that horizontal boundaries fulfill people's natural desire to relate to others who are like them in some way. Whenever people form functional groups, a bonding occurs among members that solidifies the group and its unique identity. When many organizations today contain hundreds or thousands of people, bonding in smaller groups within the organization makes it easier for people to get to know and accept those with whom they work most closely. However, such groupings also tend to validate people's tendencies to stereotype the world outside their groups, dividing the universe into camps of "we" and "they." We easily support those in "our" group and easily find fault with those in other groups of race, belief, or function. This tendency is sibling and clan rivalry writ large.

Indicators of horizontal bonding are highly visible in most organizations: the marketing people all go out for drinks together, the secretaries have their own table in the cafeteria, the chemists have their own jokes. These indicators also signal that horizontal boundary setting is occurring. Some of these boundaries are useful, but some prevent necessary cross-fertilization of ideas and information.

Haywire Horizontal Boundaries

When the factors of size, role clarity, specialization, and control led to success, the horizontal division of labor was seldom criticized. The new success factors of speed, flexibility, integration, and innovation, however, make horizontal boundaries as problematic as vertical boundaries. Moving across a maze of functional boxes inevitably creates delay, indecision, uncoordinated actions, and least-common-denominator products and services.

We are living in a time when there are more variables than most companies can predict, and when control of those variables is temporary at best. To create an organization that can handle these variables, companies must take proactive steps to create permeability not only up and down the hierarchy, but also across the horizontal spans. Failure to do so can lead to the five typical dysfunctions designated below, which we call haywire horizontal boundaries.

Warning Signs of Haywire Horizontal Boundaries

- Slow, sequential cycle times
- Protected turf
- Suboptimization of organizational goals
- The enemy-within syndrome
- Customers doing their own integration

SLOW, SEQUENTIAL CYCLE TIMES

When multiple departments or divisions must be consulted or included one by one to create new product or respond to a customer, cycle times can seem to take forever. For example, in all too many traditional manufacturing firms, research and development people design a new product and then turn the design over to engineering to create prototypes. Because engineering may not fully understand or trust R&D, it redoes the design before finalizing the engineering specifications. The design is then turned over to manufacturing, which does another redesign to make the product more "producible" and sends the manufactured product to marketing. But marketing is unable to sell the product because it is nowhere close to the specifications that customers require. Thus, this process of "throwing ideas over the wall" not only takes years and untold resources but may result in a failure. Sociologist and consultant Bruce Phillips found that the sequential development process of the big three U.S. carmakers in the early 1980s added literally years to Detroit's ability to bring new cars to market and meant new cars were based on customer requirements as much as six years out of date.[2] This was taking place when Japanese manufacturers were able to design and produce models in half the time.

When work flows from function to function, the assumption is that each specialty will add some special value. Since each function is also assumed to operate in its own way, collaboration is not possible. Furthermore, each function must wait until the previous function has done its thing, so the receiving function can build on the sending function's contributions. Meanwhile, weeks go by and the customer waits.

In an organization with permeable horizontal boundaries, a different logic begins to emerge that takes advantage of opportunities for functions to work in parallel. It is often surprising to managers how many work processes they once viewed as sequential can be accomplished simultaneously.

For example, at SmithKline Beecham R&D, as throughout the pharmaceutical industry, drug development is a long and expensive process. Reductions in cycle time can provide significant patient and financial benefits. Yet for many years, SmithKline Beecham operated under the assumption that large portions of the drug development process, particularly the handling of clinical trial data, were necessarily sequential. Based on this assumption, SmithKline Beecham's clinical operations unit was composed of numerous specialty functions: clinicians who set up trial parameters, statisticians who created data analysis protocols, operations people who arranged clinical sites, systems people who arranged collection of data, data-entry specialists who coded data into computer systems, clinical quality specialists who checked data accuracy, biometrics experts who analyzed data, and regulatory specialists who put data into formats acceptable for FDA submissions. Each specialty operated semiautonomously, taking work from the previous group and passing it on to the next, and all too often at the end of the sequence, problems were discovered that required significant backtracking or even a restarting of the cycle. As a result, the phase of drug development from clinical trial to FDA submission took an average of eight months, with many projects taking significantly longer.

To shorten the cycle time, SmithKline Beecham challenged the logic of sequential drug development. For example, it replaced the multitude of functional clinical operations departments with what it termed DARTs—Data Analysis and Reporting Teams. Each DART contained all the kinds of functional experts needed to support the clinical operations cycle for a new drug from beginning to end. DART members were charged with the goal of working together, in parallel, to take as much cycle time as possible out of the clinical operations process. In very short order, the teams began to find collaborative opportunities. For example, by designing the research protocol around FDA submission requirements from the beginning, they eliminated weeks of reformatting and additional data collection. By creating more standardized data collection methods, they eliminated data-entry time and errors. Using these ideas and many more, it took the DARTs less than a year to reduce the average cycle time significantly at a time when the number of projects also dramatically increased.

PROTECTED TURF

Once horizontal boundaries become ensconced, people vie to protect their department's power and resources. Any change in process is viewed as antagonistic to the status quo rather than useful to the organization, and departments end up spending more time protecting turf than securing or satisfying customers. For example, in a new research organization established by NASA, a number of preexisting scientific, educational, engineering, and satellite production departments were brought together under one executive to facilitate interdisciplinary collaboration on some common scientific problems. Within the first week, the hottest issue of debate among some department heads was not how to pull together the research programs but who would control the scheduling of conference rooms.

Issues of turf are classic signs of rigid horizontal boundaries. Such issues usually stem from the logic of specialization. If a group is established to do a particular task and is assessed and rewarded for the performance of that task, then it has a vested interest in maintaining control over it. If the group gives up parts of the task, it may raise questions about whether it is needed. If it gives up some degree of control over the task by letting others participate, then it may not be able to ensure that things are done "right." So the rational thing to do is to protect its turf, to maintain the resources and authority necessary to perform its particular specialty.

Today, this view is myopic. It ignores the overall process of which the group is a part. Loosening horizontal boundaries restores the broader process perspective. Turf issues decrease and reconfigurations of the overall process become more possible.

For example, as we discussed in the last chapter, in Consolidated Edison's power generation plants, as at many utilities, years of tradition have made functional boundaries particularly solid. In a workshop aimed at reducing the backlog of equipment maintenance orders at Con Edison's Waterside plant, a team of managers and union people mapped out the overall equipment maintenance process. The map clearly showed that a major bottleneck was the maintenance planning function, which prioritized maintenance requests, laid out the proper equipment repair sequence, and identified the tools and equipment needed for the job. The planning function saw its role as specifying the job plan in detail and ensuring safe maintenance procedures, but by doing every job, big or small, with the same level of detail, and without input from plant operators and mechanics, it was slowing down the overall process and creating a huge backlog.

Mechanics and operators had complained about these precise problems for years prior to the workshop. In response, the planning function had insisted that its control over planning meant that the equipment deficiency would be correctly identified and no repair shortcuts would compromise safety. During the workshop, the various groups were able to view the entire process for the first time and reach agreement on the need for collaboration. From this perspective, they all accepted a number of experimental steps: joint planning of jobs by operators, mechanics, and planners; an express process for handling small, standard jobs; and an agreed turnaround time for planning larger jobs. Owing to these and other steps, the plant's maintenance backlog was significantly reduced in six months, and a more productive, less turf-oriented relationship grew up among maintenance, operations, and planning.

SUBOPTIMIZATION OF ORGANIZATIONAL GOALS

A third warning sign of haywire horizontal boundaries occurs when functional specialists begin to view their localized goals ahead of the organization's goals in order to optimize their own achievements and rewards. For example, in one organization, a group of research engineers successfully produced several dozen patents each year and took great pride in this accomplishment. Unfortunately, their patents rarely, if ever, led to commercially successful products; nor did their efforts help the company to improve existing products or manufacturing processes. From their perspective as engineers, they were successfully achieving functional goals, but those goals had begun to override the company's interests of producing products and solving problems for customers. The engineers had suboptimized themselves as resources. In short, they made the mistake cautioned against in the saying, "Never confuse the end of the ditch with the horizon."

Even when shifting from functional to organizational goals seems like an obvious need, it is often a wrenching change. For example, when Gary Weber became vice president of technology for PPG's Glass Group, the group's Harmarville Research Center had been through a 40 percent staff reduction and was struggling with adjusting the workload to the reduced staff. At the same time, the center was asked to adapt to a major shift of business strategies—from introducing value-added products to reducing costs through manufacturing process improvement. This additional change was met with resistance and skepticism. Town meetings were used as a means to air people's concerns and communicate the need to change. Through these meetings, it became clear that many people were firmly locked into long-standing functional and professional goals that did not match what the company needed. Only after continued dialogue and debate, coupled with some reorganization of responsibilities and cooperation of local management, did Harmarville turn in the right direction so that all staff were aimed at the same horizon.

THE ENEMY-WITHIN SYNDROME

A fourth warning sign of horizontal calcification is internal organizational strife. Whether over major or trivial issues, these conflicts are almost always divisive and energy draining. A frequent result is the enemy-within syndrome, as groups see "bad guys" lurking within the organization who are out to "get them." The syndrome is visible in many businesses in which departments feud over resources, prerogative, and power. We know of several organizations that have canceled important projects because of interdepartmental conflict over design or marketing concepts, despite market demands for the product. And we have seen more than one group intentionally sabotage another to gain power or territory for itself. By way of illustration, one of us recently consulted with a major airline seeking to improve baggage-handling services in one of its hub airports. While reviewing baggage-handling procedures, he learned that the airline had two separate teams of people working at the airport, and each had its own territory. There was a station manager and staff, who handled luggage check-in and ticketing, and there was a ground crew team, whose members handled loading luggage onto the planes, transferring bags between planes, and off-loading arrivals. Although the station departure people had lots of ideas for improving the baggage-handling process, and were even willing to help between flights, the ground crew managers and staff did not want any of their help or input. Similarly, when the station manager was asked for his recommendation about how to improve customer satisfaction, he responded, "Get the customers to carry their own bags! Don't let those [ground crew] people touch them."

The enemy-within effect produced by horizontal boundaries is one of the most debilitating organizational problems; it is like a cancer in the organizational body. Turf wars and squabbles are nearly always highly charged because they originate at an emotional, gut level that is not subject to management redirection. That is why John Etling, president of General Re, distributed "no turf" buttons to his senior management team at a time when he was trying to implement a major, customer-focused quality effort. (The buttons showed a bright green chunk of lawn with a red diagonal line going through it.) His view was that the only way to deal with internal battles was to call attention to them but do it with a sense of humor. This is certainly a better alternative than viewing the organizational world as full of enemies. If all the bullets are spent on fighting within, there may be none left for the competitors beyond the walls.

CUSTOMERS DOING THEIR OWN INTEGRATION

As task specialization increases inside large organizations, customers commonly end up handling the integration of products and services, which is the fifth warning sign of haywire horizontal boundaries. In such situations, accountability for customer satisfaction is spread out over many different functions. Consider the analogy of a men's clothing store with five departments: suits, shirts, ties, socks, and shoes. When a customer wants to buy a complete outfit, he not only has to deal with five salespeople but also has to make sure by himself that the colors and patterns match.

That analogy is not far from the way IBM sold computers for twenty years, with dozens of divisions specializing in mainframes, minis, and microcomputers or focused on information systems, payroll systems, and so on. IBM customers had to figure out how to blend the various products. The insurance industry also has been based largely on the nonintegrated model. Customers often receive calls from two or three salespeople at a time, with one selling life insurance while another sells automobile or home or business insurance. In their early days, most software companies fell into the specialization trap as well, compiling stand-alone word processors, spreadsheets, and databases that the customer had to learn to use one at a time. Microsoft and Lotus, among others, now recognize that customers want complete software solutions and have started offering their software in "suites" that integrate several functions.

Integration, as we described earlier, is one of the success factors for organizations moving into the twenty-first century, because it allows them to be more responsive to customers and to react more quickly. For example, we now see banks scrambling to offer one-stop service for all the customer's financial needs; computer vendors putting together packages of hardware, software, and training systems; and media and telecommunications firms planning to provide consumers with fully integrated home systems for television, data, news, movies, and interactive communications all on one cable line.

The retail business of Fidelity Investments is another example of an organization that has worked hard to cross horizontal boundaries so customers do not have to integrate products on their own. For many years, as Fidelity grew its business, each product line operated as an independent, entrepreneurial entity—seeking out its own customers and serving them in its own ways. While this fueled a tremendous period of growth, it also forced individual investors to do their own integration of Fidelity's many mutual funds and products such as annuities and discount brokerage. Customers had to construct their own portfolio strategies and deal with a vast array of Fidelity service representatives and contact points—all the while being further solicited for business by other Fidelity groups.

In 1992, Roger Servison, the head of Fidelity's retail marketing company, realized customers were becoming overwhelmed and frustrated by the administrative process. Moreover, many lacked the skills and sophistication to develop an integrated investment strategy. To change this situation, he began meeting with his peers, who ran the various parts of the retail business, and his own product managers, who drove the various mutual funds. Together, they formulated a vision for a more integrated retail business and started dozens of projects aimed both at making it easier for the customer to do business with Fidelity and at helping the customer with an integrated investment strategy. One project, for example, standardized the customer applications for different products, reducing their number from over three hundred to three. Another project pulled together a database that delivered integrated sets of performance reports and investment information for customers. Still other projects created tools for investors developing their own portfolio strategies.

The net result was a significant increase in customer satisfaction ratings and a 2 percent improvement in overall market share after almost ten years of market share stability. Clearly, when Fidelity made its horizontal boundaries more permeable, customers saw the difference.

Centralization Versus Decentralization: The Swinging Pendulum

When the warning signs of haywire horizontal boundaries appear, most organizations react by immediately changing the organizational chart. They apply structural solutions to behavioral or process challenges. They attack specific symptoms rather than the underlying dynamics of the symptoms. Like the little Dutch boy with his finger in the dike, executives who take the structural route usually find there are not enough fingers to plug all the holes.

Consider the following typical scenario. Imagine that an organization begins to perceive that its horizontal units are not functioning properly—poor communication, turf battles, and the like are compromising customer responsiveness and simultaneously draining resources. Management decides the organization is too widely dispersed, too functionalized, and too expensive; and decides to tighten its belt by eliminating redundancies and weeding out unproductive people and departments. Or perhaps the organization fails to get a new product designed and into the market on time. Again, management decides that the problem reflects too many committees and units working too slowly in sequence or that internal strife between units caused a breakdown in communication and decision making. And again, the typical response is to rein in horizontal spread through centralization of resources and decision making. All operations are judged by how efficiently they are organized, and the various engineering, research, marketing, and other horizontal functions are combined to increase operating efficiencies. People are shifted around or laid off; resources are reassigned, field offices are consolidated, and so on. Predictably, these moves lower costs, reduce redundancies, and perhaps even increase productivity—in the short term.

However, after that short breathing space, the organization begins to feel out of touch with the marketplace. Too many of its resources are now at the head office, and not enough expertise is close to the customer. Employees in the field and, more importantly, customers begin to see the organization as slow and unresponsive. The various lines of business complain they are not receiving enough priority from the centralized functions, a lack that slows their ability to innovate, to produce product, and to service customers.

The organization has resolved some resource problems, but it has sacrificed speed and flexibility. Gradually, it once again generates a swarm of operating units, business units, strategic planning units, poles, planets, product groups, and product centers. Responsiveness and speed go up but so do costs, sometimes astoundingly. Customers like the speed but find themselves once again doing their own integration of products. (If only Norman Rockwell were alive to capture the scene of that special moment when three or four representatives from the same company, who have never met, are being introduced to one another by a customer in the customer's waiting room.) The organization reverts back to a decentralized structure and decision making. A few years later, the original problems resurface, and the organization regroups a third time.

The debate whether centralization or decentralization is the best solution to horizontal boundary problems has dominated management literature for more than forty years. In theory, the dilemma goes to the heart of how an organization with multiple specialties can control and integrate its different disciplines while allowing them to maintain independent integrity and functionality. In reality, however, the debate has become a faddish game, in which organizations swing back and forth like pendulums. More than one consulting firm has earned a fine living by recommending that a decentralized organization be centralized and then, a few years later, coming back to recommend decentralization. Each solution appears rational—until the (predictable) problems arise.

In recent years, the matrix organization has sometimes been implemented as a solution to the centralize or decentralize debate. Theoretically, a matrix organization is both centralized and decentralized, and employees are given some combination of functional, product, and geographic accountability. For example, at any one time, an employee may be responsible for a function (say, engineering), a product line (say, laundry detergent), and a geography (say, Asia-Pacific).

The matrix is ingenious in theory but confusing in practice. Russell Ackoff accurately describes the problems with the matrix organization.

> In matrix organizations, employees have two bosses. One is the head of the input (support or staff) unit of which they are a part; the other is the head of the output (line) unit to which they are assigned. [These two units] jointly determine [an employee's] chances for promotion and his salary increase, and they determine performance goals with him. . . . This property of the design produces what might be called "organizational schizophrenia." When an employee's bosses do not agree or have different value systems, the employee does not know how to behave. This can be very stressful. The decision regarding to whom to pay attention is usually made politically rather than in the best interests of the organization.[3]

In short, the concept of the matrix is flawed for a number of reasons. In addition to producing the inherent schizophrenia Ackoff describes, it blurs accountability for results, allowing an employee to choose between conflicting priorities and to blame the priority not chosen for problems and delays. As a recent *Conference Board* report notes, "General managers have long complained about their inability to hold one person accountable for business successes and (especially) failures."[4] In addition, the matrix organization often becomes cumbersome and costly. When all points of the organizational compass feel compelled to contribute to decisions, decision making is slow, and travel, meeting, and communication costs high.

In recent years, Digital Equipment Corporation was perhaps the best-known example of a matrix organization. Under founder Kenneth Olsen, DEC's matrix promoted high levels of involvement and collaboration in decision making, but it also allowed functions to stonewall, capsize, or veto major decisions, making agreement on major programs and strategic directions very difficult. At a time when the computer industry was rapidly changing, DEC was unable to move quickly. Every decision required a committee and intense consultation back and forth between product groups, functions, and geographies. Enormous costs were added as each group build up its own support structure rather than share with others. DEC came close to self-destruction. Only after abandoning the matrix, under new CEO Robert Palmer, was it able to move forward more quickly on a recovery plan.

Reframing the Question: From Structure to Process

We believe that the question, Should we centralize or decentralize? is the wrong question for organizations to ask. Therefore, the answer to it will never be right. Instead of looking for structural solutions to what is fundamentally a process challenge, organizations should be asking how to permeate horizontal boundaries and improve speed, flexibility, integration, and innovation.

To reframe the question, management must first view the organization not as a set of functional boxes but as a set of *shared resources and competencies* that collectively define the organization's range of activities. Only then can management address the more fundamental question: *How does the organization create **processes** to ensure that all its shared resources and competencies—arrayed across the horizontal spectrum—create value for customers?*

Framing the issue this way shifts the focus from a mechanical to an organic model of the organization—from, on the one hand, organizing, influencing, and bringing together a collection of separate functions to, on the other hand, transforming inputs to outputs through series of processes and subprocesses to which people with different skills and disciplines contribute. Management must shape these processes efficiently, in a way that maximizes customer satisfaction and builds capability across the firm.

In his recent work on organizational design, Jay Galbraith, a professor at the University of Southern California, coined the term the "front/back organization."[5] In an organization's "back room" are many shared resources and competencies. They may be arrayed by function, product, or geography—it doesn't matter. In the "front room" are customers who have unique and special demands. Finding *processes* to move these resources from the back room to the front room when they are needed, in whatever configuration is needed, is the true challenge. This kind of front/back movement—done quickly, flexibly, creatively, and tailored to each customer—is what boundaryless horizontal behavior is all about.

Loosening horizontal boundaries, then, calls for integration, not decentralization; process, not function; and teamwork, not individual effort. When the organization is viewed integratively as composed of shared resources, it puts an end to the structural questions about power, authority, and priority raised in the centralize/decentralize debate. Shared resources are not about which horizontal function has power but how the organization uses processes to mobilize resources, solve problems, and meet customer needs. In other words, process is more important than function. Process deals with how value is added to goods and services and activities. It is not about how much attention is paid to a functional leader.

Making It Happen: Principles for Creating Horizontal Harmony

In our view, there are five key organizational principles (listed in the following box) that companies need to keep in mind in order to develop permeable horizontal boundaries and integrate shared resources.

Principles for Creating Horizontal Harmony

- Keep the focus on the customer.
- Show one face to the customer.
- Form and re-form teams to serve the customer.
- Maintain a competence pool.
- Share learnings across customer teams.

KEEP THE FOCUS ON THE CUSTOMER

The boundaryless horizontal organization begins and ends with customers, however defined. Its entire focus is to anticipate and serve changing customer needs. Moreover, it works to see itself from the customer's point of view. The boundaryless horizontal organization is effective when all employees understand and feel the needs of the customer and all internal processes aim to form and strengthen external customer relationships.

SHOW ONE FACE TO THE CUSTOMER

Once the focus is on the customer, the second principle is to make it easy for the customer to access resources, products, and services across the horizontal spectrum. This requires organizations to reverse the lens, view themselves from the customer perspective, and provide customers with a single, simple, consistent point of access to what the organization offers. For example, a large computer firm with multiple product lines recently realized that it was not unlikely for representatives of up to six of those product lines to be meeting with a customer. At worst, each of the six individuals did not even know what the other five were working on with the customer. At best, the multiple representatives presented the customer with a confusing array of possibilities for interacting with the firm.

This does not mean that only one company representative should interact with each customer. On the contrary, mobilizing the horizontal resources may mean that many more skills and talents can be brought to bear to serve the customer. However, to truly satisfy that customer, either one person or one process-point must have the prime accountability for making sure that the customer gets what he or she needs.

In some cases, a specific individual is targeted as the customer manager. This person's job is to be thoroughly schooled in how the customer operates and to give advice about what the customer needs before the customer knows he or she needs it. This person also corrals the resources of the firm to serve those customer needs as fluidly and responsively as possible. In other cases, the single face the organization shows to the customer might be a process-point, such as an 800-number. Particularly in large-scale retail operations, it is impossible for each customer to have a single person tending to his or her needs. However, it is possible to have a consistent "window" that the customer can easily enter and where the information about the customer and his or her needs resides. A good example is Fidelity's 800-number service. No matter which service representative answers the call, the same information about the customer is available, and a consistent way of talking with the customer is used.

FORM AND RE-FORM TEAMS TO SERVE THE CUSTOMER

Once the organization has focused on customer needs and provided one face for customer contact, actual customer service is provided by fluid teams that form and re-form. These teams are composed of the competencies and resources the customer requires to meet current and perhaps future needs. They draw upon the appropriate skills and resources wherever these may reside in the organization. In that sense, the teams are ad hoc, temporary, or even "virtual"; although for large or complex customers, they may be semipermanent. Each team is dynamic: as additional customer needs are identified, additional resources and competencies are added, and the team is re-formed again.

Furthermore, these teams are not necessarily part of an organizational structure. They handle processes across functions more than responsibilities within functions. Team leadership roles are shared, depending on the needs of the customer. The teams may include individuals from multiple functions within the corporation and, through alliances and subcontracts, even individuals who work in other firms. Finally, the teams are measured by their ability to use resources from inside the firm to add value for customers outside the firm.

MAINTAIN A COMPETENCE POOL

To staff fluid and dynamic customer teams, successful organizations maintain a pool of competent people (resources) with the skills to meet customer requirements. These resources may be arrayed by function (manufacturing, marketing, sales, engineering, administration), product, or geography. But they derive their legitimacy from becoming part of a customer team. Resources that reside in functional or product silos and are not needed on customer teams become quickly acknowledged as irrelevant and are likely to be removed from the resource pool.

One implication of the competence pool principle is that functional leadership (for example, the head of engineering or finance) must constantly assess and refresh the competence of people in their disciplines and match that competence with existing and emerging customer needs. For example, at the World Bank, sector managers provide career development guidance for technical specialists involved in country development projects, because they must ensure that these specialists maintain cutting-edge skills in their disciplines. The bank can then match people with certain skills to projects that require them.

SHARE LEARNINGS ACROSS CUSTOMER TEAMS

The final principle for permeating horizontal boundaries is to create a learning process. As multidisciplinary teams work across boundaries to serve customers, they gain tremendous insights into those customers, into team members' specialties, and into processes for working together. Those learnings must be captured and leveraged. Otherwise, the boundaryless horizontal process becomes very expensive and inefficient, requiring constant relearning of the same lessons. To avoid losing critical ideas, information, insights, and competencies, the organization must establish mechanisms by which teams and other groups share best practices and learnings. Again, a further message is that functional leadership must include both within-discipline and cross-discipline learning.

The Service Model of Horizontal Harmony

The idea of a boundaryless horizontal organization is embedded in the heritage of almost all service firms. And the principles we have been discussing are among those that have guided professional service firms for decades.

For example, one of the Big Six public accounting firms begins its work with a focus on customers (principle 1). Customer needs are identified through surveys, focus groups, and constant interactions with the customers. Dedicated customer managers (principle 2) lead the accounting effort for major clients. These customer managers are generally senior partners who know the customers' business well enough to give the client advice whether the client asks the underlying question or not. They generally stay with large accounts for a long period of time to ensure continuity, and they form multiple relationships within the accounts to ensure stability.

Customer managers have the responsibility to pull together resources to meet clients' financial reporting needs (principle 3). These resources form a customer team dedicated to both the constant and transient needs of the customer. Many team members come from the resource pool of the accounting firm. Some may be aligned with a particular function (capable at information systems or manufacturing for example), some may be aligned with products (capable with particular auditing requirements perhaps), and some may be aligned with geographies (capable with financial requirements in different global markets for example). The team formed by the customer manager may also include experts from outside the accounting firm if client issues require special expertise. Membership on the team is not permanent, of course, because the client needs constantly change. However, the team's primary challenge is always to create processes for shifting inner resources and competencies to the outer customers.

Inside the accounting firm, employees work in what may seem like traditional roles. Some may work primarily in a function, some in a product line, and some in a geography. However, all employees realize they are really shared resources that may be mobilized for a team at any time (principle 4). Employees with expertise but without the ability to translate that expertise to customer value are identified and replaced. Finally, each team in the firm shares best practices with other teams, so that all clients benefit from the knowledge and ideas gleaned from particular clients (principle 5).

Other professional service firms have used the boundaryless horizontal organization just described for a number of years. Law, advertising, and consulting firms follow the model when they assign a senior partner as the "relationship manager" for an account. This person's job is to diagnose and anticipate the needs of the account and to garner resources from inside and outside the firm to ensure that those needs are met quickly and effectively. Movie studios use the boundaryless model when the producer pulls together a temporary team of writers, directors, cast members, editors, and other resources to produce a film. Some team members come from the producer's organization, most come as subcontractors, united around a particular project. Advertising agencies organize around boundaryless processes designed to produce creative and responsive advertising campaigns for customers. Construction and engineering firms organize around large clients to ensure that these clients' needs are met over time.

Horizontal Harmony in Other Organizations

Other companies than service organizations are rapidly emerging as users of horizontal organizational logic. Consider the following examples:

Microsoft.   Microsoft recently reorganized around key customers. Entitled "Re-engineering for Opportunity," the reorganization shifted product units into groups geared toward specific customers and toward passing Microsoft's product expertise along to customers. Customer units designed to build relationships now exist for each customer account and customer group (for example, end-users, organizations, and original equipment manufacturers). The memo introducing the reorganization stated: "People within these customer units will live, eat, and breathe with their customers."

Chubb & Son Insurance.   Chubb & Son has one of the most profitable histories in the insurance industry. Its traditional organization has used the principle of "dual accountability" for many years, meaning that accountability rested with both product lines and branch managers. However, Chubb found that customers often thought the system difficult because multiple Chubb employees made sales calls on them. Each represented a unique product line and was not fully integrated with other product lines. Chubb is now experimenting with the shared resource organization in five regions. Working to organize around customers, Chubb is assigning customer managers to the large accounts and working to ensure that each manager knows his or her customer needs and integrates all the Chubb resources toward serving those needs. In this way, the customer has one primary Chubb relationship.

Baxter Healthcare.   A leader in the hospital supply business, Baxter offers over 20,000 products to hospitals around the world. To manage customer relationships more effectively, Baxter has assigned specific employees to form long-term relationships with hospitals. These relationships began with traditional market research, surveys, and focus groups to find out what customers wanted. The relationship became more intimate when Baxter gave many of its hospital customers computers and software to connect them on-line to Baxter's distribution network so Baxter could track and fill customer orders. However, true customer intimacy came when Baxter representatives offered hospitals the full range of Baxter resources. Customers could attend Baxter training programs and participate in performance appraisals for Baxter employees, while Baxter employees gave hospitals expert assistance in creating their own effective teams. For example, Frank LaFasto, who has spent seventeen years at Baxter in various human resource positions, now spends about 30 percent of his time with customers, facilitating team-building and problem-solving sessions. Through these multiple contacts, Baxter has formed strong partnerships with preferred accounts.

Each of these examples illustrates the five basic principles of a boundaryless horizontal organization—and the important shifts that can occur when resources are deployed to serve customers. Again, the key is not to focus on structural means of bringing disciplines together. Rather, structures shift when flexible processes mobilize the resources of the firm to meet customer needs.

Creating Horizontal Harmony: Overcoming the Immune Response

No new organizational form or process emerges without bruises, and replacing haywire horizontal boundaries with more harmonious and permeable processes is no exception. In many organizations, professionals, specialists, and other functional experts find great comfort in their functional identities. They relate most closely to their functional counterparts, assess their careers and achievements against functional goals, and maintain high degrees of loyalty to their functional leaders. In short, their functions are their homes, the places where they speak a common language and where they feel most comfortable.

Given the emotional and psychological power of functional roots, many professionals and functional experts view attempts at change as threats or attacks. Listening to the customer might mean doing things differently than the functional "right" way; working with other disciplines might mean learning new languages or ways of thinking; and working in changing teams might mean losing that sense of home, becoming disconcertingly rootless. In short, while the changes described in this chapter might make good logical and business sense, people's existing emotional attachments may spark considerable anxiety or resistance.

To overcome this resistance and fight through inevitable immune responses, leaders can take the four preparatory steps listed below. (Additional fundamental actions are described in Chapter Five.)

Preparatory Steps for Overcoming Resistance to Horizontal Change

- Create new mental models.
- Encourage and teach teamwork.
- Define measures of shared resources success.
- Restructure quickly.

CREATE NEW MENTAL MODELS

Perhaps the greatest barrier to the success of a horizontal boundary transformation is a lingering mindset from the past. A mindset is almost impossible to give up unless there is a new mindset to replace it. People in closed functional boxes need to know what things will look like when their boxes open up or even disappear. What will be different? The two methods for creating new mental models that we have found helpful are these: send employees to visit companies that are models of boundaryless horizontal behavior and create a boundaryless model on a small scale in your own organization.

For example, early in 1994, executives at the World Bank, as part of an organizationwide change effort, realized that the bank's human resource function needed to be better aligned with the bank's operations organization, HR's prime "clients." One aspect of this alignment was to create flexible human resource teams that could mobilize a variety of HR disciplines to meet changing needs of operations managers and staff. Since the basic HR approach had been unchanged for a number of years, the proposed shift was viewed by some people with both skepticism and confusion, and few really understood what it meant. To view a tangible model, teams of HR and client personnel visited organizations with teams similar to those proposed for the World Bank, including Chase Manhattan Bank, Northern Telecom, and Hewlett-Packard. These visits and subsequent discussions about them helped management refine its thinking and generated enough support to allow the bank to move ahead.

At Carrier Corporation, former CEO William Frago wanted to create a boundaryless process for sharing and leveraging product systems expertise across this global company. Because this was likely to involve dismantling and reallocating a number of large divisional and functional units and changing the mindset of many valuable professionals, Frago decided to begin overcoming resistance by starting with one vice president who had formerly headed a large division. He asked the vice president to pull together a very small team of engineers, purchasing, quality, and financial people and to focus the team on creating a common technology platform, across the worldwide Carrier organization, for room air conditioners.

At first, the vice president and many of his peers were in shock. They found it difficult to get rid of the notion that to be a senior executive you needed to be in charge of an entire product system and have hundreds of people reporting to you. Both a vertical and a horizontal boundary mindset prevented them from recognizing that the larger issue was to contribute to the company by improving its processes. Eventually, however, through international cooperation among Carrier divisions, this VP saved the company millions of dollars by standardizing technology components. Once a new mental model of product systems leadership, focused around contribution to results and development of cross-disciplinary processes, was operating in one area of the company, Frago was able to expand it over the next year to include the offerings of all Carrier's product systems.

ENCOURAGE AND TEACH TEAMWORK

Boundaryless horizontal organizations require exquisite, flexible teamwork. Because teams will change as business needs change, organizational members must be able to join and lead teams quickly to solve particular problems. This is especially true in corporations that have multiple business units forming in Eastern Europe, China, Indonesia, India, and other emerging markets in which change is especially rapid and flexibility is survival.

The best way to encourage and teach teamwork is to give people experience on real teams working on real business problems and to use those teams as learning vehicles. This was the approach that Roger Servison took at Fidelity Investments. Realizing that the various professionals in the retail organization would need to work extensively in teams, rather than the traditional functional silos, he and his senior team set up a short-term skunk works. They identified six key business opportunities that could be solved only through cross-functional effort and assigned a part-time cross-retail team to each one. Subjects ranged from reducing direct mail costs to increasing use of automated customer services. Servison then asked one of us to lead a "launch" workshop to help the teams get started on their projects and on learning how to operate effectively as teams. Once the teams were underway, trainers from Fidelity's corporate HR organization helped them continue to reflect on their team dynamics. At the end of sixty days, one of us again held a workshop in which the teams pulled their conclusions together and reflected on their learnings. They met with Servison and his senior staff, reported their conclusions, and began implementing. Within ninety days, the teams were producing results (for example, direct mail costs were reduced by 60 percent). More importantly, a large number of people had learned what it meant to work in a flexible team.

DEFINE MEASURES OF SHARED RESOURCES SUCCESS

As a third preparatory step, executives can set the stage for horizontal boundarylessness by setting desired measures that can only be achieved through a process of sharing resources. We have found these three measures particularly useful:

◆ *Higher customer satisfaction:* assessed by collecting data from surveys, focus groups, targeted interviews, or other customer focused information
◆ *Lower cost of services:* assessed through productivity measures or budget reductions
◆ *Reduced cycle time:* assessed through speed of responses and greater productivity

Measures of success must be established at the beginning of an effort if they are to shift processes. In essence, they serve as goals, stakes driven into the ground that people can reach only through loosening horizontal boundaries.

RESTRUCTURE QUICKLY

In some situations, organizations may need to restructure or consolidate before they can devise processes for weaving together horizontal resources. The need arises particularly when multiple units do essentially the same types of work. Then the similar activities must be pulled under the same umbrella—either to generate some immediate savings or at least to identify processes employed and competencies that exist—before you start figuring out how best to transform the activities.

A key success factor in such consolidations is to move quickly once the idea has been articulated. In most downsizing efforts, rapid, bold decisions invite employees to focus on the future not on the past. The time from announcement to actual practice should be as short as possible, even if many details and processes cannot be completely worked out before the change occurs. Likewise, in moving toward a model of shared horizontal resources, it is better to implement changes quickly so that employees always know their status within the organization.

The creation of a boundaryless horizontal human resource organization at Northern Telecom depicts how consolidation might be performed. The company needed to create a shared service center for HR, revising functions and reducing personnel from approximately 750 down to 390, after which it would be in a position to leverage certain processes across the organization. To carry out the consolidation, the company employed a large-scale conference process. First, to develop a vision for the new HR service group, forty people representing many HR roles and HR internal customers sequestered themselves for three days. During this time, they kept all other employees apprised of the progress toward the new service group through teleconferencing and memos. With a vision established, another large group met two weeks later in a second conference to design the new organization to fit the vision. At this point, employees wanted to know who was to be included in the new organization. As a result, just one month after the process started, every person was told what was going to happen to his or her job. People could then get on with the process of implementing the new vision or of finding new jobs (with Northern Telecom's help). In less than three months, the new structure was up and running, teams were designing new horizontal processes, and approximately 300 people who needed new jobs had been placed inside and outside of Northern Telecom.[6]

Getting Started: How Haywire Are Your Horizontal Boundaries?

In this chapter, we have discussed the evolution of horizontal boundaries and the ways in which they go haywire and cause organizational dysfunctions. We also have provided a vision of a boundaryless horizontal organization. The next chapter is designed to help you translate this vision into a series of discrete action steps so that the expertise in your company can be leveraged toward achieving customer goals and internal cross-fire can be eliminated or minimized.

At this point, we suggest that you reflect for a few moments on the nature of your current horizontal boundaries. The following questionnaire (Questionnaire #3) can help you assess the extent to which such boundaries may be haywire and the extent to which your organization already has processes to share resources. Part 1 of the questionnaire asks you to map your organizational functions according to importance to key customers and degree of collaboration with other functions. Part 2 asks you to identify warning sign behaviors in your organization. Part 3 asks you to identify the degree of horizontal harmony in your organization.

Questionnaire #3

Stepping Up to the Line: How Congruent Are Your Organization's Horizontal Boundaries?

PART I: MAP RELATIONSHIPS

Instructions: In the space below, identify ten or more functional disciplines or specialties that exist as different units in your organization.

Now use the following table to note the ways in which these units contribute to key customers and collaborate with each other. This will produce an informal map of the horizontal groups in your organization.

Organizational Unit	Professional Disciplines in the Unit	Extent of Collaboration with Other Functions (High, Medium, Low)	Contributions to Customers	Effectiveness of the Function as Viewed by the Customer (High, Medium, Low)

PART 2: IDENTIFY WARNING SIGNS

Instructions: Assess your organization on the following warning signs of haywire horizontal boundaries. Use the scale next to each statement to indicate the extent to which the statement characterizes your organization's behavior, circling a number from 1 (not true at all) to 5 (very true). Also, make a note of an example that supports your assessment.

	Not true at all			Very true	
1. Organizational processes tend to be slow and sequential instead of fast and parallel.	1	2	3	4	5
2. Functional groups are more concerned with protecting their turf than with serving the customer.	1	2	3	4	5

	Not true at all				Very true
	1	2	3	4	5
3. Functional groups and disciplines place greater priority on meeting their own functional goals than on contributing to overall organizational achievements.	1	2	3	4	5
4. Functional groups and disciplines regard each other with suspicion, blame each other for problems, and operate as though the enemy is within the organization.	1	2	3	4	5
5. The customer needs to integrate our products and services.	1	2	3	4	5
6. Our organization tends to swing back and forth between centralization and decentralization every few years.	1	2	3	4	5

PART 3: ASSESS HORIZONTAL HARMONY

Instructions: Identify the extent to which your organization applies the five principles for creating horizontal harmony. Use the scale next to each statement to indicate the extent to which the statement characterizes your organization's behavior; circling a number from 1 (not true at all) to 5 (very true).

	Not true at all				Very true
1. The focus of attention is always on the customer.	1	2	3	4	5
2. The customer has a single point of contact with our organization.	1	2	3	4	5

3. We form and re-form teams to serve the customer.   1   2   3   4   5

4. We have an extensive pool of competence that we can draw upon for customer teams—and we keep that pool refreshed.   1   2   3   4   5

5. We have active and robust processes for sharing learnings across customer teams and across functions.   1   2   3   4   5

Questionnaire Follow-Up

Ask a group of peers from different disciplines and functions within your organization to review this questionnaire also. Then discuss everyone's responses to see if you and your peers have a shared view of your organization's horizontal health or dysfunction. The resulting information will give you a more solid foundation on which to construct an action program, using the ideas in Chapter Five.

5

Integrating Resources to Serve the Customer

To create boundaryless horizontal organizations, companies must see themselves as sets of shared resources and competencies that are mobilized, in different ways at different times, to meet customer needs. The challenge is to create processes by which this mobilization occurs quickly, effortless, and proactively.

Imagine that your organization is composed of virtuoso musicians, each playing his or her own instrument. These musicians are the functions and disciplines. In order to make music, they need to blend their expertise. But as we stated in Chapter Two, this blending must be more along the lines of improvising jazz than of playing classical music from a score. The needs of customers change so fast that one day, one customer may need the music of a sax, a clarinet, and a trumpet; another customer might require a piano in that mix; and tomorrow, some completely different ensembles may be needed. None of the players has any scored music, nor is there a conductor; yet they all must improvise together in a way that the customer finds pleasing.

Our goal in this chapter is to provide five specific *improv vehicles* (listed in the following box) for facilitating harmonious behavior across horizontal boundaries. Again, not all of these vehicles may be appropriate for your situation at this time. The ones that are appropriate may not be of equal importance. Together, however, they will help you frame an action strategy to create and maintain harmony on the horizontal level.

Improv Vehicles for Permeating Horizontal Boundaries
- Orient work around core processes.
- Tackle processes through targeted teams.
- Turn vertical dimensions (information, competence, authority and rewards) sideways.
- Create shared services for support processes.
- Develop organizational learning capability.

Orient Work Around Core Processes

Shared resources and competencies are tied together by processes that transform organizational materials and know-how (inputs) into products and services that meet customer needs (outputs). Therefore, orienting work around core processes is the first improv vehicle that executives can use to make horizontal boundaries permeable. This orientation shifts the emphasis from engineering work or systems work, which tends to be internally focused, to cross-functional process work, which by definition is externally customer focused. Orienting work around core processes in the four ways described below also supplies the foundation on which all the remaining improv vehicles will build.

Orienting Work Around Core Processes
- Define core processes.
- Set customer-focused stretch objectives for each process.
- Assign process leaders.
- Remove process barriers and streamline process flows.

DEFINE CORE PROCESSES

Processes cut across an organization and represent the flow and transformation of information, decisions, materials, or resources to serve customers. Processes common to many firms include:

- *Commercialization of technology:* the processes by which ideas become products and services
- *Order fulfillment:* the processes by which customer requirements are entered into the organization and satisfied
- *Purchasing:* the processes by which supplies are ordered and acquired
- *Servicing:* the process by which customer complaints and needs for information and training are fulfilled

Firms also have processes that focus on internal customers. For example, the development of employee competence is a process serving all units of the organization, as are internal communication, employee payment processing, and many others. In general, however, these are not core but support processes—necessary to keep the organization going but not directly focused on meeting customer needs. As we will discuss later in this chapter, support processes can often be managed in different ways than core processes—for example, through shared service groups, outsourcing, or automation.

Every organization has its own definition of core processes. For example, the World Bank's operating regions, which work with developing countries to reduce poverty, define some of their core processes as developing-country assistance strategies, economic and sector analytical work, project development and approval, and portfolio (or project) supervision. Fidelity Investments focuses on processes for customer acquisition, servicing, and retention and for investment management.

To define your company's core processes, ask: Who are our key customers? What are the flows from input to output that add value to these customers? What are the main products or outputs that our customers look to us to provide? What steps are necessary to produce these outputs?

SET CUSTOMER-FOCUSED STRETCH OBJECTIVES FOR EACH PROCESS

Once core processes are defined, executives must evaluate each one according to external customer measures more than internal management measures. For example, one manufacturer of large transformers traditionally measured "parts shipped on time," defining "shipped" as "left company property." The business scored an average of 95 percent on this measure. In reality, however, when a transformer's scheduled delivery date arrived, the transformer was often placed on a flatbed rail car adjacent to the plant. It could sit there for weeks, still being worked on by company employees, but because the railway siding was not on company property, the unfinished transformer passed the test of having been "shipped." When a customer-focused process measure was put in place, there was a better indictor of timeliness: "products received by the customer on time." Under this measure, the business's success rate fell to about 75 percent.

Typical customer-focused process measures are reduced cycle time, decreased costs through more integrated logistics processes, and increased responsiveness through fewer steps in meeting customer needs. To develop measures like these, go to your best source of data—customers themselves. Ask them how *they* measure and assess your effectiveness and what it would take to delight them. Then look at your organization and test whether you are measuring indicators that align with your customers' expectations. For example, most airline passengers have experienced the joy of boarding a flight prior to the scheduled departure time, then having the plane roll away from the gate exactly on time only to stop on the tarmac fifteen feet away, whereupon the passengers are told that their arrival airport is closed or maintenance has reported a problem and that they are not going anywhere for quite a while. They are victims of the definition of "on-time departure" that says, "left the gate within fifteen minutes of schedule." Although passengers would much prefer to do their waiting in the terminal, the industry's performance measures do not recognize that expectation. Like the transformers, the passengers have been shipped "on time."

Putting the right measures in place, of course, is only the starting point. Setting ambitious stretch goals for the achievement of process improvements is equally critical. Without such stretch goals, people think about maintaining the numbers rather than changing them. Stretch goals force fresh thinking about the processes themselves. For example, the president of a major drug company recently told his R&D organization to reduce from ten years to four years the cycle time from "first human test" of a new drug to "FDA approval." Before he set this seemingly impossible goal, R&D managers were already working very hard to streamline the existing process, but they were not questioning the construction of the process itself. Once the six-year improvement goal was seriously laid out, a host of new ideas for constructing a "drug development factory," for using information technology in new ways, and for outsourcing portions of the process began to receive serious consideration. Although it is too early to see results, the change in managers' thinking alone has been palpable.

ASSIGN PROCESS LEADERS

Once executives have identified core processes and customer-focused measures and stretch goals, the next step is to assign clear accountability to process leaders. A process leader is equivalent to the lead person in a jazz band, who not only plays an instrument but gets the other instrumentalists to "jam" together. The lead person also arranges for a place to play, makes sure the music gets started, and often sets the beat.

Similarly, process leaders are responsible for shepherding the flow of information, materials, or resources across boundaries within the firm, while in many cases, they also play a functional role. For example, in 1994, Hewlett-Packard identified order fulfillment as one of the firm's top three "hoshin," or priorities. An order fulfillment manager was then placed in charge of ensuring that this process was managed and improved throughout the corporation. The manager reported to the executive committee and had the ability to work across all product, functional, and geographic boundaries to make sure that the order-fulfillment process worked effectively. Another example comes from GE Capital's Commercial Equipment Financing business, where "innovation"—creating and implementing new products and services—was identified as a core process. To make sure that innovation was treated as a process across the different functions and product groups, a senior marketing person was designated as "innovation coordinator," with authority to bring groups together, run workshops, cross-fertilize with ideas, and report to the management committee on other steps it should take. In addition, she was charged with organizing an improvement effort to significantly increase the percentage of revenue generated by new (less than five years old) products and services.

REMOVE PROCESS BARRIERS AND STREAMLINE PROCESS FLOWS

Since orientation around processes is only valuable insofar as it leads to tangible improvement from the customers' perspective, one of the jobs of the process leader is to remove process barriers and/or streamline and reconfigure process flows so others can meet the stretch goals.

A number of tools exist for improving process flows. For example, town meetings of process participants, like those described in Chapter Three, can be employed to remove process barriers that are quick hits, items easily agreed on for removal. GE Capital used the town meeting process to take weeks out of its internal process for purchasing office materials, computer supplies, and contractor services. Participants in the session represented GE Capital businesses that used the purchasing process and the GE Company's corporate purchasing and payment processing functions. By sitting down together for two days, these people discovered a number of surprises: that virtually all purchases, whether for twenty or twenty thousand dollars, were subject to the same process; that almost all purchases required five or six approvals; and that all purchases required extensive paperwork (in green, pink, and yellow multiple copies) even though the same information existed in an electronic database. Participants quickly agreed on changes in approvals, eliminated the paperwork copies, and created an "express" process (requiring no approvals) for purchases under $2,500. They then appointed a process leader to coordinate more extensive changes. Figure 5.1 shows how radically the overall process was simplified after several more town meetings.

Figure 5.1. GE Capital Purchasing Process Map.

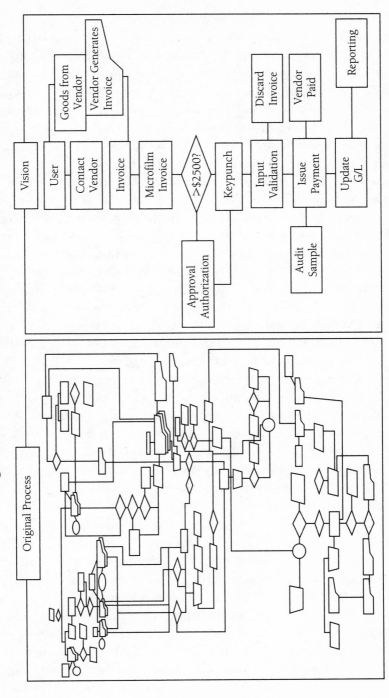

Other tools to improve or reconfigure process flows come from the methodologies of quality control, total quality, and reengineering—for example, process mapping, flowcharting, root-cause analysis, pareto charts, and statistical process control.[1] In our view, the key to using all of these tools is to combine them with the steps outlined previously, that is, a measurable, customer-focused stretch goal, a cross-functional team, and a process leader to pull it all together. Otherwise, they will be used as a small child uses a hammer—the child will find something to pound but is unlikely to build anything constructive.

An overall improvement effort undertaken by J. P. Morgan & Company exemplifies the effective use of a number of process stream-lining tools. In 1993, Morgan was trying to grow some of its key cash and securities processing businesses significantly by installing electron-ic communications tools directly into customer sites—thus giving cus-tomers direct access to and control over transfers, funds flows, and information. Morgan was able to sell the service, but it was taking up to six weeks to complete installation, creating customer satisfaction prob-lems right from the start.

To resolve these problems, Morgan management pulled together a "client access implementation re-engineering" team (CAIR). Led by a product manager, the team included representatives from technical ser-vices, systems, client administration, product development, and client relations. The team created a "responsibility matrix" (Exhibit 5.1) that specified who was responsible and who else was involved for each process step. The team also developed a process map of the installation needed for an upcoming client. (The team's map is shown in Exhibit 5.2.) Team members then brainstormed ways of cutting the time required in half. Ideas included prefilled forms (so customers could check off information rather than write it in), customized training mod-ules for customer users based on their own usage patterns, a program on diskette to download technical specifications from the customer environment, and simulation of the customer environment at Morgan so that system bugs could be worked out before installation.

After these innovations, a model installation was completed success-fully in a record seven days, weeks faster than anything done previous-ly. Equally important, the installation received a high satisfaction score from the customer. In the following months, the CAIR team identified further innovations and eventually created an ongoing process for

Exhibit 5.1. J. P. Morgan & Co. Responsibility Matrix.

Task	IC	TL	SLS	SM	CSR	CTS	LEG	CST	CSH
1. Sell Access									
• Negotiate with client									
• Complete contract									
• Complete licensing agreement									
• Establish accounts									
• Set up billing procedures									
• Agree on the schedule with client									
2. Assemble Implementation Team									
• Designate team leader									
• Select team									
• Conduct launch meeting									
• Assign responsibilities									
• Clarify expectations									
3. Analyze Client Business									
• Send technical survey to client									
• Collect in-house "intelligence" about client									
• Determine client H/W requirements									
• Determine client user profile									
4. Prepare Client Training									
• Determine training requirements									
• Review training curriculum with client									
• Compile training material									
5. Configure and Test System									
• Set up hub									
• Set up CWS									
• Set up Host									
• Set up BWS									
• Test system									
6. Install CWS and Test System									
• Confirm client visit									
• Install CWS software/hardware									
• Test CWS software									
7. Train Client									
• Provide overview and introduction to system									
• Train security administrator									
• Train systems administration									
• Train for instruction									
8. Follow-up with Client									
• Send implementation									

NOTE: Coding for key players' levels of involvement: R = responsible for completing the task; P = participant in the task; I = needs to be informed when task is completed; A = needs to approve task.

Exhibit 5.2. J. P. Morgan & Co. Implementation Process Map.

Phase I

Request for Implementation	Complete Documentation	Analyze Client	Prepare Client Training	Submit Documentation

Request for Implementation

Complete access request for implementation—RFI and submit to IC (Sales)

Assemble implementation team (IC)

Complete Documentation

Complete contracts (CSR, Legal)

Complete licensing agreement (CSR, Legal)

Establish custody and DDA accounts (CSR)

Send start-up materials to client (PC)
• Technical survey (scan for viruses)
• Business survey
• Account forms
• User forms

Set up billing procedures (IC)

Analyze Client

Clarify implementation requirements with client (IC)
• Documentation
• Technology
• Time
• Training

Collect in-house "intelligence" about client business (IC)

Conduct business analysis telephone conference with the client (IC)

Determine client hardware requirements (IC)

Determine client user profile (IC)

Determine client support structure (CSR)

Prepare Client Training

Determine training requirements (IC)

Review training curriculum with the client—and assure staff availability on scheduled site visit (CSR)

Prepare training agenda and verify with client (CSR)

Compile training material based on client's business needs (CSR)

Submit Documentation

Technical survey (IC)

Business survey (IC)

Accounts (IC)

User profiles (IC)

Billing (IC)

Security and systems administrators (IC)

Communications set-up (HUB)

Contract(s) (CSR)

Licensing agreement (CSR)

Phase II

Configure System (In-house)	→	Test System (In-house)	→	Install and Test System (On-site)	→	Train Client	→	Follow-up With Client
Disseminate documentation to Hub Admin, CTS and BIC (IC)		Test System end-to -end (CTS)		Confirm client visit, training schedule and set-up (CTS)		Provide overview and introduction (CTS)		Send implementation survey to the client and follow up (IC)
Set up Hub (HUB)		Scan CWS software ("Unzipped") for viruses		Install CWS software (CTS)		Train on security administration (CTS)		Track volumes (CSR)
Set up CWS (CTS)		Prepare CWS software		Scan client PC(s) for viruses		Train on systems administration (CTS)		Track straight-through rates (CSR)
Set up Host(s) (BIC)		Create and store CWS back up (CTS)		Test CWS Software (CTS)				Ensure revenue is being collected (CSR)
Set up BWS (BIC)						Train on instructions and reporting based on client's business needs		Send overall access survey to client and follow up (IC)
						Train client on support structure/contacts (CTS)		Relay client feedback to Product Development (CTS)
								File implementation report (CTS)

NOTE: IC = implementation coordinator; CSR = client service representative; CTS = client technical services; HUB = hub administration; BIC = branch implementation coordinator.

doing every installation, no matter the size or complexity, in less than two weeks.

In this way, the Morgan team succeeded in reorienting one part of the firm's business around a core process. Team members had successfully applied the first vehicle for creating the boundaryless horizontal organization.

Tackle Processes Through Targeted Teams

Once an organization focuses on processes instead of organizational or functional units, teaming becomes a critical improv vehicle for bringing together the right resources to manage and improve these processes. While some processes can be managed by soloists playing virtuoso music by themselves, most processes require a carefully chosen ensemble to blend specific different instruments together.

The concept of teaming is not new, but it is often misunderstood. In the popular business press, teams have often been billed as the answer to every organizational problem—one more magic bullet that will slay the competitive dragon. The reality, however, is much more complex. Yes, teams are in many ways the lifeblood of organizations with permeable horizontal boundaries. As they bring skills together to accomplish processes, they increase employee commitment, productivity, and feelings of ownership; increase a firm's range of ideas; and create a beneficial social ambiance.

But teams are not appropriate for every kind of work; nor are all teams the same. For example, consultants Jon Katzenbach and Doug Smith make a useful distinction between "working groups" and "teams."[2] Working groups have a common leader and members may meet to share information and make common decisions, but each person is individually accountable for achieving results. Groups do not do real, hash-it-out work together. Team members, in contrast, have shared goals and shared accountability. They produce something together and no one member can succeed in meeting the team goal unless the others also are successful. In addition to shared goals, we would add that effective teams:

◆ Share in a horizontal process that includes a number of different disciplines, functions, or skills.
◆ Have an agreed-upon way of working, a modus operandi, that cuts across the boundaries.
◆ Have shared measures of success and ways of rewarding success.

We have seen numerous companies invest considerable resources in team-building activities, team facilitation, team psychometric testing, and more, with the well-intentioned aim of improving team functioning. Yet in many cases, the "teams" did not have shared goals or collective outputs that depended on joint work. Rather, they were collections of people with various kinds of organizational relationships.

Many senior management "teams" are working groups. Members run their semiautonomous businesses or product lines in parallel, not through a horizontal process that cuts across the entire organization. And there is no collective work product. The final financial results, the goals, are merely aggregated numbers, totaled up from each individual unit.

Moreover, it is often appropriate for senior management to form a working group rather than a team. Part of the success of GE Capital as a financial services conglomerate has been CEO Gary Wendt's insistence that his business leaders do not need always to operate as a team. Instead, he wants each one to be individually accountable for delivering the numbers for his or her own business, even if that means occasionally competing in the marketplace with another GE Capital business. Integration across businesses comes from sharing best practices and competitive information, particularly through quarterly executive council meetings. In this way, Wendt keeps his business leaders totally focused on their own operations. Within most of their own businesses, however, these same leaders work very hard to foster cross-horizontal teams around core processes. For example, GE Capital Aviation Services (GECAS), one of the world's largest aircraft leasers, is organized around regionally based "deal teams." These teams include regional marketing people; underwriters; financial, legal, operations, and servicing people; and others as needed, so that GECAS can bring together resources from the functional organization for a particular customer or for a particular deal and then re-form these resources for the next deal.

To assess the effectiveness of cross-functional teams in your own organization, you can use the Team Effectiveness Checklist (Exhibit 5.3). This checklist contains a number of self-diagnostic questions that test whether your team is really a team and the extent to which your team has the ingredients in place to make it work successfully. We suggest that you answer the questions and discuss the scores in collaboration with other team members.

Exhibit 5.3. Team Effectiveness Checklist.

Instructions: Answer each question by placing the appropriate number of points in the space provided: 5 = to a great extent; 3 = sometimes; 1 = hardly at all.

Part 1. Teams need to be organized around horizontal processes that include different disciplines, functions, or skills.

____ 1. To what extent is there one key process that provides the focus for our team?

____ 2. To what extent does our team represent all of the functions or disciplines that contribute to this process?

____ 3. To what extent is our team composed of the skills needed to maintain and improve this process?

____ 4. To what extent does our team have the ability to add or delete competencies?

Part 2. Teams need to have a shared view of what is to be accomplished, a goal toward which all team members contribute.

____ 5. To what extent is there a specific goal (or goals) that our team needs to accomplish?

____ 6. To what extent do our goals align with and contribute to the overall business goals and objectives?

____ 7. To what extent are our team goals clear and defined in simple terms, so that all team members understand what the team is trying to do?

___ 8. To what extent are our team goals shared among all users of the team's output?

Part 3. Teams need to have agreed-upon ways of working that cut across boundaries.

___ 9. To what extent has our team defined how it will solve problems, make decisions, and handle conflict in the team?

___ 10. To what extent does our team have a process for dealing with poor performance or discipline issues within the team?

___ 11. To what extent does our team dedicate time to assessing team members' ability to work as a team?

___ 12. To what extent is our team clear about roles, about who does what to accomplish team goals?

___ 13. To what extent do all members of our team feel empowered to voice their opinions so that the team makes better and more informed decisions than individuals acting alone?

Part 4. Teams need shared measures of success and ways of rewarding achievement.

___ 14. To what extent are our team's goals measurable and operational?

___ 15. To what extent do all members of our team feel personal responsibility for team results?

___ 16. To what extent do team members share in the rewards earned by our team?

___ **Total score**

Scoring: Interpret your score as follows:

- *65 or more.* Your team is most likely a true team and is functioning reasonably well. You might want to focus on the few key scores that were lowest or the category that received the lowest scores and do some fine-tuning.
- *45 to 65.* There are probably some significant weaknesses in the way your team is functioning. Look to see if the weaknesses are across the board or if there are targeted categories that need immediate attention.
- *Below 45.* You should examine whether your team is really a team and whether team members understand what it means to be a team. The material in the next section on types of teams might be particularly helpful.

When using teams as an improv vehicle to cross horizontal boundaries, it also is necessary to consider the type of team that should be created. Organizational theorist J. D. Thompson noted many years ago that there are three basic types of teams, each one appropriate to different kinds of cross-functional situations.[3] Selecting the right type is as critical as deciding whether to have a team or not.

The three types that Thompson defined are pooled, sequential interdependent, and reciprocal teams. Table 5.1 is a tool we have found useful for targeting the right type of team to a situation and effectively crossing horizontal boundaries. It is critical to use the right type of team if horizontal boundaries are to be loosened rather than solidified.

The following examples illustrate how targeted teams work in practice.

Pooled teams.   In pooled teams, individual team members doing their individual tasks have no direct connection with each other. They do, however, have a common goal (which distinguishes them from working groups), and the team outcome is determined essentially by adding up team members' quotas or outputs. USAA Insurance is an example of the pooled team approach to customer service among the new breed of 800-number insurance agencies. These agencies have gained rapid market share recently by consolidating claims services—previously provided by local agents and several head office support functions—into teams or representatives available through an 800-number.

At USAA, each customer who calls in is assigned to a team and to a person on that team. Every time the customer calls in after that, he or she is transferred to that primary person, who answers questions and can process an entire claim, thus maintaining a feeling of personal service. If the primary person is unavailable, however, another team member can handle the call because each transaction with the customer is dutifully recorded in the database so that any team member can review the case and be up to date on that customer. In other words, each team member is responsible for managing his or her own group of customers. The team and the technology provide back-up. The net result is that the customer always feels that he or she is getting personal attention, and USAA finds that even without on-site agents, customer satisfaction is as high as industry norms.[4]

Many companies have struggled with providing customer service because, rather than pooled teams, they use sequential interdependent

Table 5.1. Targeted Teams: How to Choose What Is Right for You.

	Pooled	Sequential interdependent	Reciprocal
Definition	Individual work added together to achieve a common goal	Individual work tied together in sequence to achieve a common goal	Collective work to achieve a common goal
Criteria for Using	When the same processes can be performed simultaneously by multiple team members	When a process can be divided into sequential tasks or subprocesses	When the process is constantly changing or needs to be uniquely applied for each situation or customer; when there is a need for creating something new
Horizontal Boundary Issues	Need for common training, materials, and procedures Each member needs to carry his or her own weight How to manage variation in output	How to manage hand-offs Can some tasks be performed in parallel? How can the process be speeded up?	How to replicate and learn from different applications How to assign and manage roles and responsibilities
Examples	Piece work Bowling team	Assembly line	New product development Hospital operating room Basketball team

teams, and customers who call in are handed off from function to function. The sales process is also one that lends itself to a pooled team approach, because it allows each salesperson to use his or her own approach to achieving the sale.

Sequential interdependent teams.   The members of a sequential interdependent team depend on each other in a "line." One person's output becomes the next person's input, as in an assembly line. People work essentially alone, but they have a common goal. Because people are dependent on each other for input, the critical issue for team effectiveness is the management of the interfaces. At Eastman Kodak, a sequential interdependent team approach was used to reinvigorate the Black & White Film Division. As we described earlier, new manager Stephen Frangos found his division weighted down with old technology, older equipment, rather traditional functional processes, poor performance, and bad morale.

To revitalize the division, Frangos formed a number of sequential interdependent teams organized around key manufacturing and business processes. They were given increased responsibility for managing their end-to-end processes, for making decisions that affected their operations, and for reengineering their work flows. They then spent time setting work norms, defining process and business goals, agreeing on hand-off procedures, and improving work processes. As a by-product, the teams also became social forums for employees to share concerns and celebrate successes. Through the revitalization effort, the Black & White Division not only turned around its financial performance but transformed its culture. Employees became reenergized. They felt more commitment to their job and work.[5]

Reciprocal teams.   The members of reciprocal teams have a common goal but do not have a routinized work flow. Instead, they work collectively together. Reciprocal teams are found in hospital operating rooms when a group of doctors must work in a highly synchronized and unified manner to save a patient even though each situation is unique. New product development teams and problem-solving task forces are also usually best organized as reciprocal teams.

Harley-Davidson used a reciprocal team approach to sustain a companywide turnaround, after the firm's market share dropped from over 60 percent to 25 percent in the late 1970s, and Harley managers took over the ownership of the firm in 1982. Over the next decade, the company experienced a dramatic turnaround through new product development and creative marketing. The Harley motorcycle became a symbol of freedom, an emblem of a life-style shared by customers of all ages and social ranks. But Richard Teerlink, president and CEO, Harley-Davidson Inc., knew that to bring Harley to a new stage of success in the 1990s much more creativity and innovation would be needed. He wanted to create an organization that avoided internal politics and boundaries, that sharpened its focus on innovative products that gave added value to customers, and that empowered employees. With these goals in mind, he and his top managers created a team-based organization to replace the traditional hierarchical structure.

The new Harley organization was envisioned as three overlapping circles: create demand, produce product, and provide support. The "create demand" team integrated all activities related to customers: market research, customer service, distribution, and customer contact. The "produce product" team focused on engineering, manufacturing, and assembling the product. The "provide support" team consisted of the staff support functions—finance, information services, human resources, legal, and so on.

Because these teams were reciprocal, they were not hierarchically focused. Each team voted on its team leader, set goals as a team, and operated collectively to achieve the goals for its area of operation. It also shared accountability and rewards for the performance within its domain.

At the intersection of the three overlapping circles was the Long Range Strategy Group. It included Teerlink and Jeff Bleustein, president and COO of Harley-Davidson Motor Company. Each circle team also nominated two members to serve on the committee. Thus, the concept of reciprocal teamwork was the dominant logic in the new Harley organization—an organization that helped Harley ride beyond its performance in the early part of the decade.

Turn Vertical Dimensions Sideways

Once the organization is oriented around processes and has targeted teams in place to manage and improve these processes, the same four dimensions that had to be digitally tuned in the vertical dimension—

information, competence, authority, and rewards—come into play again. In order to enhance the effectiveness of the process and team approach, they need to be tuned sideways—across functions, disciplines, and product groups—amplifying the music played by the teams. Reconceiving these dimensions then, so that they expand and reverberate across horizontal boundaries, is the third improv vehicle that can help create horizontal boundarylessness.

The specific tools and techniques for moving these four dimensions sideways, across different types of process teams and structures, are described below.

Tools and Techniques for Moving Four Dimensions Sideways

Information: Share databases across functions; conduct cross-functional meetings; publish cross-functional newsletters, videos, and other communications; co-locate related functions.

Competence: Use cross-functional rotation planning; transfer best practices and create common culture at a corporate "university."

Authority: Encourage team decision processes; use working team huddles; set up cross-functional steering committees.

Rewards: For pooled teams, use individual rewards; for sequential interdependent teams, combine individual and team rewards; for reciprocal teams, use team objectives, team measures (including 360-degree feedback), and team rewards.

MOVING INFORMATION SIDEWAYS

There are four primary ways that we have found to move information sideways, across horizontal boundaries. First, information may be shared across functions by creating common databases. Hewlett-Packard employees use a database to share information updates and new ideas across product groups. The World Bank "all-in-one" system allows teams to set up e-mail distribution lists so that all member-to-member correspondence, meeting notes, and progress reports can be easily shared. SmithKline Beecham R&D uses groupware technology to set up databases by subject so that people from different functions or locations can contribute to a dialogue in a specific area.

Second, information can be shared across boundaries in cross-functional meetings. Motorola holds an annual conference, attended by executives from almost every functional and business group, for sharing the best learnings from quality teams across the company. The conference is also a motivator and a reward for the teams.

Third, it is important not to forget traditional written and videotaped information sharing. These are among the ways that AT&T disseminates learnings from its annual award process for best practices in human resources.

Finally, simply physically moving people together is a powerful tool for encouraging greater horizontal information exchange. When NASA wanted to study the global water cycle and its effect on climate variations, one of the first steps was to co-locate a number of scientists, educators, and flight engineers in an interdisciplinary center.

MOVING COMPETENCE SIDEWAYS

The two primary vehicles for moving competence across horizontal boundaries are rotation planning and cross-functional training.

Rotation planning is, of course, the intentional movement of people from one function, process, or product group to another. The goal is to increase each individual's competence by broadening his or her experience and to increase overall organizational competence as groups are cross-pollinated with the skills and experience of the rotated employees. For example, Baxter Healthcare's succession planning process encourages the rotation of individuals across product and functional boundaries, and Unilever moves employees across product lines and around the world to ensure that competencies flow across functions.

Cross-functional training, in which people from different disciplines, functions, and product groups train together, produces two types of learning. On the one hand, people engage in informal exchanges of ideas and techniques; on the other hand, the common experience encourages a common organizational culture and language. Motorola and its famous university are perhaps the best example of using training and development experiences to engender cross-functional competence. For example, when Motorola wanted to expand operations in China, Motorola University was its forum for sharing competencies around competing in China. Managers from product lines that would market in China, managers who had experience entering international markets, and managers who had functional expertise on competing in China were brought together to share experiences, ideas, and approaches.

MOVING AUTHORITY SIDEWAYS

Authority or decision making can be moved across horizontal boundaries in a number of ways.

The first vehicle is to enhance team decision making by giving teams the authority to make decisions about their work processes and by agreeing upon consultation routines. For example, each of Harley-Davidson's three circle teams has the authority to make decisions about processes within its circle. However, if the decision affects another circle, the first circle must systematically touch base with those who would be affected before enacting the decision.

Another tool for encouraging horizonal decision making is what we call the *huddle*. Originally developed by Wal-Mart, the huddle brings people together from different functions or from different steps within a process, usually on a regular basis, for very quick and disciplined on-the-spot decision making. At the World Bank, a team of HR generalists and HR specialists that supports two operating regions with organization development, training, group facilitation, and so on, huddles for thirty minutes each morning to share client information and make immediate decisions about policy positions, client support, and individual cases. Once a week, the huddle is expanded to include the support team that processes transactions. At these expanded huddles, immediate decisions are made about streamlining or eliminating various transaction processes that have come up during the week.

A third vehicle for enhancing horizontal decision making is the cross-functional steering committee. In Motorola's communications sector, this committee is composed of the leaders from engineering, manufacturing, finance, marketing, quality, and so on, and is the primary forum for making critical decisions about new product development projects. Whenever new product development teams arrive at an important decision point (which material to use for a part, which vendor to use, whether to change a technical design, how to position a product in the product line, how to price a product, and the like), the project "prime" calls together the steering committee. The committee's job is to make a decision that is owned by all functions across the horizontal spectrum.

MOVING REWARDS SIDEWAYS

As teams become more cross-functional, reward systems must change correspondingly. In our view, each type of team requires a different strategy if rewards are to be motivational. Because people in pooled teams work individually, individual measures and rewards or commission systems make sense. People who go beyond what would be ordinarily expected can be rewarded, while good workers will not be penalized because another person has not contributed his or her full share.

The reward system for sequentially interdependent teams probably needs to be a combination of individual and team incentives. People need incentives both for doing their own piece of the work effectively and for managing the hand-offs and interfaces that make a difference to the achievement of the collective team goal. At the same time, sequentially interdependent teams often perform well in the context of gainsharing plans that include an entire plant or work site. In this case, the incentives to work together may outweigh the loss of individual incentive, particularly if the collective plan provides line of sight, meaning that individuals can see how they personally contribute to the team's objectives and how they are rewarded when the team succeeds.

Reciprocal teams are the most highly cross-functional and require rewards systems to match. When it is impossible to measure how much each individual contributed, then team-based rewards are needed for achievement so that each team member receives bonuses, recognition, trips, and the like equally.

Create Shared Services for Support Processes

The core processes described earlier are bolstered and facilitated by a number of support processes.[6] Usually resident in staff functions such as personnel, legal, and finance, these support processes often create unnecessary rigidity in horizontal boundaries because they are oriented toward control rather than service or because the demand for them is greater than the resources they can make available at an effective cost.

Shared services, as the name implies, is the consolidating of staff service functions within an organization and the fourth improv vehicle for loosening horizontal boundaries. In divisionalized companies, each operating unit likely has dedicated support processes. Shared services merges these separate activities into one function that crosses units. For example, at AlliedSignal and Amoco Corporation, the shared service includes the majority of the business services: law, finance, information systems, human resources, real estate, and security.

In addition, in many companies, the same teams or individuals that manage core processes also provide various kinds of support processes, a service that deflects their energy from the core processes. For example, the manager of a new product development team might also be responsible for handling employment verification for the team members, signing off on or filling out forms for changes in employment status, and hiring part-time workers. In a shared services environment, these activities are unbundled, or separated out, from the core processes.

When support processes are both *shared* and *services,* the organization removes support redundancies and overlapping work and allows people to concentrate on their core process responsibilities. This can produce tremendous productivity gains. At the same time, when the emphasis is on service instead of corporate control and functional turf, far better support is provided to those core processes.

Furthermore, the vehicle of shared services is not an alternate form of centralization. It is the opposite of centralization because, as one manager of a shared services unit summed it up, "the user is the chooser of the services offered." Corporate does not control who uses what services. It is a *pull* not a *push* system. The distinction is critical and leads to a number of other differences, which are summarized in Table 5.2.

The shared services process begins when executives examine organizational support processes with the aim of identifying common or similar services. Clearly, the large corporation that found it had three separate payroll processing systems feeding separate and differently formatted information into the corporate accounting system uncovered a major shared services opportunity. The company that found it had over twenty different "training registration and tracking" services but no way of pulling together good data about training utilization had discovered a less dramatic but still highly useful shared services opportunity.

After identifying such opportunities, executives should ask: Would pulling together these common support processes potentially add greater speed, flexibility, integration, and innovation to the organization at less cost? If a number of support processes pass this test, the next issue is to determine the appropriate type of shared services to use.

TWO TYPES OF SHARED SERVICES

Organizational support processes fall into two types—transaction based and transformation based—which require different modes of delivery. Management should consider two primary criteria in determining the appropriate way to deliver each process: how often is the support process used across the organization and what expertise is required to provide the support. The matrix in Figure 5.2 shows the relationship between these two criteria and whether a shared services approach is recommended at all, and if so, which one is recommended.

Table 5.2. Differences Between Centralized and Shared Services.

Centralized Services	Shared Services
• Control the field.	• Are controlled by process users.
• Retain power at the top of the hierarchy.	• Disburse power and influence.
• Push activities to the field.	• Allow process users to pull resources from corporate.

Figure 5.2. Selecting a Shared Services Approach.

	Low	High
High	Create service centers (high-tech)	Create centers of expertise—in-house or outsourced (high-touch)
Low	Allow each unit to manage on its own	Outsource or contract service outside

Frequency/Volume of Process Across the Organization

Technical and Organizational Expertise Required

Transaction-Based Activities Performed in Service Centers

Transaction-based activities are largely routine administrative tasks with standardized service requirements that can be common across numerous business locations. They are also usually high-volume activities. For a human resource group, for example, they include administering benefits policies, changing individual compensation arrangements, payroll processing, keeping vacation records, tracking educational assistance and training, organizing corporate charitable campaigns, managing relocation activities, handling travel reimbursements, responding to job application requests, and providing company information and employment verification.

Because transaction-based services are information-intense and routine, they lend themselves to support provided by well-trained administrative personnel or given through highly automated channels such as 800-numbers, voice mail, e-mail, interactive voice response, voice recognition systems, and video teleconferencing—especially in organizations where transaction frequency is high. In such cases, the shared service function can easily be located in a single physical area, a *service center.* Requests for benefits information, employment status, salary ranges, and positions available are all easily handled by a service center equipped with voice mail and teleconferencing.

When Northern Telecom created such a service center for human resource information inquiries (as one aspect of the consolidation described in Chapter Four), for instance, it went from seventy people across seven locations to fewer than forty people in one location, saving over $1 million per year with an initial investment of only $500,000. Northern Telecom also discovered that about 30 percent of all human resource information inquiries could be managed satisfactorily without face-to-face intervention.

Sometimes, automation even allows users to take care of their own support. At Northern Telecom, managers and staff can enter their own personal data (change of address, marital status, number of children, and so on) directly into the service center computer system from their own work stations.

A service center should be designed not only to manage support process transactions but also to continually reengineer, streamline, and improve support processes. As processes are brought into the central center, they can more easily be put under the microscope and examined for usefulness. When the World Bank HR service center unbundled tasks previously done by dozens of different personnel officers, it found that a number of them were unnecessary. For example, personnel officers had been listing open positions in each division in "vacancy reports" when the same information was readily available elsewhere.

Of course, when a support process requiring little expertise is not often called for, the service center approach may be inappropriate—like using a 20-gauge shotgun to kill a fly. In such cases, it may be more cost- and customer-effective for each business unit or core process team to handle the transactions on its own. For example, in an organization that rarely uses temporary clerical support, making such support a service center function would probably be seen as bureaucratic and meddlesome rather than helpful.

Transformation-Based Activities Performed in Centers of Expertise

Transformation-based activities are nonroutine and nonadministrative activities that tend to involve unique situations and call for person-to-person contact, deep knowledge, and individual expertise. For example, transformation-based activities in an HR context include staffing, career planning and development, compensation, communication (PR and media), employee and union relations, and organizational development. Other expertise-based services in an organization might include tax accounting, security planning, real-estate strategy and planning, and systems development.

Sharing transformation-based services requires a high-touch rather than high-tech approach. The specific vehicle is a *center of expertise*. Staffed by experts in the appropriate support processes, the center can leverage their advice across the company, somewhat as an in-house consulting function would. A center of expertise is most appropriate when each business location or unit cannot afford to hire its own full-time expert, but the combined volume of work across the organization will support one or more full-time experts.

PPG, for instance, established ten Centers of Human Resource Expertise to provide highly professional support to its strategic business units, none of which could have afforded to maintain this level and range of expertise on its own. Center names were chosen to be understandable to customers: Productivity/Employee Satisfaction, Measurement, External Factors, Leadership, Work Processes/Operating Methods, Safety and Environment, Workforce Skills, Organization Structure, and Business Strategy. Each center is staffed with one or two experts who can offer advice and counsel on specific business problems and work on projects for the SBUs.

Management should also consider whether the expertise needed is generic (applicable in most companies) or organizational (requiring deep knowledge of a specific company). Setting up a pension plan, administering it, and managing the funds are highly specialized skills, but they are generic. They can be applied in almost any kind of setting. However, providing good staffing advice requires organizational as well as special expertise. The expert should have in-depth knowledge of what a business unit is trying to achieve, the skills it needs, and the pool of talent available.

Most often, degrees of both types of expertise are desirable. In general, however, when there is a high volume of support process work that requires only generic expertise, an outsourced center of expertise is worth exploring. For example, Continental Bank outsourced its systems development and maintenance activities after determining that the skills required were sufficiently generic to be done by an IBM subsidiary.[7] Many other organizations have outsourced such services as security, language training, food preparation, travel management, and insurance. When expert support requires considerable organizational knowledge, then the center of expertise is usually more effectively kept in-house.

Finally, centers of expertise should not be created if the frequency of support required in either generic or organizational expertise does not warrant it. In such cases, organizations should either contract out the services as they are needed or use consultants. For example, the retail side of Fidelity Investments periodically requires strategic development of internal communications approaches and materials. To bring both technical skill and organizational knowledge to bear on this part-time need, Fidelity works with the same communications consultant each time, on a long-term retainer arrangement.

SHARED SERVICES IN ACTION: AN EVOLUTIONARY APPROACH

Starting in the late 1980s, Albert F. Ritardi, vice president of corporate administrative services at AlliedSignal Corporation, began a multiyear transformation of the services unit from a traditional functional staff group to a series of shared services. His three-phase process illustrates what it takes to use shared services as a vehicle for permeating horizontal boundaries.

When Ritardi first took over Corporate Administrative Services, it had a corporate staff of several hundred people who managed corporate activities ranging from pension services (for both current and retired employees), 401(K) savings plan administration, the human resource information system, aviation services, corporate travel, corporate real estate and facilities, corporate transportation and distribution, corporate payroll processing, and corporate security. Some functions supported corporate headquarters staff while others focused on the entire corporation. All, however, were performed along traditional lines—through establishment of policy and procedures, monitoring of those procedures, and hands-on implementation of day-to-day tasks. Costs were high and the service mentality low. In fact, many of the service people felt the key to doing their jobs better was to get the operating people to "cooperate" better.

Given the potpourri of functions, the first phase of Ritardi's effort was what he called "census reduction and traditional problem solving." In essence, he took the existing functions and tried to make them work better and less expensively. He consolidated some units and tightened up certain policies and procedures (vendor contracts for example) to gain immediate cost reductions.

In the course of doing this, Ritardi realized that the services really fell into two categories—centers of scale (our service centers) and centers of expertise—and that he needed to treat the two categories differently. He found that centers of scale could reduce costs through consolidation, standardization, process changes, and technology. Therefore, he made activities such as payroll check processing, travel services, transportation and distribution systems, and human resource transactional processes such as corporate benefits administration into centers of scale. Centers of expertise, Ritardi realized, could improve service through leveraging advice across the company and getting business units to pay (charge-back) for center services. He applied this approach to real-estate and property tax consultation, facilities management, benefits consultation, and the development of HR systems applications, among other services.

After two years of work, Ritardi had reduced the unit's overall headcount by 40 percent and saved the corporation $12 million. However, by this time, he understood that the support processes in the unit represented only a fraction of the support processes performed in the corporation. AlliedSignal was a conglomerate of businesses, with three semiautonomous sectors: Aerospace, Automotive, and Engineered Materials. And in each sector, many of the very same support processes that Ritardi's organization managed for corporate staff were being duplicated for sector personnel. For example, he found that Corporate Administrative Services managed only 30 percent of the company's total pension services, only 10 percent of the payroll, and only 20 percent of the security services. Even aviation services were duplicated. Each sector had its own corporate jets.

Armed with this information, in 1991, Ritardi began the second phase of his efforts: "consolidation and performance improvement." With the support of AlliedSignal's new chairman, Lawrence Bossidy, Ritardi set out to bring the corporate and sector support processes together as shared services. To start, he abandoned the viewpoint of the traditional organizational chart and, instead, focused on processes. For each key support process, he and his people identified where in the corporation this process was handled most effectively and efficiently. Then, where it made sense, Ritardi orchestrated a shift of all instances of the process to this location. For example, it was determined that the aerospace sector had already invested considerable time and resources in developing a state-of-the-art payroll processing system. Rather than create a new corporate payroll processing function, AlliedSignal made the aerospace sector the owner of the payroll process for the entire corporation, receiving a fee from the other sectors and from corporate for the payroll service. Then the other sectors and corporate shut down their payroll processing organizations.

In many cases, Corporate Administrative Services became the owner of the process, either because it had the best way of doing it or because the process required a consistent corporate perspective or would be a distraction to a business unit. In a few other cases, responsibility was shared between the corporate centers and the sectors. For example, the corporate center of expertise for security services oversaw the creation of an outsourced master contract and established guidelines for each business, but many businesses argued that they had local considerations that required process management closer to the situation, and thus they kept control of the performance of the service.

During the course of the consolidation, Ritardi also focused on performance improvement. Particularly as processes achieved greater scale and critical mass, more technology and process improvements were possible. For example, 800-number national customer service response and help lines were established for processes such as savings plan administration, pension delivery, and HR systems and staffing. The overall result was another $12 million of real-cost savings as well as significant customer service improvement.

By the end of 1993, however, Ritardi realized that despite all the consolidations and cost savings, processes were all-too-often performed in much the same way as before. Customer service was still not a high enough priority, and true reengineering of the processes had only just begun. Thus, he began a third phase of transformation: "reengineering for customer service."

While the full results of this phase are not yet complete, the outlines are certainly in place. Each center of scale and center of expertise is rigorously reengineering its support processes, and $18 million of potential savings from such reengineering has already been identified. One reengineering goal is to create global platforms for support processes that will give AlliedSignal consistent support worldwide while it maintains the ability to tailor support processes for each business or location.

Another aspect of this phase of work is Ritardi's vision of grouping the shared service centers into a single global business services initiative. The Global Business Services Organization, created in early 1994, includes a financial business services group, a human resource business services group, an administrative business services group, and a data center/network services group. These four groups will share their own support organization that will provide them with applications development, reengineering help, communications and customer service help, and the like. They will also receive input and guidance from a shared services "board of directors" consisting of the three AlliedSignal sector presidents and the two senior corporate officers responsible for the finance and human resource processes of the corporation.

By envisioning the value of shared services, Ritardi clearly created a vehicle for providing support to AlliedSignal's core business in a flexible and cost-effective way that cut across horizontal boundaries. And there is much more to come. Ritardi now says: "Yogi Berra was wrong in saying that 'it ain't over 'til it's over.' It's never over!"

Develop Organizational Learning Capability

To this point, we have reviewed four improv vehicles for quickly and flexibly pulling together different combinations of skills and disciplines—the jazz ensembles—that cross the horizontal boundaries of an organization. The last vehicle is developing organizational learning capability.[8] This is the "sound system" that connects these various ensembles together so they can benefit from each other. Without it, each new ensemble will be starting completely from scratch—with no knowledge of its various predecessor's musical ability, no experience to build upon, no riffs and patterns to serve as starting points.

In our definition, *learning capability* is the ability of the organization to learn from the lessons of its experience and to pass those lessons across boundaries and time. Without this capability, the organization will tend to recreate its own solutions rather than leverage its investments in change and improvement. People will spend too much of their time on figuring out necessary styles and rhythm by watching internal colleagues (who are also trying to figure it out) when they should be focusing on the customer.

Our definition also distinguishes between *learning* and *learning capability*. We mean to broaden the scope of learning to an evolutionary process that includes both first-order and second-order learning. This distinction originates in the work of Chris Argyris and Donald Schön of Harvard University.[9] *First-order learning* involves improving the organization's capacity to achieve specific, known objectives; *second-order learning* reevaluates the nature of the objectives and the values and beliefs underlying them. For example, creating a new product involves first-order learning; redesigning the process by which new products are created requires second-order learning.

GENERATE AND GENERALIZE IDEAS WITH IMPACT

The process of developing learning capability can be captured in a simple conceptual formula.

$$(G_1 \times G_2)II = LC$$

In this formula:

> LC is *learning capability.*
> G_1 is *generate:* the process of continuously creating, acquiring, adapting, or improving upon ideas at all organizational levels.
> G_2 is *generalize:* the process of building upon ideas and sharing them across time and space and across hierarchical and functional boundaries throughout the organization.
> II is *ideas with impact:* ideas that add value to the firm's stakeholders over a long period of time.

Idea generation without idea generalization is not true learning capability. Many managers experiment and innovate, trying new marketing, manufacturing, and organizational arrangements. Often an individual initiative works, but if it is not generalized to other situations, locations, or customers, then true organizational learning has not occurred.

Similarly, ideas without impact do not create true learning capability. A firm that spends large portions of its training budget to ensure that managers know how to follow procedures, fill out forms, and create accountabilities is not creating ideas with impact. Any old idea will not do. Organizations with learning capability are able to distinguish between ideas that serve to maintain boundaries and the status quo and ideas that push boundaries and stimulate real change. That is why our formula *multiplies* by II. If the idea has true impact, the generalization of the idea will create value far beyond a one-time application. But if the idea has no impact, then no amount of generalization will make a difference.

Motorola is an example of a company that has effectively used learning capability as a key to competitive success. Starting in the mid 1980s with the advent of its Organizational Effectiveness Process (OEP),[10] Motorola made learning capability an explicit improv vehicle for crossing horizontal boundaries and adding value. The process was launched in April 1983 when chairman Robert Galvin announced to company officers at their annual meeting that despite record earnings, Motorola was becoming slow, ponderous, and bureaucratic. He called for a "renewal" of the company, but did not specify what that meant or how it was to be achieved. That, he said, was up to the officers to figure out. As it turned out, what they created was a powerful iterative learning capability that continues to drive Motorola's success more than a decade later.

Galvin and his team shaped the OEP effort not around a set of directives but a "framework" that outlined which issues every officer and business unit should work on. The framework included thoughts about business strategy, structure, management process, and performance goals. Each business unit was to translate this framework into a series of action projects, or experiments, that would give the officers some tangible experiences in organizational renewal. They were to be the sparks that would ignite specific ideas with impact. Some early projects were separating out the high-end and low-end salesforces of the cellular communications business, accelerating the product development process for mobile radio products, creating worldwide product responsibilities for the semiconductor sector, and creating new venture teams to explore untapped markets in the communications sector.

To make sure the ideas generated were generalized beyond a single business unit, each general manager was required to write a yearly paper reporting on his or her experiments and what was learned from them. This process is still used and the papers are still discussed by the senior policy committee and in other management forums. In addition, Motorola uses the annual officers meeting to review progress and learnings, and it produces videotapes and other training programs to spread the word whenever an innovation seems to have application elsewhere.

The result of this generalization process has been the rapid spreading of ideas within Motorola. For example, an "experimental" new product development process that was tried in the Mobile Division in Fort Worth, Texas, rapidly became a model that is now used throughout the company. In short, Motorola's success has been due not only to its creativity but to its intentional development of learning capability.

In our experience, building learning capability is one of the most powerful actions executives can take to ensure long-term competitiveness and success. The three specific steps that follow develop this capability.

Steps for Developing Learning Capability

- Build a commitment to learning.
- Understand and foster an organizational learning style.
- Encourage an idea generalization culture.

BUILD A COMMITMENT TO LEARNING

People must be taught why learning is critical, and this teaching will require a strong organizational effort. The need for learning can be framed intellectually (it develops competence, capacity for change, ability to compete, and so on) or affectively (it improves oneself), but learning must be backed by commitment from the organization. If it is just a "nice to do" activity, it will fall by the wayside in the face of other priorities. The commitment to learning can be fostered through such activities as these:

Make learning a visible and central element of the strategic intent.   For example, Harley-Davidson made "intellectual curiosity" one of its five core values. It expects all employees to challenge the status quo and look for ways to improve. In Chairman Richard Teerlink's words: "All employees must be willing to question why things are being done they way they are. Open-minded review of every aspect of an organization is essential for success."

Invest in learning.   The number of dollars and the scope of time invested in training programs to create learning strategies, learning activities, and sharing best practices across functions and divisions are powerful signals to employees about commitment to learning.

Measure, benchmark, and track learning.   Process measures can build the learning commitment. For example, when employees track cycle time on processes such as payables, inventory turnarounds, and order-to-remittance, they are also tracking their ability to respond—a measure that can encourage the learning of improvements. Similarly, benchmarking external competitors on the same process times can yield useful comparisons that produce learning opportunities.

Create symbols of learning.   Awards and events to reward performance encourage the dissemination of ideas throughout an organization.

UNDERSTAND AND FOSTER AN ORGANIZATIONAL LEARNING STYLE

In addition to creating a commitment to learning, organizations also need to learn how to learn. To gain a better understanding of how organizations learn to learn, two of us, aided by a colleague, collected data from over 380 businesses around the world.[11] Analysis of the data revealed four learning styles. Each has implications for developing learning capability.

Learning through continuous improvement.   Managers in organizations geared to continuous improvement generate ideas through a constant determination to improve on what has been and should be done. They work to master each step in the improvement process, using suggestion systems, task forces, reengineering design teams, flowcharting, and the like. At the same time, these continuous improvement learners tend to have more bureaucratic cultures and a lower capacity for change than other learning types. Thirty-four percent of respondents identified this method as their dominant style.

Learning through competence acquisition.   Some organizations demonstrate public commitment to learning by acquiring competence (new talent or ideas) from either inside or outside the company—rotating people into new divisions or buying companies or individuals with certain skills. Firms in this category tend to have a narrower range of new ideas than other learning types, although they are more competitive. Evidently, when the competencies acquired are about how to produce change, organizations respond by being more competitive. Twenty-five percent of respondents identified this learning method as their dominant style.

Learning through experimentation.   Other businesses focus on trying out new ideas right away. They tend to be the first in their industries to market a new product or try new manufacturing tactics. GM's Saturn plant, for example, experiments with new organizational arrangements and manufacturing technologies. These companies are usually willing to try new ideas before they are fully tested. They act quickly, knowing that the risks may be high. Our research indicated that such firms faced a higher probability of having difficulty in finding enough alternatives before acting and of not having complete cognitive maps before acting. However, overall, the experimenters have the highest capacity for change. Twenty-one percent of respondents identified this method as their company's dominant learning style.

Learning through boundary spanning.   A final group of companies generates ideas by going outside organizational boundaries and learning what other companies do. Benchmarking best practices is commonplace. For example, Digital Equipment Corporation used benchmarking to revise its human resource practices, while Samsung, Motorola, Whirlpool, and Boeing have sent hundreds of employees to Japan to learn from Japanese manufacturing technologies. GE formed a consortium with Toshiba, United Packaging, and other noncompetitors to share best practices. However, our research showed that this kind of company often generated too many alternatives (learning possibilities), resulting in difficulty with coordinating, sharing, and implementing the new concepts. Boundary spanners also had the lowest overall capacity for change, perhaps because their managers tend to look outside for ideas but do not always make change happen inside the firm. Fifteen percent of respondents identified this method as their dominant learning type.

Understanding these learning styles and knowing which may work best for an organization's strategy, culture, and context (industry and market position) can help leaders find more innovative, creative ways to generate and generalize ideas. Note, however, that learning styles, like personality types, are seldom pure; businesses may and should adopt multiple learning styles. We suggest you talk with your colleagues about which learning style predominates in your organization and whether you feel this style is sufficiently robust. Then, identify at least one other style that would be worth fostering to expand your learning range and also identify steps to encourage that style. For example, if your organization tends to focus on continuous improvement, looking within for opportunities to improve, then set up a best-practices field trip to another company and expose people to learning through boundary spanning.

ENCOURAGE AN IDEA
GENERALIZATION CULTURE

A public commitment to learning and an understanding of organizational learning style will flourish only in a supportive culture. Figure 5.3 depicts a management architecture that encourages the growth of such a culture through the design of the six domains discussed below.

Develop a shared mindset.   When managers build a culture focused on learning capability, they acknowledge the value of learning and explicitly encourage individuals to share ideas across boundaries. They can work to build commitment to learning into the shared mindset of the company through:

◆ Welcoming inquiry and analysis of all decisions
◆ Not punishing failures that are the result of overreaching
◆ Encouraging a norm of reciprocity (two-way feedback)
◆ Building dialogue into decision-making processes
◆ Avoiding a one-best-way mentality that discourages individuals from learning from each other

Figure 5.3. Creating a Learning Culture.

1. Shared Mindset (Organizational Culture) To what extent does our culture promote learning?			
2. Competence	*3. Consequence*	*4. Governance*	*5. Capacity for Change*
To what extent do we have individual, team, and organizational competencies that facilitate learning?	To what extent does our performance management system encourage learning?	To what extent do our organizational structures and communication processes facilitate learning?	To what extent do our work processes and systems encourage learning?
6. Leadership To what extent do leaders throughout our organization demonstrate a commitment to learning?			

The mindset for learning is a critical dimension. Organizations must consider that learning can occur along a continuum from superficial to substantial. Substantial learning does not occur until organizational initiatives (for example, continuous improvement or reengineering) reshape the fundamental values and culture of not only employees but the organization as a system. A commitment to learning also recognizes how regular small failures foster learning while constant successes restrict ideas and cause complacency and risk aversion. Small failures have a positive influence on long-term performance by increasing risk tolerance and problem recognition and encouraging deeper information processing. Leaders need to avoid punishing people for failures (unless they are of a persistent and avoidable pattern); instead, they must milk failures for learnings.

Build organizational competence.   As we have discussed, competence relates to the ways in which managers encourage the development of knowledge, skills, and ability. In the context of creating a culture that supports learning, specific actions that leaders can take include:

◆ Rotating assignments across divisions systematically
◆ Hiring knowledgeable outsiders into key positions
◆ Hiring and/or promoting people with a demonstrated capacity to learn
◆ Outplacing nonlearners and telling people the reason for it
◆ Building training programs and required ongoing education experiences around the sharing of best practices
◆ Using "postmortems" to learn from experience: What did you learn? What will you do differently as a result?

These actions will affect who is moved into, up, and through the organization and how individuals are trained within the organization to develop competencies. They will build learning capability systematically to replace habits of random learning.

Clarify consequences.   Perhaps the most powerful shaper of a learning culture is the creation and clarification of consequences for learning or not learning. As we discussed earlier, people tend to do what they are rewarded for and to avoid what they are punished for. When managers offer desirable consequences for learning, they enhance a learning culture. Actions that attach positive consequences to learning include:

- Evaluating learning actions and outcomes during performance appraisals
- Asking multiple stakeholders to appraise performance (with a 360-degree performance review for example)
- Rewarding employees when they learn from postmortems of mistakes
- Giving special recognition awards to managers who anticipate competency needs and learning strategies
- Encouraging and rewarding experimentation
- Tying bonus and incentive systems to learning
- Holding people accountable for results but not punishing specific experimental initiatives that may fail along the way

Shape governance processes.   Governance processes are organizational structures, decision-making processes, and communication strategies. Specific management actions that shape these process so as to encourage learning include:

- Building a fluid organizational structure that is flexible and adaptive
- Developing and using ad hoc cross-functional teams
- Establishing centers of excellence and rotating jobs in and out of the center to transfer know-how
- Supporting routine, fluid, and informal interaction with subcontractor suppliers and other outsiders
- Creating a campaign to show how ongoing learning is different from but linked to training and education
- Publishing learning "dysfunctions" openly; that is, not picking on individuals but, instead, publicizing behaviors and habits that the organization defines as learning dysfunctions
- Encouraging external benchmarking and communication
- Sharing information and successes

All these activities urge managers to share ideas across boundaries rather than to stockpile them.

Build capacity for change.   Employees' view of organizational change processes is another key influence on the culture of learning. Management activities that encourage the development of a change orientation include:

◆ Rejecting business that locks the company or unit into old, non-growth patterns
◆ Building flexible and current information systems
◆ Establishing a physical setting that encourages flexibility
◆ Creating ties with idea sources such as universities

Build leadership for learning.   The ultimate test of organizational learning capability is the extent to which leaders are able to learn and teach others to learn. Actions that build leaders who can create learning capability include these:

◆ Teaching leaders to coach
◆ Teaching leaders to facilitate
◆ Selecting leaders who teach

As leaders become more comfortable engaging in these activities, they will model the learning culture, and they will foster the movement of ideas from one unit to another.

Putting It All Together: Harmony on the Horizontal

In this chapter, we have reviewed five improv vehicles for loosening horizontal boundaries. With these vehicles, leaders can bring together the different resources that are shared in an organization, focus them on customer needs, and create an ongoing process of change and learning, without getting mired in the horizontal boundary issues of territory and turf.

An example of how these improv vehicles can be used together is Fluor Daniel, Inc., an international construction and engineering firm. The dominant feature of the Fluor Daniel organization is the existence of approximately thirty (the number is variable) "enterprise units" (operating companies) organized around the core construction process of the firm and representing the interface between Fluor Daniel and its clients. Managers of enterprise units coordinate and control projects for their group of clients. Then, for each major project—a pulp and paper mill in New Zealand, a petrochemical plant in the Philippines, or a power plant in Indonesia for example—a project manager pulls together the resources necessary to accomplish the project, many of them from the Fluor Daniel resource pool of technical, operational, and administrative competencies.

Learning capability is a critical issue for Fluor Daniel because what happens with one customer gives Fluor Daniel a competitive advantage with other customers, *if the company can leverage learning*. For example, from their experience in the Philippines, Fluor Daniel executives learned a great deal about winning government support for industrial development, about working with employees from non-Western backgrounds, and about working in political and cultural environments very different from those in the United States. These lessons were invaluable to Fluor Daniel when the firm entered Indonesia. It did not have to relearn all the lessons of creating a new business in a new setting because it was able to generalize learning from previous experiences that contributed to a successful entry into the Indonesian market.

Fluor Daniel generates ideas by encouraging project managers to solve customer problems creatively, collaborating with both the customers and other project managers. It then generalizes those ideas by building linkages between project managers. Thus, the corporate role is not only to set strategic direction and policy but explicitly to share best practices. Corporate managers have the opportunity and obligation to observe innovative client solutions and transfer the insights to other managers.

Other policies at Fluor Daniel also encourage the generalization of ideas. Staffing moves laterally, and employees are moved from one project to another not only to provide technical expertise but to share innovative ideas. Training and development courses are built on internal best-practice cases so that managers share insights and innovations. Organizational communications talk about employees who have shared ideas and improved competitiveness. Client managers share questions, and answers are shared through electronic media so that learning across clients occurs.

As Fluor Daniel, Motorola, J. P. Morgan, AlliedSignal, and the other organizations described in this chapter illustrate, permeating horizontal boundaries is not a one-time activity. Creating fluidity across disciplines and functions is an ongoing process. It requires constant attention, experimentation, tuning, and learning. Sometimes, as happens in a jazz ensemble, the music does not work the first time out. Sometimes there are discordant notes or missing instruments or uneven rhythms. Sometimes the musicians do not even get along. But if there is a willingness to keep playing, to try new arrangements, then the beat will go on.

To keep the horizontal harmony going, we suggest that you think through the five improv vehicles described in this chapter, and use them to construct an explicit strategy and work program for making your horizontal boundaries more permeable. The following questions are intended to stimulate your thinking and start a dialogue with your colleagues:

◆ Which improv vehicles might be most helpful to your organization in loosening horizontal boundaries?
◆ What progress have you already made in implementing or testing improv vehicles? In other words, to what extent have you already oriented around processes? To what extent do you use targeted teams? Do you have shared service organizations for support processes?
◆ In which part of your organization might it be possible to test some of the ideas in this chapter? Is there a unit, division, or location that can become a learning model for other parts of the organization?

The first two sections of this book have dealt with the boundaries within an organization: the vertical boundaries that create distinctions of status and rank and the horizontal boundaries that create distinctions of territory. By making these boundaries more permeable, you can accelerate your organization's success through speed, flexibility, integration, and innovation. However, your organization does not operate in a vacuum. It is part of a chain of organizations—customers, suppliers, regulators, and others who influence and affect its ultimate success. Creating boundaryless relationships with these external organizations is the subject of our next section.

PART 3

Free Movement Along the Value Chain

Crossing External Boundaries

6

Toward Partnership with Customers and Suppliers

Like the medieval lords who built moats and walls around their castles, many organizations have constructed artificial boundaries between themselves and the outside world. While these boundaries do not consist of water and bricks, they are just as difficult to surmount. More importantly, just as social evolution made castle walls obsolete, the new success factors of speed, flexibility, integration, and innovation are making boundaries between organizations less relevant. In fact, hiding behind such boundaries today can be more dangerous than venturing outside.

This is not to say that organizations should immediately eliminate all external boundaries and form partnerships, alliances, joint ventures, and collaborations with everyone around them. That would be chaotic and counterproductive. And it would negate the external boundaries' positive effects: a focus on a manageable (bounded) set of business competencies and priorities, and a sense of identity with others who share a common purpose. However, by making specific external bound-

191

aries more permeable, organizations can dramatically increase speed, flexibility, integration, and innovation. In addition, the more that strategy, technology, management practices, resources, and values flow back and forth naturally between organizations, the less necessity there is for crisis-generated breaches of the outer wall.

Our purpose in this chapter is to make the case for loosening external boundaries—the forces that divide organizations from their customers, suppliers, and other external stakeholders. To do so, we focus on the concept of the *value chain* and the process by which organizations are linked together to create products and services that have more value combined than separate. We will begin by contrasting the traditional view, in which every company aims to maximize its own success as a unit in the value chain, to the boundaryless view, in which each company aims to maximize total success across the value chain. Then we describe a number of barriers that prevent organizations from breaking down the external boundaries and moving toward the boundaryless approach. Finally, we present a diagnostic instrument that assesses where your organization stands in terms of breaking down external boundaries. Chapter Seven then outlines specific practices leaders can use to break through external boundaries and strengthen an entire value chain.

Note that while vertical and horizontal boundaries are the floors, ceilings, and internal walls of the organizational house, external boundaries describe not just outside walls but the community in which the house stands. The objective of loosening internal boundaries is to create a more effective individual organization, one that is more capable of dealing with customers, suppliers and other external entities. The objective of loosening external boundaries is to create not only more effective individual organizations but to make stronger interactive groups out of organizations that share a value chain. However, the specific actions we describe will still be at the level of individual firms.

The Value Chain: The Traditional View

All companies function as links in chains of entities that produce and distribute products or services to end-users. Many companies are in the middle of a value chain, receiving materials, components, and services from some companies (suppliers or vendors) and selling products or services to other companies (customers). Along the way, other external entities such as government regulators, investor groups, investment analysts, and even competitors influence the work done.

The overall purpose of this chain of interorganizational relationships is to maximize profit or contribution by producing higher value than the competition. That higher value is defined by product functionality (meeting market needs), low cost, high quality, and minimal time to market. The prototypical example of a value chain is the automobile industry, especially in the West. Most car models require at least 10,000 parts, up to 75 percent of them manufactured by independent suppliers.[1] In addition, the direct customers of most automobile companies are also independent businesses (dealerships). Finally, environmental groups, government regulators, and others influence the process all along the chain.

Since early in the twentieth century, most companies, especially in North America, have viewed their participation in the value chain from an independent, legalistic perspective. Cooperative arrangements beyond the minimum required level with other organizations not only have been met with suspicion but have been discouraged or even forbidden by decades of antitrust laws and regulations. As a result, each organization in the chain has been encouraged to view itself as an independent legal entity, focused on the maximization of its own profitability, even at the expense of its customers and suppliers. Consultants John Carlisle and Robert Parker describe the traditional relationship between members of a value chain as a "sophisticated form of haggling in hopes of making their own piece of the transaction pie larger than the one received by the other party."[2]

This traditional every-company-for-itself attitude leads to the following five types of value chain boundaries, which unintentionally destroy competitiveness by reducing speed, flexibility, integration, and innovation.

Strategies and plans are developed independently. In the traditional mode, organizations establish their own market targets, production plans, schedules, billing procedures, product development cycles, resource allocations, and so on, without consulting other members of the value chain. Often, this results in some links of the chain being out of sync with other links. For example, when an automobile company introduces a new design but gives suppliers late notice of design changes, it is virtually impossible for the supplier to meet requirements because it is already geared up to produce the original design.

Information sharing and joint problem solving are limited.   Companies with a traditional value chain perspective tend to withhold from each other such information as real cost of materials, in-process quality problems, profit margins, and all manner of problems viewed as dirty linen. The tendency is to try to solve such problems independently, without letting others in the chain know a problem exists. This result is often a suboptimal or untimely solution or, when a problem is not resolved, an unpleasant surprise for other members of the value chain.

To illustrate: when a tool and dye shop that built custom equipment had trouble achieving proper tolerances in a line of precision machinery, management hid the problem, trying to solve it internally. After two weeks of unsuccessful industrial engineering studies and experiments, management told the customer the machinery would not be shipped on schedule. This event, like a thrown rock sending ripples through a pool, spread severe disruption through customer production schedules. Finally, in desperation, management brought a materials supplier in, who quickly discovered that a different grade and composition of metal would solve the problem.

Accounting, measurement, and reward systems are separate and unsynchronized.   Traditionally, each entity in a value chain has its own set of measures, rewards, and ways of accounting for performance. It is not uncommon, for example, for a customer to emphasize and reward quality while the producer emphasizes and rewards volume, productivity, or cost management. In one industrial business, a number of productivity investments were funded at the expense of several quality programs. The producer's margins improved, but a key customer soon canceled all contracts until quality performance was upgraded, making the productivity gains moot.

Salesforces push products on their terms.   When each member of a value chain aims to maximize its own profitability, salespeople naturally focus on pushing product, urging customers to take more products at times and prices best suited to the seller. They devote much less time to listening to the customer, determining specific needs and requirements, and working collaboratively with the customer on the best use of the products. Often, the customer ends up with a proliferation of products that it does not fully use or truly need.

In a large decentralized bank, for example, different computer vendors had introduced a variety of technologies and systems, each one designed to meet a specific need. However, none of the vendors helped the bank managers think about an overall architecture, communications strategy, or common standards. The result was a jumble of systems that could not be integrated and an eventual decision to spend millions of dollars building new systems from scratch.

Resources are utilized inefficiently.   Residing throughout any value chain are tremendous pools of resources, expertise, and technical and operational knowledge concerning all facets of production, sales, distribution, finance, and general business. Yet in the traditional mode, each entity in a value chain tends to use its own resources, without any mechanism for tapping into the resources of others. For example, in the late 1980s, a large bank financed a number of leveraged buy-outs and then watched the borrowers struggle to succeed. Only after the loans went into default, thus compromising its own balance sheet, did the bank provide the borrowers with financial and management expertise.

The Search for an Alternative Model

Today, given the potentially negative consequences of traditional value chain boundaries, many companies already are looking outside themselves to the entire web of institutional relationships of which they are a part. They want to figure out how to strengthen the web, not just their own strand. In a 1991 Dataquest and Arthur Young survey of 700 start-up and fast-growth companies, nearly 90 percent reported forming strategic alliances with other companies.[3] Similarly, alliance expert Robert Lynch reports that the health care industry alone tends to spawn over 550 alliances each year.[4] One pharmaceutical company, for example, has nineteen current partnerships with biotechnology firms. Other industries, such as software, electronics, and retail, also are generating large numbers of formal and informal cross-company relationships, and a best-practices study of highly successful companies, commissioned by General Electric in 1990, also concluded that a focus on customer-supplier partnerships was one of the keys to future competitive success.

The concept of cooperative relations between independent companies, however, is not new. In fact, the growth of many of today's industries was fueled by cooperative arrangements between firms that were too small or lacked sufficient skills to mount major ventures on their own. The shipping industry developed through alliances of shipbuilders, insurance underwriters, manufacturers, and trading companies. The electric power industry developed through consortiums of inventors (such as Thomas Edison), investors, power generating companies, and equipment manufacturers. (That is why the world headquarters for GE Lighting is to be found in Cleveland's NELA Park—NELA is an acronym for National Electric Lighting Association.)[5]

Today, however, the number of strategic alliances, partnerships, and joint ventures is multiplying at a rate far greater than ever before—a trend Peter Drucker predicted in 1982, saying that "the multinational of tomorrow will be comprised of autonomous partners, linked in a confederation rather than through common ownership."[6] As product life-cycles shrink, global competition heats up, the cost of innovation spirals up, customers demand more, and everything moves faster, companies are realizing that they cannot keep up by working alone. They need to join forces to drive technologies, expand distribution, enter new markets, ensure sources of supply, and match end-user expectations.

At the same time, successful companies are abandoning traditional methods of competing by buying majority interests in key suppliers and controlling outside suppliers and customers through limiting information, antagonistic negotiations, or outright threats. The costs are too great and the risks too high. Instead, these successful companies are finding ways of cooperatively integrating with suppliers and customers. As consultants Richard Normann and Rafael Ramirez noted in a 1993 *Harvard Business Review* article: "Increasingly the strategic focus of successful companies is not the company or even the industry but the *value-creating system* itself, within which different economic actors— suppliers, business partners, allies, customers—work together to *co-*

produce value. Their key strategic task is the *reconfiguration* of roles and relationships among this constellation of actors in order to mobilize the creation of value in new forms."[7]

Moving the Value Chain from East to West

Adding to the pressure for looking at the value chain differently is the fact that many competitors in the Far East do not operate in the traditional mode. As University of Massachusetts professor Michael Best notes: "The primary goal of industrial policy in Japan is to promote . . . the entrepreneurial firm, consultative buyer-vendor relations, and inter-firm associations."[8] Thus, Far Eastern companies, as members of *keiretsu,* engage in extensive cooperative arrangements, joint ventures, and even government-sponsored arrangements with other members of a value chain—described to us by one Japanese manager as "a river with many branches that flow together." Their cooperative efforts often produce better products faster and with less cost than do the independent ways of working of traditional Western companies.

MIT researchers James Womack, Daniel Jones, and Daniel Roos, in their groundbreaking study of the Japanese automobile industry, describe how "each *keiretsu* consists of perhaps twenty major companies, one in each industrial sector. . . . There is no holding company at the top of the organization. Nor are the companies legally united. Rather, they're held together by cross-locking equity structures—each company owns a portion of every other company's equity in a circular pattern—and a sense of reciprocal obligation. . . . Among the key companies in every group are a bank, an insurance company and a trading company. Each of these has substantial cash resources that can be made available to the members of the group."[9]

Some North American organizations have tried to emulate aspects of the Eastern arrangements between producers and suppliers, for example by pushing the just-in-time (JIT) inventory concept. Unfortunately, when techniques like JIT are forced on suppliers who lack an overall view of the value chain, the result, as Best describes, is that JIT "becomes an instrument for parent firms to shift the costs of holding inventory to supplier firms."[10] When some links in the chain cannot handle the extra cost or the reduced margins, they collapse and weaken the overall chain. This is an example of what MIT professor Peter Senge calls "shifting the burden," which produces a temporary improvement in one location that only masks a more fundamental weakening of the entire system.[11] Such ineffective cost shifting was a concern expressed by many suppliers to General Motors during the José Ignacio Lopez purchasing regime—especially when GM purchasing people tore up existing contracts and simply demanded lower prices. It is also a concern for the suppliers of struggling retailers. For example, K-Mart Corporation, according to the *New York Times,* is on "an all-out offensive to force its manufacturers to carry the burden of its current problems on their books." As the *Times* goes on to report: "K-Mart . . . is asking toy manufacturers to carry goods they ship to it on their books as inventory. . . . 'They are asking the manufacturers to take steps they can't possibly agree to,' said Sean McGowan, an analyst at Gerard Klauer Mattison & Company. . . . Not only would agreeing to such payment terms force toy makers to do the same for their other customers, Mr. McGowan said, it would also squeeze the toy makers."[12]

Unfortunately, shifting the burden seems to be all too common as Western companies struggle with lagging competitiveness. Costs, quality requirements, inventories, and administrative procedures are increasingly pushed back along the value chain without a full understanding of the implications. Rather than collaborate with other members of the value chain on systemic solutions, many companies continue to go it alone—developing their own productivity programs, competitive awards, and quick fixes for symptoms. When they do think of themselves as links in a value chain, their aim is to force other links to conform to what they think is needed.

In short, even though many organizations have realized that a new approach to the value chain is needed, they often focus more on the mechanics of interorganizational relationships than on the underlying assumptions. To loosen external boundaries and fully leverage the power of the value chain, companies must internalize a new set of assumptions for customer-supplier relationships.

Refocusing the Lens: A Rising Tide Raises All Boats

In our view, successful companies in this decade and beyond will be those that take a systemic, boundaryless view of their participation in the value chain. They must acquire an entirely new mindset, abandoning the legalistic view of organizations as independent entities linked only by market forces and learning to see themselves as parts of an integrated system much like a vertically integrated company with multiple owners. From this perspective, companies can see that a rising tide raises all boats, that success will come from improving the overall profitability and continuing vitality of the value chain as a whole, rather than just their own bottom lines and organizational health.

Carlisle and Parker describe the boundaryless view of the value chain in this way: "If customer and supplier firms can recognize their common ground in a shared interest in capturing the customer sale which actually nourishes them both, it should be possible for them to work creatively and effectively together to capture that sale for 'their' product."[13] Possessing this recognition becomes critical when companies face the new generation of competitor whose strategies for winning are based on customer service, quality, cycle time, and constant innovation rather than low cost and technical excellence alone.

The company that loosens its external boundaries will follow the new cooperative and systemic organizational model that is contrasted to the old model in Table 6.1.

BUSINESS AND OPERATIONAL PLANNING ARE COORDINATED

In the successful value chain, all members collaborate in both strategic and operational business planning. The goal is not only better product development and production planning, but also common or coordinated administrative and operational procedures such as billing, customer service, purchasing, shipping, and inventory. One member might even

Table 6.1. Changing Value Chain Assumptions for Boundaryless Organizations.

Old Model (Each Organization Aims to Maximize Its Own Profit)	New Model (Each Organization Aims to Maximize Total Value Chain Success)
1. Strategies and plans are developed independently.	1. Business and operational planning are coordinated.
2. Information sharing and joint problem solving are limited.	2. Information is widely shared and problems are solved jointly.
3. Accounting, measurement, and reward systems are separate and unsynchronized.	3. Accounting, measurement, and reward systems are consistent.
4. Salesforce pushes products on salespeople's terms.	4. Selling is a consultative process.
5. Resources are inefficiently utilized.	5. Resources are shared.

take on certain administrative functions for several others, resulting in huge opportunities for chainwide cost reduction.

The gains that can be won from such a collaborative approach are illustrated by a manufacturer of premium road and racing bicycles. In the summer of 1990, the company redesigned its product line with an eye toward capturing significant share in the fitness market. Guided by significant consumer input, the company created a prototype bike that was lighter but stronger than the existing products and that users could ride longer with less fatigue. Excited by the new product, the salesforce aggressively signed up dealers and took a high volume of orders for delivery during the spring 1991 selling season. Once company managers saw they had designed a winner, they geared up for manufacturing and assembly. The only problem was that the company had designed the new bike without consulting or collaborating with the key parts suppliers. Senior managers were shocked to learn that several suppliers critical to the braking systems could not produce the required parts in time for the spring delivery dates. The company's only alternative was to go to other suppliers, whose costs were significantly higher and whose product required extra assembly time and labor costs when it reached the bike company. The new bike debuted successfully, but produced no profit margin to speak of. With that lesson in mind, managers designed the following year's bike with vendor collaboration from the beginning. This approach resulted in much higher margins for both the bicycle company and its suppliers.

INFORMATION IS WIDELY SHARED AND PROBLEMS ARE SOLVED JOINTLY

As members of a system, participants in a boundaryless value chain share information much more freely than before. A production problem in one part of the chain is everyone's concern, and the best resources from throughout the system are applied.

For example, GE Appliances has worked for several years to speed up production processes, achieve more flexible and responsive manufacturing, and improve overall quality. A key component of the effort is close and strategic collaboration with key parts suppliers. If suppliers can respond more quickly to changes in production schedules and product designs and manage parts inventories more effectively, then GE Appliances can produce major appliances faster and tailor production more quickly to customer requirements.

To achieve these ends, GE Appliances wanted to develop close information systems linkages with suppliers, so that production, inventory, sales, specification, and scheduling data could be fully coordinated, making the production chain as seamless as feasible, with suppliers an integrated part of the process, not just an input. Four key suppliers were selected to pilot the information systems link. Initially, they found that the data they received were insufficiently detailed and difficult to interpret. Based on this feedback, GE Appliances supplemented the data link with a monthly data package of more specific analyses and recommendations for action. The approach was then expanded to the twenty-five largest suppliers. Now, GE Appliance engineers work continually with suppliers to improve quality and accelerate the flow of materials through the production process.[14]

ACCOUNTING, MEASUREMENT, AND REWARD SYSTEMS ARE CONSISTENT

A key requirement for a boundaryless supplier-customer relationship is a common score-keeping and incentive system so that everyone in the value chain works off the same numbers, speaks the same language, and aims toward the same set of goals. Successful value chains have jointly accepted methods of determining costs, margins, and investments. Agreed-upon performance goals for each organizational unit are derived from those methods. A matching reward system motivates people to achieve the systemwide objectives.

For example, when a manufacturer of auto parts reviewed its sales goals with its leading nationwide distributor, it discovered a subtle but significant disparity in priorities. The manufacturer wanted to emphasize margin goals, but the distributor had created a sales incentive program based completely on volume, regardless of margin. As a result, sales of low-margin products were far ahead of plan, while sales of higher-priced products lagged and were the subject of constant price change requests. A joint manufacturer-distributor team then developed sales goals for specific product categories, and a sales incentive program with one level of rewards for total sales volume and higher payouts for sales of high-margin product categories.

A similar dynamic became clear some years ago in what was then the Jones & Laughlin Steel Company (now part of LTV Steel). In a project to reduce "mixed steel" (that is, a mixture of right and wrong types of steel sent to a customer), the company realized that its workers had no incentive to keep the different grades of steel separate. In fact, since workers were paid for tonnage, their goal was to produce as much steel as possible, as fast as possible, and ship it out. Whether the right or wrong grades of steel were shipped, the workers still got paid. Only when J&L lined up its measurement and compensation systems with those of its customers, measuring correct shipments and including that measure as one factor in the pay plan, was it able to significantly improve its quality record.

SELLING IS A CONSULTATIVE PROCESS

In the boundaryless world, successful companies engineer a significant shift in the role of their salespeople. Instead of pushing product, salespeople increasingly consult to the customer, helping customers crystallize supply requirements and find optimal ways to meet those requirements and best utilize purchased products. In short, salespeople create a pull for product, because as William Frago, former CEO of Carrier Corporation, points out, "You can get much more movement by pulling on a chain than by pushing on it." At the same time, salespeople become conduits into their own companies for customer feedback about desired operational and product delivery improvements and product development and enhancement ideas.

In the Minneapolis branch of IBM, the notion of consultative selling helped a number of salespeople shift their behavior patterns and achieve striking results. In one case, a potential customer was having trouble determining whether to purchase a new manufacturing system. The IBM representative then helped the customer form an interfunctional team to establish criteria for selecting the system. That assistance not only made the sale more timely and efficient, it also ensured that the customer bought what was needed and not what the salesperson wanted to push. In another case, a financial services customer wanted to buy imaging technology but was blocked by the huge capital investment needed for the system and all its peripheral equipment. However, the salesperson and the customer were able to construct a modest experiment with one piece of imaging technology, at low cost, using all the customer's existing peripherals. Then the salesperson helped the customer transition to imaging technology a step at a time. This spread out the costs and had an extra benefit of giving the customer time to absorb the new technology much more effectively.

RESOURCES ARE SHARED

Finally, a systemic view of the value chain allows twenty-first-century companies to deploy resources and expertise more efficiently throughout the chain. For example, the developers of a state-of-the-art distribution system in one company might work as consultants to upgrade distribution in other parts of the value chain.

In the synthetic fiber manufacturing industry, the sharing of engineering resources with customers such as carpet and apparel mills has become a critical success strategy. The customers benefit by getting help in using new fibers, which may have altered physical properties that cause them to react differently in weaving machines. Customers learn how to calibrate their weaving equipment to work most effectively with various fibers and how to distinguish equipment problems from fiber consistency issues. The fiber producers benefit by hearing more immediate feedback on their products, increasing the use of their fibers, and hearing ideas for new products and enhancements.

A number of companies now provide training for their customers or suppliers. Whirlpool offers customers and dealers extensive management, sales, and technical service training. The Federal Aviation Administration (FAA) offers pilots training in FAA standards and guidelines. A division of Greyhound that services airlines provides training for its customers in safety and flight services. And Marriott Corporation develops specialized training in customer service approaches that it offers to selected customers.[15] All these examples illustrate how resources in one part of a value chain can be applied to other parts.

Barriers to Boundaryless Customer-Supplier Relationships

While the new, boundaryless view of customer and supplier relationships may sound logical and attractive for many companies, getting there is not so easy. The six substantial barriers listed below can undermine such radical change efforts. Before diving headlong into the waters of cross-company collaboration, it is important to be aware of these barriers, to be able to recognize them, and to develop strategies for swimming around them.

Customer-Supplier Relationship Barriers

- Legal and regulatory tradition
- Competitive confusion
- Lack of trust
- Difficulty in letting go of control
- Slowness in learning new managerial skills
- Complexity

LEGAL AND REGULATORY TRADITION

The first barrier to boundaryless external relationships is the long-standing legal tradition that companies in related industries should remain totally independent or else face legal or antitrust limitations. Thus, U.S. commercial law encourages company autonomy rather than collaboration, which is often viewed as collusion or restraint of free trade.

While boundaryless relationships clearly must be pursued within the framework of current laws, it is worth observing that respected MIT economist Lester Thurow, in a discussion of U.S. competitiveness vis-à-vis the Japanese, suggests that perhaps the antitrust structure has outlived its usefulness.[16] Consider this example: early in 1993, in the midst of highly speculative and preliminary explorations by TCI, Time Warner, and Microsoft of how cable television, software, hardware, and telecommunications companies might work together, Representative Edward Markey of Massachusetts, chairman of the House Subcommittee on Telecommunications and Finance, sent a letter to federal regulators warning that an alliance between TCI, Time Warner, and Microsoft could "close the market to competitive entrance."[17] Such an alliance might eventually need to be scrutinized. But in our view, the time when dozens of companies from multiple industries were first trying to make sense of the opportunities being presented by the emerging data superhighway was far too early to be ringing the monopolistic alarm bell. If, in the early days of this and similar important explorations, executives feel that every cross-company meeting or preliminary discussion will be subject to regulatory scrutiny, then they may shy away from potentially productive alliances, not wanting to lose time, resources, and goodwill through battles with government regulators.

The point is that the regulatory environment, while changing slowly (witness the U.S. government's encouragement of an industrywide automotive partnership to build electric cars), is still skeptical or even hostile toward intercompany collaboration. Thus, not all boundaryless arrangements will be viewed as having pure motives, and some may require costly lobbying or time-consuming justifications to dissuade regulatory bodies from seeing restraint of trade.

COMPETITIVE CONFUSION

A second barrier to boundaryless relationships between suppliers and customers is that they have the potential to force companies to place their bets with one value chain as opposed to another or, at least, to cause confusion about who is an ally and who is not. For example, an automotive parts producer that forges a highly collaborative relationship with one automobile company might be precluded from similar relationships with competitive automobile manufacturers. Therefore, the potential payoff from the strategic relationship must outweigh the potential loss of business from other sources and the risk of relying on a concentrated customer base.

This is the dilemma that many suppliers to Wal-Mart have faced in recent years. Having created state-of-the-art telecommunications and information systems that connect them directly to data from Wal-Mart stores, they can now manage inventory, order processing, and payments quickly and electronically at far-reduced costs. However, when these suppliers think about transferring these same business practices to K-Mart, Home Depot, and similar companies, their first consideration is that Wal-Mart might reduce their share of business if they form a similar alliance with a Wal-Mart rival.

Competitive confusion also arises when business rivals find themselves competing in some arenas but pursuing joint ventures and cooperative arrangements in others. These dual roles are an increasing source of confusion in the computer and telecommunications industry. An article in *The Wall Street Journal* describes how:

> Competitors cooperate in one digital arena while banging heads in another. TCI, for example, wants to use the extra capacity on its cable system to offer telephone and data services in competition with the Bell operating companies. Time Warner wants to do the same thing. Yet both Time Warner and TCI are allied with telephone companies in other digital projects. US West, in turn, has allied with Time Warner in the U.S. but with TCI in England. "You very much have to accept that you are going to compete against a company in some places and cooperate in others," says Chuck Lilly, the US West executive in charge of the company's cable, cellular and publishing units.[18]

A similar competitive confusion crops up in large corporations with multiple business units. For example, GE Motors is a major supplier of small motors to Maytag, and as part of a value chain partnership, also provides technical and process improvement training to Maytag. Yet Maytag is an arch rival of GE Appliances in the dishwasher and refrigerator markets. Similarly, PPG Industries' flat glass business unit supplies raw glass not only to the PPG automotive fabrication business unit but also to that unit's competitors. For companies that want to establish boundaryless relationships with customers and suppliers, identifying these potentially contradictory relationships and weighing the trade-offs is a major but essential task.

THE TRUST BARRIER

Most traditional companies have long histories of internal conflict between functions or departments. Across companies, the chasms caused by lack of trust can be much deeper. Yet the boundaryless world requires a great deal of cross-company interdependence if the overall value chain is to succeed. That interdependence is based on trust.

As most students of Japanese business have pointed out, the successful relationship between Japanese suppliers and customers is based much more on trust and cooperation than is the typical relationship between comparable units in the production chain of the West. We have watched this Western trust barrier in action in numerous work sessions between suppliers and their customers. In almost all these sessions, at some point, one party makes demands on the other based on individual interest rather than joint, value chain interest. If the supplier and customer do not have enough trust to conduct a healthy dialogue about the demands, problems result that raise the trust barrier further. For example, in discussions between an insurance company and a pension customer, the customer requested a number of ad hoc reports and customized processing procedures. The insurance representatives, trying to please the customer, agreed to everything, despite the problems that their operations and systems colleagues would face in meeting the requests. Later, the insurance personnel referred to the customer as "unrealistically demanding." The customer, in turn, was continually frustrated by the difficulty of getting reports that had been agreed to.

Alliance consultant Robert P. Lynch observes that extreme lack of trust between alliance partners can produce these very ugly results:[19]

◆ The "Fake": competitive companies pretend to be interested in an alliance only to get information about the potential partner.
◆ The "Steal": companies take competitive technology and information after an alliance breaks up.
◆ The "Squeeze": financial constraints force one alliance partner to turn over data or technology to the other.
◆ The "Float": alliance partners get cold feet and leave the joint venture in limbo.
◆ The "Bleed-Through": one partner takes processes produced in the partnership and applies them to a joint venture with a competitor.

The overall message is that while boundaryless relationships depend on trust between organizations, such trust does not exist a priori. It must be nurtured and encouraged, so that lack of it does not poison relationships and weaken the entire value chain.

THE CONTROL BARRIER

Most Western companies are used to having total control over their destinies (or more accurately, the illusion of control). In the boundaryless world, however, executives must become comfortable with *control sharing*—collaborative, collegial, consultative arrangements with a range of business partners. When external boundaries are loosened, no one member of the value chain will be able to dictate arbitrary terms and conditions to others. With limited numbers of strategic partners, companies cannot afford to force a one-sided agenda that might weaken the chain by causing a partner to walk out or collapse. Instead, each partner is responsible for setting its needs in the context of a web of relationships and for working to meet those needs in ways that strengthen the entire web.

A small manufacturer of high-quality, custom-rolled aluminum is a good example of a company that has made substantial gains by overcoming issues of control with key suppliers and customers. In the early

1990s, this company successfully increased rolling mill productivity by 20 percent, through focused reductions of horizontal barriers between such groups as production control, maintenance, and quality assurance. The productivity boost was equivalent to an extra shift's worth of output; however, it compounded a larger issue that had plagued the company throughout its long history: it was unable to deliver all orders on time. Over the years, it had learned to accept an 80 percent on-time delivery rate as normal. With the extra productivity, however, this customer service level became unacceptable, leading both to customer dissatisfaction and to increasing inventories.

To break its long tradition of accepting a less-than-exceptional delivery record, the company tried an experiment: it would have a model week. During that model week, managers and employees would do everything possible to achieve 100 percent on-time delivery performance. Sales would not promise product that could not be delivered; production control would plan schedules more than a week in advance; manufacturing would think through new ways of loading the annealing furnaces. After several weeks of preparation, the model week began. And much to the amazement of almost everyone, 100 percent on-time delivery was achieved. Then it was sustained, not just for one week but for two. Then reality hit.

Just when management and staff were feeling that they really could control their own destiny, they discovered that a critical, single-source supplier had sent a batch of material with unacceptable structural defects in the metal structure. Previously, the company would merely have returned the material, made some angry phone calls, accepted the upset of key delivery schedules, and waited for a new shipment. Now, with customer-satisfaction time ticking urgently away, managers and staff realized they had no real control whatsoever over on-time delivery. They were completely at the mercy of their suppliers. They could change this reality only by breaking through previously unbreachable boundaries between themselves and their suppliers.

To surmount these boundaries, a company team asked the supplier who had sent the defective material to join in a number of working sessions aimed at achieving a consistent level of on-time delivery above 95 percent. These working sessions uncovered the fact that the structural variations were traceable to an earlier supplier in the value chain who was providing the raw materials used to make the aluminum alloy. The session participants then determined that certain material formulations produced different molecular properties in the alloy and that these properties had an effect all the way through the end-use customers' manufacturing processes. That realization led the company to approach on-time delivery in a whole new way. Instead of trying to control just its own "internal" piece of the value chain process, it focused on creating a collaboration with suppliers and customers that would control the entire process from beginning to end. The result was a sustained on-time delivery rate that has stayed above 95 percent for over two years.

THE SKILL BARRIER

The fifth barrier to boundaryless relationships between members of the value chain is organizations' need to develop a new set of managerial skills. For many years in traditional organizations, managers have achieved results by using the levers of authority, reward, and punishment and of control of resources. To a large extent, these same methods have been applied to customer and supplier relationships as well. Prices, specifications, timing of deliveries, support services, and so on were all a result of often rancorous negotiations, ultimately backed up by threats of doing business elsewhere or raising prices.

In the boundaryless relationship with customers and suppliers, these traditional tactics are counterproductive. The same behavioral shifts that we described earlier for developing new vertical and horizontal collaborations with employees and colleagues apply to developing external organizational agreements as well. As Peter Drucker put it more than a decade ago, the new shape of the corporation "will totally change what is demanded of management. The critical skill in the new multinational—for most businessmen a brand new one—will be that of coordinating units that cannot be commanded but which have to work together."[20]

More specifically, managers must spend more of their time at the interface between links in the value chain, managing relationships there rather than negotiating terms and conditions. In this role, managers need superb listening skills, a variety of problem-solving techniques, and an ability to build consensus.

To illustrate: a large industrial company that services the automotive industry has mustered three different marketing groups to deal with Detroit, one for each major product line. All three product lines produce parts critical to automotive manufacture, all enjoy a long-standing reputation for product reliability, and all three are competitively priced. Yet one of the three marketing managers has consistently produced better results than the others—more volume, longer-term contracts, more favorable pricing, earlier involvement in product changes, and the like. For some time, senior management attributed the difference to weaker competition in the one product area. Upon closer examination, however, management realized that this one marketing manager was going about his job in a fundamentally different way. Instead of dealing with the automakers' purchasing departments, this manager had developed relationships with their key people in engineering, product design, and manufacturing. In fact, he and his staff spent most of their time in plants rather than Detroit offices, they often brought in technical experts to help in the plants, and they enjoyed full membership in product design teams. In other words, this marketing manager's success was not due to random chance. It was due to his systematic application of a different set of management skills, focused much more on building relationships and solving problems than on negotiating prices and delivery dates.

THE COMPLEXITY BARRIER

The final barrier to boundaryless relationships between customers and suppliers is the sheer complexity of the undertaking. No matter how straightforward the business interests and the content of the collaboration, there always are a multitude of variables that can influence success, and many of them cannot be fully controlled or predicted in advance. They include shifts in the business climate, changes in government regulations, and developments or frustrations in technology. Collaboration also requires an ongoing match between the business goals and needs of the partners, a fit between company cultures, and the right chemistry among the key players who will be working together.

The ultimate failure of a strategic partnership between copier makers Savin and Ricoh is a good example of the ways complexity can break down a previously successful relationship. Savin was built in the 1960s by American entrepreneur Paul Charlap, who joined forces with Israeli inventor Benny Landa to develop a copier that used liquid toner instead of the black powder toner that Xerox employed. The technological shift allowed the Savin copier to use less energy (the powder needed to be heated to become liquid) and be much more reliable (the powder tended to get into the machinery and cause breakdowns). Savin had no manufacturing capability, so to get its invention to market fast, it built a relationship with the Japanese camera company Ricoh. Ricoh would produce the machines that Savin would distribute and service. The arrangement worked spectacularly well for several years. In the late 1970s, Savin had significantly cut into Xerox's market share and had one of the best distribution networks in the United States. Then, in the 1980s, the complexity factor came into play.

First, external business strategies began to change. Xerox, responding to the threat from Savin and other manufacturers, focused heavily on quality and reliability improvement as well as new product development. Then, Savin's partner changed its business strategies. Ricoh, seeing a huge market opportunity, began to sell its own copiers under its own name, setting up a competing distribution system to Savin's. And Savin, seeing its success threatened, began to invest heavily in developing technology for color photocopying with liquid toner. At the same time that Savin was investing much more of its capital in R&D and its own manufacturing, the dollar-yen exchange rate deteriorated significantly, forcing Savin to pay much more to Ricoh for copiers and spare parts. During the ensuing cash squeeze, Savin allowed its distribution base and service levels to deteriorate, causing further cash problems. Negotiations with Ricoh became increasingly frustrating; there was little common ground between the U.S. managers and the Japanese company. Finally, when the color technology failed, Savin collapsed into bankruptcy. Ricoh, with its years of experience making and selling copiers, was now positioned to enter the U.S. market on a major scale. After several years of bankruptcy proceedings and a series of ownership changes, Savin was eventually bought by Ricoh.

Robert Lynch, in talking about the high failure rate of technology-based partnerships and noting that their success diminishes with increasing complexity, says, "When explorations into new technologies are coupled with the development of new products for new markets, it is like solving a triple simultaneous equation with three unknowns."[21] Managers who are moving toward boundaryless relationships must be alert to complexity and realize that the relaxing of external boundaries may allow the dynamics of a relationship to shift rapidly. It is not enough merely to establish a customer-supplier partnership; that is only the beginning. Once initiated, the partnership must be continually recalibrated, adjusted, tested, assessed, and reworked. Otherwise, as happened with Savin and Ricoh, the complexity may become overwhelming.

From There to Here, from Here to There/Funny Things Are Everywhere

Given the extent of external boundaries and the barriers to crossing them, getting from here to there for most companies will often seem like the Dr. Seuss tale from which we have taken the title of this section,[22] as companies are beset by things of all sorts in their paths. Although stories appear daily of companies engaging in joint ventures, alliances, and partnerships, many of these new arrangements stumble and struggle and often founder and fail. For every successful new boundaryless arrangement between companies, there probably are at least as many that are unsuccessful. Here are two additional examples.

In the late 1980s, GE Lighting researchers developed a new light source with vast potential for use in automobile headlights. Called "discharge forward lighting," the technology provided much more focused, energy-efficient light from a significantly smaller source than before. It presented a possibility that automakers could completely redesign automobile front ends with lighter weight materials and fewer costs. The opportunities for enhanced beauty, safety, fuel efficiency, and cost effectiveness seemed significant.

Given the vast potential, GE Lighting searched for and found a joint venture partner among its customers. The partner would get a head start with the new technology in exchange for sharing in some development costs. For the next two years, GE and its partner struggled to create a commercially viable product but found it difficult to resolve the host of technical factors. For example, the auto company insisted that the cost of the discharge forward lamp had to be equal to or less than that of the halogen lamp it would replace. GE, however, argued that the appropriate comparison was between the entire old and new lighting systems, including electronics, wiring, and housing. The complexity barrier was writ large as the partners attempted to deal simultaneously with technical, commercial, aesthetic, and cultural issues. After two years of work, GE Lighting began to look for alternative partners, and the existing partnership was dissolved.

Additional difficulties that might surface in cross-institutional relationships can be seen in the 1993 proposed joint venture between Blockbuster Video and IBM to develop and launch a computer network that would store and download compact discs on demand at Blockbuster stores. A store customer would select entire disks or specific songs from a music catalogue. The selections would be immediately downloaded onto a blank disk, so the customer would never have to leave the store without finding a particular number. For Blockbuster, the system would have allowed diversification from video rental into retail music without the company's having to build up a big inventory. For IBM, the project would have promoted the development of a system requiring sophisticated high-end computers, an IBM specialty.

For both companies and consumers, then, the idea looked powerful, and it was announced with some fanfare. But Blockbuster and IBM had failed to bring in other key members of the value chain—the music producers. Companies like Sony and Time Warner reacted with concern, worried about losing proprietary rights over their music, losing control of production and packaging, and easy pirating of recordings. Faced with these trust and control barriers, as well as the venture's technical complexity, Blockbuster and IBM did not take the project forward.[23]

However, while individual companies must still struggle with the complex strategic issues of when to pursue partnerships and with whom, the real question is not *whether* cross-organizational partnerships, alliances, and joint ventures are worthwhile. As the twenty-first century approaches, they seem to be occurring in almost every industry sector at an increasing rate. The more difficult question in the long run is *how* to make these boundaryless relationships successful—how to get over the barriers of legal and regulatory tradition, competitive confusion, lack of trust, difficulty in letting go of control, slowness in learning new managerial skills, and complexity, and how to forge a new model of collaboration between independent but linked companies.

Getting Started: How Well Linked Is Your Organization's Value Chain?

In this chapter, we have painted a broad picture of how successful companies will create much more permeable boundaries between themselves and their partners in the value chain through joint planning, greater information sharing, development of common measures, a more consultative sales process, and increased sharing of resources. The result will be significantly faster and more focused product development, streamlined manufacturing and distribution, lower-cost support systems, more flexible responses to market shifts, and an overall competitive advantage in relation to competing value chains.

Developing looser external boundaries, however, will not be easy. There are plenty of challenges along the way, including overcoming regulatory traditions, sorting through competitive confusion, building trust with partners, learning to let go of total control, and managing the complexity of multi-organizational business efforts. Currently, barriers such as these cause at least as many failures and frustrations as successes.

In our experience, however, it is possible to make progress, no matter the starting point. That is the subject of Chapter Seven. Before you turn to that chapter, we suggest that you get a fix on the relationships with customers and suppliers that your company has today. This knowledge will help you select from Chapter Seven the actions that will be most effective given your current stage of external boundaryless development.

We have described five external boundaries that define customer-supplier dynamics: planning, information sharing, measurement, the sales process, and resource utilization. Like all organizational boundaries, each of these boundaries represents a continuum of possibilities, ranging from the impermeable (here, a traditional, go-it-alone mode) to the highly permeable (here, a mode of considerable sharing and collaboration).

Your company may be at a different point on the continuum of each external boundary. The rigidity or looseness of each boundary will also vary in relation to the particular customer or supplier that is on the other side of it. However, since the five boundaries are to some extent interdependent, it is unlikely that your position on one boundary will be vastly different from your position on the others. For example, it is difficult to engage in a great deal of information sharing without also increasing collaboration in other areas. If such a collaboration imbalance were to occur, it would point to the possibility that trust was localized in one relationship between individuals rather than widespread and that the overall relationship was in fact fragile.

The following self-diagnostic instrument (Questionnaire #4) allows you to locate your company on this continuum for each of the five external boundaries. To improve the accuracy of your answers, we suggest that you have a specific customer, supplier, or value chain partner in mind as you score yourself.

Questionnaire #4

Stepping Up to the Line: How Well Linked Is Your Organization's Value Chain?

Instructions: Diagnose your company's progress toward a boundaryless relationship with customers and/or suppliers in your value chain. Select a strategically important customer/supplier (or category of customer/supplier) in your value chain. Circle a number on each scale to reflect where your customer/supplier relationship now stands.

	Traditional				**Boundaryless**	
I. Strategies/operating plans	Developed independently	Shared	Coordinated		Developed jointly	
•Marketing plans	1 2 3	4 5	6 7	8	9	10
•Product development plans	1 2 3	4 5	6 7	8	9	10
•Production/inventory planning (including who owns inventory)	1 2 3	4 5	6 7	8	9	10
•Distribution/transportation planning	1 2 3	4 5	6 7	8	9	10
•Information systems planning	1 2 3	4 5	6 7	8	9	10

2. Information sharing/problem solving	Highly guarded	Selective sharing as needed		Joint sharing/ problem solving		Two-way understanding		Integrated data systems/processes on common issues	

2. Information sharing/problem solving	Highly guarded	Selective sharing as needed		Joint sharing/ problem solving				Integrated data systems/processes on common issues	
• Cost structure	1	2	3	4	5	6	7	8 9	10
• Profit margins	1	2	3	4	5	6	7	8 9	10
• Quality/production problems	1	2	3	4	5	6	7	8 9	10
• Problem-solving methods	1	2	3	4	5	6	7	8 9	10
• Market information/feedback	1	2	3	4	5	6	7	8 9	10

3. Accounting, measurement, and reward systems	Related	Understood but unconnected		Consistent but separate				Interconnected	
• Accounting procedures	1	2	3	4	5	6	7	8 9	10
• Quality measures	1	2	3	4	5	6	7	8 9	10
• Costing systems	1	2	3	4	5	6	7	8 9	10
• Rewards and incentives	1	2	3	4	5	6	7	8 9	10
• Communication processes	1	2	3	4	5	6	7	8 9	10

4. Sales processes	Independent/ differing views	Selective collaboration		Two-way understanding				Consultative partnership	
• Establishing sales goals/quotas	1	2	3	4	5	6	7	8 9	10
• Assessing customer needs	1	2	3	4	5	6	7	8 9	10
• Determining optimal product usage	1	2	3	4	5	6	7	8 9	10
• Providing product feedback	1	2	3	4	5	6	7	8 9	10
• Setting terms of the deal	1	2	3	4	5	6	7	8 9	10

5. Resources/Skills	Separate		Called upon in emergency		Transfer of knowledge			Shared resources/ colocated		
•Technical expertise	1	2	3	4	5	6	7	8	9	10
•Financial expertise	1	2	3	4	5	6	7	8	9	10
•Organizational/management skills	1	2	3	4	5	6	7	8	9	10
•Information systems	1	2	3	4	5	6	7	8	9	10
•Training	1	2	3	4	5	6	7	8	9	10

Questionnaire Scoring

Add up the numbers from each boundary to find your total score. (For example, total boundarylessness—which is probably not possible—would score 250, that is, 10 points on each of the twenty-five scales.) Interpret the numbers as follows:

- *75 or less.* You are probably just getting started on developing a boundaryless relationship with the customer or supplier. Your main challenge is to tune in to the needs of the other organization and find where the opportunities for further collaboration lie.

- *75 to 150.* You have made good progress on the relationship and are probably poised to build momentum toward long-term collaboration. Your challenge is to create action experiments that can generate results and provide further experiences of success.

- *More than 150.* You have experienced a good deal of success in the relationship, and are probably ready to design mechanisms for sustaining progress in the long term. Your challenge is to align and integrate systems and structures and to institutionalize the boundaryless relationship.

Questionnaire Follow-Up

You can also use this instrument in a group of people who are in contact with the particular supplier or customer you have in mind or who are affected by the relationship with that supplier or customer. Asking members of the supplier or customer organization to participate as well will add greater richness and candor to the assessment. One way to facilitate the follow-up discussion is to place an enlarged copy of the blank instrument on the wall and ask people to record their answers on the enlargement using small colored stickers. The resulting visual map of areas of agreement and disagreement can be the starting point for a discussion of how to move the relationship forward most productively.

Both the group discussion and your personal analysis can focus on these follow-up questions:

- On which external dimensions have you made the most progress toward a boundaryless relationship? What have you done to make this progress? What has worked particularly well?
- On which dimensions are you lagging the most? Why are they the most difficult? What have you tried and what barriers have you run into?
- How far do you need to move on each continuum to successfully strengthen this part of the value chain and increase your competitive capability? Which dimensions are most critical to your progress? Where do you want to focus your efforts?
- Is the relationship with the chosen supplier or customer representative of your overall situation in your value chain? Are there ways to leverage learnings from this relationship elsewhere, or vice versa? Are there more broadly based changes that need to occur?

7

Strengthening the Value Chain

In Chapter Six, we introduced the concept of the value chain, the process by which a network of organizations creates products and services of greater value than those that can be produced by any organization alone. We argued that a mindset focused on strengthening the value chain is critical for increasing overall speed, flexibility, integration, and innovation in individual organizations and in the value chain as a whole.

Our goal in this chapter is to describe a number of specific actions (digital switches) that companies can use to lower external boundaries that have become barriers and to forge a new pattern of relationships with customers, suppliers, regulators, and other external entities. We anticipate that organizations will employ a number of these actions simultaneously, building on those that work and creating new approaches based on second-order learning. Organizations may also identify some actions that will work best with particular types of customers or suppliers or in certain situations.

Before we begin, however, we should make clear that our focus is not the *business strategy* of alliances, partnerships, and joint ventures. A rich literature already exists on how to select an alliance partner, how to evaluate the fit between potential partners, how to assess the potential payoffs and risks, and how to structure an alliance and set up the architecture of cooperation in terms of management agreements, decision making, and so on.[1]

Instead, we concentrate on how organizations can overcome the barriers described in Chapter Six, building the relationships, the mindset, and the attitudes necessary for success in boundaryless collaborations between members of the value chain.

The actions we describe for tuning your organization's performance in relation to its external boundaries are divided into three categories: getting started actions, building momentum actions, and sustaining progress actions. Questionnaire #4, in the previous chapter, will help you to choose the action category with which you should probably start and to decide which particular actions are appropriate for your organization now.

Getting started actions are for organizations in the early stages of building boundaryless relationships across the value chain. These companies need to break old patterns and introduce employees to the external focus. Therefore the proposed actions will identify opportunities for strengthening an entire value chain by getting the people in your company to consider how it is to do business from the various viewpoints of customers and suppliers.

Building momentum actions are for companies in the middle of the boundaryless continuum who want to create tangible successes upon which to build further collaborations. The key here is to design some short-term, relatively low-risk experiments in strengthening the value chain. Such experiments can give your organization and your value chain partners the experience of success in getting better results through collaborative, cross-institutional action.

Finally, *sustaining progress actions* are for organizations that are ready to institutionalize the new value chain model. These actions expand the collaborative process, assess the learnings, consolidate the gains, and move companies to the point where quantum leaps in performance are possible through collaboration.

Table 7.1 summarizes these three categories, and lists the specific actions discussed in this chapter.

Table 7.1. Creating Boundaryless Relationships with Customers and Suppliers.

Score on Value Chain Self-Assessment	Appropriate Actions
75 or less	*Getting started.* Tune in to customers and suppliers and figure out where the opportunities are. • Arrange customer/supplier cameo appearances. • Take customer/supplier field trips. • Hold open-agenda dialogues with management teams. • Map customer/supplier needs. • Collect customer/supplier data.
75–150	*Building momentum.* Experiment with collaboration to experience success and learning. • Hold customer/supplier town meetings. • Organize cross–value chain task forces. • Share technical services. • Teach sales people to be consultants.
Above 150	*Sustaining progress.* Align/integrate systems, structures, and processes to sustain gains in the long term. • Integrate information systems. • Reconfigure roles and responsibilities.

Getting Started Actions

The actions, or tuning switches, in this category are aimed at giving all employees a better understanding of the overall value chain of which their company is a part. With this broader perspective, people are more likely to identify opportunities for improvement. There are five principle actions, listed below, that can change people's perspectives:

Five Getting Started Actions

- Arrange customer/supplier cameos.
- Take customer/supplier field trips.

- Hold open-agenda dialogues between management teams.
- Map customer/supplier needs.
- Collect customer/supplier data.

ARRANGE CUSTOMER/SUPPLIER CAMEOS

One of the easiest and most powerful ways to build an external focus is to bring in customers, suppliers, alliance partners, or other members of your value chain to speak to your organization. We have often been shocked by how little contact many people in organizations have with their external customers or suppliers and how little they understand the pressures, preoccupations, and priorities of key "outsiders."

There are as many subjects for these presentations as there are customer and supplier issues, but we have found that these three topics can form the core of any customer's or supplier's presentation:

- *What is my business:* How does it work? What are the key performance measures and goals? Who are my customers and competitors?
- *What are the keys to further success for my business:* What do we need to do differently? What changes are occurring in the markets that cause us to lose sleep? Where are the risks and problems?
- *How can you help me be more successful:* How can we do business together in more effective ways? If we were one business instead of two, what would we do differently? How can we reduce overall transaction costs or eliminate paperwork or speed cycle times (and so on)?

The gains that can result from such cameo appearances were illustrated when GE Lighting invited several independent distributors (sellers of commercial lighting products) to speak at an internal company meeting on the subject "What It's Like to Do Business with Us." In one of the speeches, a customer casually mentioned that GE shipping schedules were not synchronized with his company's monthly receiving, booking, and inventory accounting schedules. He noted that while orders were pretty consistent each month, products would arrive at different times— presumably due to manufacturing changes, carrier availability, and the like—leading to fluctuations in his inventory levels, periodic stock outages, over-ordering, late payments, disputed bills, and a host of other administrative efficiencies. He suggested that perhaps GE Lighting could work with customers on a fixed schedule of deliveries.

Over the next six months, the head of GE Lighting's distribution organization responded by collaborating with a dedicated trucking company and several customers to create an experimental procedure for fixed delivery schedules from one warehouse. Much to GE Lighting's surprise, the new procedure not only made it easier for the customers, but also reduced GE's outstanding receivables and improved shift scheduling and staffing in GE warehouses. The experiment proved so successful that it was expanded to other distribution centers and eventually became standard procedure for over one thousand customers.

While not all cameo appearances of customers or suppliers lead to such dramatic changes, they do lead to everyone's dawning awareness that the world looks different from different parts of the value chain and that successful cross-organizational interactions take those different perspectives into consideration. This, of course, is a good starting point for loosening external boundaries.

TAKE CUSTOMER/SUPPLIER FIELD TRIPS

A second way to increase value chain understanding is to take people to visit customers and suppliers at their locations. Connections with other organizations in the value chain are often vague and foggy for most employees. In most organizations, only sales or purchasing people regularly get to visit customers and suppliers, and many of those meetings are restricted to isolated offices and limited numbers of participants. When senior managers visit, the meetings are all too often held in restaurants or executive suites and do not give a broad flavor of the customer's or supplier's organization. But when people are taken off their routine jobs for a day or two for a close look at another organization's business, they can develop a much deeper and more personal understanding of how their work is linked to customers and suppliers. This understanding can lead them to much more targeted efforts at value chain improvement.

A classic example of this approach took place several years ago at the Columbia, South Carolina, plant of what was then Allied Chemical

Fibers (now AlliedSignal Fibers), a manufacturer of staple fibers for the carpet and apparel industry. As a beginning step in a plantwide quality effort, management took two busloads of hourly and middle-management people to a nearby carpet mill. There, the mill workers showed the Allied people how certain fiber quality defects (known as drips and fusions) could shut down the knitting machines. Having seen, up close and personally, the impact of these defects on their customers' jobs, the Allied people zeroed in on reducing drips and fusions—without a lot of preliminary executive cajoling, convincing, or proselytizing. Everyone at all levels pitched in with ideas and actions, and defect levels began to go down within weeks. By repeating this approach and building on it over the next year, the Columbia plant not only increased customer satisfaction considerably but also reduced its own costs through eliminating a number of recurring quality problems.

It is one thing to talk to employees about the impact of quality on customers. It is a wholly different story when employees hear the same message from customers themselves and see with their own eyes how customers are affected by their work. Suddenly, the value chain is no longer an abstract concept but a reality that they can feel and touch.

HOLD OPEN-AGENDA DIALOGUES BETWEEN MANAGEMENT TEAMS

Senior management teams, too, can benefit from a greater understanding of the total value chain and their effect on others in it. In our observations, most dialogue between senior managers of companies in the same value chain is transactional, that is, it centers on a particular deal, negotiation, or problem resolution. At times, these senior managers will share common issues or best practices, such as how to deal with a difficult board, how to handle investor relations, how to set up a compensation or stock-option program. But rarely do they step back and take stock of the entire relationship, looking at how each management group can help or strengthen the other. Moreover, most dialogue between senior managers from different companies occurs in one-on-one meetings, usually between equivalent levels. These senior-level "summits" often take on the feel of diplomatic visits, complete with appropriate protocols, formalities, and ritual behaviors. The only thing missing is rich give-and-take dialogue of the sort that would lead to joint ways of strengthening the value chain.

To overcome this pattern, companies can organize *open-agenda meetings* between their top teams, that is, meetings with no issues set in advance. The purpose is to meet to share information on each company's methods of working, issues, and challenges and to begin a dialogue about how the companies can help each other be more successful (Exhibit 7.1 is a sample agenda for such a meeting.)

General Re has used the open-agenda method to open up dialogue with a number of its key customers. One session, for example, was hosted by company chairman Ronald E. Ferguson and attended by his top team and the chairman and senior officers of a large customer insurance company. Ferguson opened the meeting by emphasizing that the purpose was not to discuss any individual deals or transactions but rather to look at patterns of interaction between the companies, what was working and what could be strengthened. He then talked informally (without notes or slides) about some of the current challenges facing General Re, some of the initiatives the company had underway, and some of his concerns for the future. Each member of the General Re

---

Exhibit 7.1. Sample Agenda for Senior Management Dialogue.

- *Introduction by host executive:* key issues facing the host company and programs underway to address them; introduction of other host team members.

- *Response by visiting executive:* key issues facing the visiting company and programs underway to address them; introduction of visiting team members.

- *Discussion of the value chain:* Where are we linked? Who are the other members of the value chain? What does the end-use customer expect? What will it take for the entire value chain to prosper and be successful?

- *Work session:* What would each team like the other company to do differently to be a better customer/supplier/partner? (Each person makes individual notes; people do not respond to each remark but look for patterns and common themes.)

- *Moving forward:* Are there any joint projects or initiatives that should be started, based on the ideas presented about what to do differently? What will each company do on its own? When and how can the dialogue be continued?

---

team then introduced himself or herself and said a few words about the work going on in his or her area. Once this tone was set, the chairman of the customer company, who had come into the meeting not knowing what to expect, began to reciprocate. He informally talked about the challenges facing his company, where it was making progress, and where it was not. The dialogue had begun.

Eventually, Ferguson asked everyone in the room to write down, individually, what he or she would like the other company to do differently to be a better customer or supplier. At first, the comments were gentle, with neither side wanting to offend the other. After these first suggestions for change, however, Ferguson made it clear that he was not going to be defensive and genuinely wanted to listen. Then things heated up, and the inputs became more pointed. In the next hour, a number of constructive themes emerged. The most significant was the need for more collaborative product development, so the customer company could help shape the reinsurance product from the beginning rather than have to accept or reject a finished product (after months of General Re design work).

On the basis of this meeting, a joint product development team was established, and further working groups in areas of risk management and subsidiary ventures were also agreed upon. Even more significantly, the members of the General Re team realized they needed to significantly strengthen their understanding and appreciation of customer issues. One action that resulted was the refocusing of General Re marketing representatives. In place of simply representing General Re product lines to customers, the newly named "client advocates" were charged with discovering client risk management and risk transfer needs and then constructing the most effective response to those needs.

MAP CUSTOMER/SUPPLIER NEEDS

The first three actions for change described above require personal interaction between members of the value chain. The next two actions are analytical methods for increasing people's appreciation and understanding of customer and supplier issues.

Customer/supplier needs mapping is a powerful analytical tool. The methodology was originally derived from quality functional deployment (QFD) tools used in process control. It was then simplified and applied to clients by Richard Hilbert of GE's corporate business development staff.

The main premise of needs mapping is that a company's core business processes must be closely aligned with customer and supplier needs because processes that do not help customers or suppliers to meet their needs weaken the value chain. At the same time, however, business processes must meet such internal needs as cost, profitability, and market share. Sometimes trade-offs must be discussed.

Through needs mapping, groups of people in a company can identify the processes with the greatest leverage on various parties' requirements for success. Those processes can then be improved or reengineered, adding strength to the value chain.

Figure 7.1 is an example of a customer needs map for a hypothetical fast-food restaurant. The company's process is arrayed along the top of the matrix. The customer's needs are listed down the left-hand side. They are weighted to indicate their relative importance to the customer. A score of high (H), medium (M), or low (L) indicates how important each company process is to each customer need. For example, the first process step, taking the order, has a high impact on how quickly the customer gets his or her order, so the first cell on the chart ("Quick"/"Take Order") receives an "H" score. As shown in Figure 7.1, scores are tallied by assigning points to each score (as shown in the legend), the points value of each score is multiplied by the appropriate importance rating, and the process columns are totaled. The processes with highest total scores are those with the greatest change leverage. In the fast-food example, the process with the greatest impact on both customer and company goals is "plan capacity," that is, the decisions made about numbers and levels of staff, amounts of supplies to keep on hand, and so on. This suggests that the restaurant manager would want to find cost-effective ways of staffing adequately for peak periods and should be constantly on the lookout for changes in customer traffic patterns. The manager would probably get more benefit from these activities than from working on new and better ways to fill orders, the process with the lowest total score.

Figure 7.1. Customer Needs Map: Fast-Food Example.

Process

Customer Needs		Importance Rating	Take Order	Fill Order	Prepare Food	Store Food	Select Food	Purchase Materials	Plan Capacity	Clean	Train Employees	Advertise	Track and Report Costs
Service	Quick	5	H	H	L				H	M	M		
Service	Clean	4	L		M	L		L	M	H	H		L
Service	Friendly	1		L							H	L	
Service	Inexpensive	4			L	M	M	H	M		L	M	H
Food	Good taste	4			H	H	M	L		L	H		
Food	Healthy	3	L		H	H	H	L		H			
Business Needs	Market share	4	M	L	L		M		M			H	
Business Needs	Cash flow	5			L	M		M	H			H	H
	Total Ranking		65	50	93	94	63	62	126	82	100	94	85

NOTE: Importance rating: 5 = most important; 1 = least important. Relationship strength: high = 9; medium = 3; low = 1.

SOURCE: Figure developed by Richard Hilbert.

In 1992, GE Lighting Europe mapped customer needs to attack a number of previously intractable quality problems with a major line of fluorescent tubes produced in the U.K. A cross-functional group from engineering, manufacturing, marketing, finance, sourcing, and distribution first mapped the overall process for getting a fluorescent bulb from raw materials to the customer. These process steps were then arrayed against the quality problems, the key customer complaints. Weights were assigned to the quality problems and process steps were scored.

The results of this analysis suggested that the greatest quality improvement would come from two activities: improving a particular stage in the manufacturing process and strengthening certain aspects of packaging. After teams deployed against these specific areas and took corrective actions, including a redesigned package, customer complaints dropped significantly.

The customer needs map is effective because organizations have finite resources and must be selective in their efforts to change processes. The map is a form of mental discipline that encourages thoughtful selectivity.

COLLECT CUSTOMER/SUPPLIER DATA

The final getting started action for changing an organization's perspective on its value chain partners is to collect performance feedback from customers and/or suppliers. While this is probably the most commonly known action step and perhaps the easiest to implement, it is still tremendously underutilized. Many companies are unsure what data to collect and in what form to collect them. Some companies are also hesitant to "bother" their customers, fearing customers will resent being asked for feedback.

The truth of the matter is that it almost does not matter what questions are asked or how the data are collected. Nor is it necessary for every survey to be statistically valid. The main value of collecting customer/supplier data is not the data themselves. Rather, it is the data-collection process that is important: it forces people in the company to begin to think externally, and it sends a message to the external partners that you are interested in their input.

The following example will illustrate what we mean. Several years ago, a maker of large imaging equipment began to wonder why many customers took so long to pay. The company was particularly curious because it had worked very hard to accelerate shipping schedules and get products to customers on the "promise" date over 90 percent of the time, a significant improvement over previous performance. But if the equipment was being shipped on time, why were payments getting even further behind?

To answer that question, the company surveyed a number of customers about their satisfaction when their equipment arrived. Much to the company's dismay, customers were very disappointed. While the equipment that the company produced was arriving on time, various component parts produced by other manufacturers and critical to assembly and operation were arriving much later. The company was shipping its pieces 90 percent on-time, but customers received complete equipment less than 40 percent of the time. And until it asked, the company had been completely oblivious to the problem, which was rectified over the next six months through a concentrated effort to coordinate shipments with the other component producers.

As this case illustrates, other parties in your value chain have much to say to you about how your company does business, and it is important to seek out their views through whatever methods you can. The challenge present in all methods will be to convince your people to value the input from beyond the external boundary, to welcome it without defensiveness or skepticism. It is all too easy for managers to think that their customers or suppliers "don't really understand our business" or "just want to change things so they can take advantage of us." Getting beyond these attitudes is the underlying benefit of any getting starting action. When the readiness to listen begins to flower, a world of possibilities starts to emerge.

Building Momentum Actions

Once people in an organization learn an appreciation for the issues facing other members of the value chain, the challenge is no longer one of education, orientation, and empathy alone. Now the questions become: How do we translate this newfound understanding into tangible, sustaining action? How do we experience the short-term successes that will reinforce the value of collaboration and make it worthwhile for all value chain partners to keep the lines of communication open?

In our experience, there are four powerful actions that build an ongoing momentum, making the process of collaboration so rewarding that it cannot easily be truncated.

Four Building Momentum Actions

- Hold customer/supplier town meetings.
- Organize cross–value chain task forces.
- Share technical services.
- Teach salespeople to be consultants.

HOLD CUSTOMER/SUPPLIER TOWN MEETINGS

In Chapter Three, we introduced the town meeting process as one of the most useful tools for change ever developed for breaking down hierarchical and functional boundaries within a company. By bringing together groups of people from different parts of an organization in a safe, structured problem-solving environment, the town meeting helps them generate innovative recommendations for changing the way their work is done and challenges managers to make immediate yes/no decisions on those recommendations. Participants are then empowered to follow up on the approved ideas and make them happen.

While the town meeting was originally designed at GE to loosen up internal ceilings and walls, GE quickly realized that the process was a means of crossing external walls and strengthening relationships with customers and suppliers. In the past few years, GE businesses have initiated literally hundreds of town meetings with customers and suppliers, all aimed at strengthening the value chain in which they both participate.

For many years, for example, the Sears Kenmore brand of appliances provided direct competition to the GE Appliance business. In the late 1980s, however, Sears began selling GE brands, thus becoming a cus-

tomer as well as a rival. With the advent of the Sears Brand Central concept in 1989, Sears positioned itself as a distributor more than a propo-
nent of one brand, and the time seemed right for GE Appliances and
Sears to overcome the old sense of competition and forge a new relationship. GE Chairman and CEO Jack Welch described the town meeting process to Dick Lieberman, Sears national merchandising manager,
and found a receptive audience. As Lieberman later reflected, "the lightbulbs went on. The timing was right because Sears had undergone
recent changes: a more integrated, vertical organization; a new philosophy of everyday low pricing; and the introduction of power formats,
like the Brand Central concept in Sears Home Appliances. With the
potential to reduce unnecessary work, increase productivity and derive
more synergy out of the Sears–GE relationship, the [town meeting]
seemed a perfect fit for the new corporate direction Sears was taking."[2]

A joint Sears–GE Appliances design team identified five major areas
of opportunity to address: appliance delivery, billing procedures, inventory management, in-store merchandising, and customer/market information. The team also developed an agenda for the first session,
selected five teams of participants (one for each area), and considered
how the process could unfold beyond one session.

The first session was fraught with difficulty. Participants were used to
thinking of each other as competitors and, despite preparatory remarks
by Lieberman and Welch, came to the session with a basic sense of dis-
trust. Over the course of the three days, however, a shared sense of understanding began to emerge, and the five teams generated productive ideas.
When the ideas were immediately accepted by the Sears and GE senior
managers, the group's skepticism was replaced by a sense of accomplishment. One Sears participant later recalled: "The actual . . . sessions were
some of the most encouraging ones we've ever spent with a supplier. We
questioned procedures that had outlived their usefulness, examined ways
to remove redundancy, and tried to reduce the business equation to its
bare essentials. Although we haven't seen all the implications of the [town
meeting], it has created a mindset for progress."[3]

Following the initial town meeting, progress on the joint projects and
recommendations was reviewed at each organization's senior staff meeting. Sears then held two internal town meetings and GE Appliances held
one, all aimed at addressing issues raised by the partner organization at the

joint session. In July 1990, a second joint town meeting was held to review the first round of projects and begin a second set of more ambitious efforts, such as coordinating the production-sales-inventory systems and integrating systems across the companies. A sustaining process had been created.

Encouraged by GE's early experience, many companies since have taken to town meetings to strengthen value chain relationships with a supplier, a customer, or with multiple members of the value chain all at once.

In many instances, companies have used a *customer-supplier expectations questionnaire* (Table 7.2) as part of the preliminary session to set the stage for an open discussion. To use this tool, each participant first ranks the twelve characteristics of the buyer or the supplier relationship (as appropriate), in order of importance according to his or her own expectations. The participants then form company teams to develop a consensus ranking of the characteristics. (This step often proves to be a team-building activity for participants.) Next, each company team speculates about how the other company team has ranked the items. Then the teams share their guesses. A rich discussion usually ensues around the perceptions and misperceptions each team has about the other company, about what each company is really looking for in the other, and what each company has in mind when it speaks about partnership.

A good example of the kinds of insights that can be gained from the questionnaire comes from a session between a group of General Motors purchasing people and their suppliers. On the one hand, the GM team resorted to a strict mathematical calculation that produced a "product" very quickly—but very little satisfaction or buy-in on the part of team members. On the other hand, the suppliers argued about each item and, when they could not reach agreement on an item, agreed to disagree. They took a long time to complete the assignment but were much more personally engaged. Witnessing the different approaches gave everyone a better understanding of the style differences that might be shaping the overall relationship between the companies.

ORGANIZE CROSS–VALUE CHAIN TASK FORCES

An alternative way to orchestrate immediate successes in collaboration is to form a task force that draws its members from different parts of the

Table 7.2. What Aspects of the Buyer-Supplier Relationship Are Most Important?

There are hundreds of ways to describe an effective relationship between buyers and suppliers. The following list of characteristics or qualities has been compiled from a number of studies of salesmanship and vendor relations. All seem to be important. Your task—first individually, then as a team—is to rank the characteristics from 1 to 12, in the order you feel should be the most important to the customer-supplier relationship.

	Your Ranking	Team Ranking
Part 1: Characteristics important to suppliers		
1. Reliability. Always keeps commitments and delivers on promises.	——	——
2. Candor. Provides us with all the information we need; willingly shares information.	——	——
3. Authority. Has the authority to make final decisions.	——	——
4. Loyalty. Values a long-term relationship; sticks with us over the long haul.		
5. Trust. Believes that we have the customer's best interests in mind; does not take advantage of the relationship.	——	——
6. Openness. Is open to new ideas and alternative ways of doing things.	——	——
7. Fairness. Negotiates fair contracts; prices product fairly.		
8. Clarity. Knows what he or she wants; clearly communicates performance requirements.		
9. Organizational savvy. Gets things done effectively within the customer organization; works "the system" well.	——	——
10. Honesty. Gives us a straight answer; never misrepresents things.	——	——
11. Competence. Understands the product development process; knows what is required for us to produce a quality product.		
12. Flexibility. Is always willing to compromise in order to create a win-win situation.	——	——

	Your Ranking	Team Ranking

Part 2: Characteristics important to customers

1. Reliability. Always keeps commitments and delivers on promises.

2. Candor. Provides us with all the information we need; willingly shares information.

3. Quality. Meets our expectations in terms of product quality.

4. Consistency. Provides us with a consistent level of overall service over time.

5. Trust. Has our best interests in mind; does not take advantage of the relationship.

6. Creativity. Offers us new ideas and product improvement; develops new products to meet our needs.

7. Fairness. Negotiates fair contracts; prices the product fairly.

8. Responsiveness. Goes the extra mile for us.

9. Organizational savvy. Gets things done effectively within the supplier organization; works "the system" well.

10. Honesty. Gives us a straight answer; never misrepresents things.

11. Competence. Thoroughly understands the product features and how the product can meet our needs.

12. Flexibility. Is always willing to compromise in order to create a win-win situation.

value chain. It should operate like any other organizational task force, with a few subtle differences:

The task force should have an urgent and compelling business goal. Moreover, achieving the goal should result in a significant payoff for *all* the parties. This mutually beneficial goal is a key element for overcoming the inevitable parochial views, interests, and perspectives of task force participants.

The task force requires a clear leader.   This leader must be able to pull things together across the organizations. The leader must also be accountable for the results. Some companies prefer to have co-leaders from the different organizations, but this arrangement often reflects a trust barrier at work, with neither organization trusting that a member of the other organization can be an impartial leader. Thus, the leader (or leaders) also must be someone who can go beyond the organizational view, take a value chain perspective, and convey that perspective clearly to all team members.

The task force must engage in up-front team building.   While team building is always helpful in a task force, it is vital for a cross-company effort. Not only do task force members often not know each other, they also come into the project with different views of the problem, different assumptions about how to tackle it, and different ways of working.

The task force needs a great deal of project management discipline.   Whether team members are assigned full or part time, each organization is making a significant commitment of resources. Task force members need to be well utilized. In addition, task force members will carry the story of their collaboration back to their home organizations. If they have clear task responsibilities, feel a constant sense of progress, and receive periodic short-term feedback and reinforcement from management, they are likely to feel enthusiastic about the collaboration, and take a positive view of collaboration back to their companies. Nothing will make them feel more positive than the achievement of short-term results.

One example of a successful cross-company task force comes from PPG Industries fiberglass products group. As part of an effort to accelerate new product development and reverse a business growth slowdown, this PPG division set up several teams to tailor fiberglass applications for specific customers. One team decided to take a collaborative approach with its customer, an automotive parts manufacturer that was developing a fiberglass-reinforced plastic suspension spring for one particular model produced by a major automobile company. The spring had the potential to be lighter and stronger than a conventional metal spring, and the PPG team recognized that if the spring were successful a much broader market could be developed.

Given the potential opportunity, both companies were willing to innovate. But the goodwill did not translate initially into a successful product. No matter how PPG formulated the fiberglass, the customer was not able to create a strong enough bond to the plastic materials, leading to a series of product failures. To resolve this problem, the PPG team worked out an unusual agreement—the customer would help PPG recreate the customer's highly confidential proprietary bonding process within PPG. That agreement allowed PPG and the customer to work together to test different types of fiberglass and different conditions for the bonding process. The result was a successful new application for fiberglass, which later expanded beyond the one automobile model originally targeted.[4]

One of the best-known examples of the cross–value chain task team approach is the design of the Ford Taurus/Sable. Input from dealers, customers (such as large-volume fleet managers), and suppliers helped Ford create a car that broke all previous sales records for its class and eventually became the best-selling car in North America.[5]

In both these cases, success would not have been possible without a loosening of the traditional external boundaries of the sponsoring organization. Moreover, in both cases, project participation was in real time as part of an ongoing urgent effort. People were not asked to do isolated tasks as part of a larger project that the they knew little about. The more enduring value of these efforts, however, was that they built bridges between members of the value chain that could grow and evolve over time, making it easier for future collaborations across boundaries to occur.

SHARE TECHNICAL SERVICES

A third way to produce tangible, short-term improvements across the value chain is to extend your company's expertise to its suppliers and customers. You might offer your value chain partners help in using your products, financial management, inventory control, information systems, distribution, sales, management practices, and many other areas. Such help, of course, must be provided in the spirit of strengthening the entire value chain; it should not be offered simply as an incentive for doing further business or as a way to gather proprietary information. Also, partners must feel ready to accept such help. They should not feel forced to accept only to maintain good relationships. For example, as we mentioned before, many suppliers to General Motors felt they were coerced into accepting help when José Ignacio Lopez was the head of GM procurement. Although many of them welcomed the expertise they were given by GM engineers, they did not appreciate what accompanied that help: unilateral price reductions and the threat that if the technical recommendations were not implemented, GM would not do business with them.

There are many examples of extremely positive technical support between collaborators. As mentioned earlier, shared technical assistance has been a long-standing tradition of fiber manufacturers and carpet mills. Production and engineering experts in AlliedSignal Fibers' customer service department, for example, have received training in consulting skills so they can effectively translate their expertise into customer results. In many carpet mills, they work in such close collaboration with regular employees that they are indistinguishable from them.

Other firms use similar technical exchange tactics. Hewlett-Packard engineers work on customer project teams to ensure that HP products are used effectively. Honeywell loans designers and engineers to customers. Many financial institutions lend not only money but also financial expertise to their customers.[6]

The Swedish furniture company IKEA has one of the most extensive and successful programs of supplier assistance. Consultants Richard Normann and Rafael Ramirez report that "long-term suppliers . . . receive technical assistance, leased equipment, and advice on bringing production up to world quality standards. . . . For example, the company employs about a dozen technicians . . . to provide suppliers with technical assistance. The company's Vienna-based Business Services Department runs a computer database that helps suppliers find raw materials and introduces them to new business partners."[7]

TEACH SALESPEOPLE TO BE CONSULTANTS

As mentioned in Chapter Six, when companies lower their external boundaries, they also stop pushing product on customers. Instead, they practice consultative selling. The company representative tunes in to customer needs, shapes product offerings and configurations to meet those needs, and then works with the customer to help him or her take full advantage of the product. In this context, the job of the sales rep is less about transferring specific products or services from one organization to another and more about building a mutually beneficial collaborative relationship.

Consultative selling requires the ability to:

◆ Understand the customer (both the individual and the organization) in terms of business pressures, internal politics, competition, information access, culture, readiness to change, and so on.
◆ Map the customer organization to know who is who, what are the points of entry, who needs to be involved in decisions, and so on.
◆ Interact with the customer in ways that build the relationship, empower the customer, and develop trust.
◆ Provide products, services, and solutions in a variety of ways so as to match the unique needs of the customer.
◆ Help the customer use the products or services in creative or high-leverage ways.

Traditionally, salespeople are trained first in technical product knowledge and second in selling, that is, in making contact, presenting the product, negotiating price, and closing the deal. They are rarely trained in the skills just discussed. Therefore, a major action for building momentum across the value chain is to build such skills, through both training and on-the-job experience. If combined with appropriate changes in sales compensation, performance measurement, and management follow-up, such training can have a significant impact.

For example, in 1991, the IBM Business Professional Institute developed the "Consulting Skills Workshop," a three-day course for IBM sales reps. (The course agenda is outlined in Figure 7.2.) Its purpose was to give members of IBM's 8,000-person salesforce the skills, work methods, and strategies that would enable them to be perceived by customers as allies in the pursuit of the customer's business objectives.

Figure 7.2. Agenda for IBM's "Consulting Skills Workshop."

Day 1	Day 2	Day 3
A. Marketing in the 1990's • The Competitive Challenge B. Diagnosing Consulting Opportunities • Hidden Factors • Readiness: Identifying the Client's Issues • Demands: Making Sure the Client Makes Measurable Demands • Agendas: Mapping the Client Organization	C. Consulting Face-to-Face • Mastering Anxiety • Versatility: Preparing for Client Visits • Consultative Interviews and Meetings D. Consultative Tactics and Strategies • In a Specific Sale • Building Key Relationships	E. Moving Into Action • The Breakthrough Strategy F. Action Plan: Creating and Presenting a Work Plan for a Client • Building a Support System in the Branch

The course was offered first as a pilot program in ten IBM sales branches over a six-month period. The ticket of admission for the fifteen to twenty attendees in each session was a specific customer situation in which the rep wanted some assistance. During each course, the attendees applied their learnings from each module to the customer situations, and "consulted" to each other about the situations. By the end of the three days, each sales representative had a detailed work plan for addressing his or her situation in some new ways.

Many reps who took the pilot courses developed new business in ways they had not previously thought possible, and there were other benefits. One senior account rep, for example, related how he found a way to avoid losing a major multimillion dollar account at one company:

> I stopped by to make a courtesy call on the president, [and] he started complaining how he was still not getting the information he wanted and that huge systems expenditures had been a waste of money. In the past, I probably would have gotten on my high horse and argued with him that he had the best possible equipment and plenty of reports. But instead, I asked him what was missing. Before I knew it, we were engaged in a long conversation which made me realize that his own systems people didn't have a clue about the kind of information he wanted. I promised to work with his systems people to reconfigure some of the reporting, and help them tune in more to what he was looking for. It didn't take long at all to make some changes . . . and we went from being cast as the villain to having a much more solid relationship.

After such successes, the IBM sales organization developed a cadre of internal trainers to teach the course, rolling it out to hundreds of sales reps each year ever since.

Another illustration of introducing a consultative-selling mindset took place at the Chase Manhattan Bank. In late 1989, Chase launched a series of senior management task forces charged with transforming key aspects of the corporation prior to dramatic downsizing and shifts in the business mix. At the time, the majority of marketing efforts at Chase were product based; in essence, they pushed individual products on customers, and each customer organization often dealt with a number of Chase representatives. A change in this culture was critical if the bank was to streamline itself and increase its revenue base, and the job of one task force was to develop a more customer-focused marketing approach that would cut across the various product lines. One approach the task force developed was the half-day "Global Customer Workshop," an organized forum for sales representatives to share information about a key customer and leverage the customer relationship across lines of business.

At a typical session, reps who already did or wanted to do business with the customer reviewed the business currently being written out of each product area and identified the client decision maker for each part of that business. A large board quickly filled with an informal map of the business relationship. Everyone then put the current business aside for a moment and contributed to a list of competitive challenges facing the customer. Next, the group brainstormed ways that Chase could help the customer meet its challenges by going beyond current products. Dozens of new ideas usually emerged, to be prioritized and assigned to various participants or to teams if there were cross-product opportunities. At a session covering the bank's relationship with one large retailer, for example, twenty-seven separate opportunities were assigned for follow-up.

While each workshop produced tangible business opportunities, many of which resulted in revenue, the real gain was in changing the mindset of the marketing people so they could see the total relationship from the client's perspective. Over the following three years of downsizing and reorganization, this mindset was continually reinforced, both through further training and through changes in compensation and performance management. It has been a critical element in Chase's emergence as a stronger bank.

As these two cases demonstrate, it is possible to introduce consultative selling to a salesforce that sells directly to customers and can immediately apply the new methods. But how do you introduce consultative selling when salespeople sell indirectly, through a network of distributors? That was the question facing Kevin Sullivan, PPG director of sales for the fiberglass business, in the late 1980s. To increase distributors' sales of fiberglass products, he realized that the PPG salesforce would have to strengthen the sales and managerial skills of the distributors. This would require PPG salespeople to make a profound shift in approach, from pushing product to being teachers and consultants. To start, PPG salespeople ran some goal-setting and work-planning sessions for a few distributors, with the goal of showing them how to get a greater return on time invested in selling PPG products. They also scheduled formal follow-up reviews to evaluate progress and see what further support the distributors might need.

Very shortly, the new approach paid off. For example, one distributor that had been a low performer for PPG had been concerned that sales of his other line of products would suffer if he focused on PPG products. The sessions with the PPG sales representative helped this distributor see how to increase all his current sales while expanding his focus on PPG products. In one year, he tripled his sales of PPG fiberglass and became one of the top ten PPG fiberglass distributors.[8]

Like a number of our actions for change, consultative selling is not an event, or time-bound action, that happens at one given moment. Rather it is an evolving shift in mindset and perspective that causes people to gradually acquire an additional set of skills. Moreover, while the skills can be taught and practiced, the mindset must emerge out of leadership's conviction that the best way to be successful is to help customers be successful. If your company has evolved to the point where this premise is a given, then consultative selling can be a powerful action for change, deepening ties across the entire value chain. In addition, your organization is probably ready to move to the next level of boundaryless external relationships and to institutionalize partnership arrangements.

Sustaining Progress Actions

Once companies have generated tangible successes in partnerships and collaborations, they face the challenge of sustaining their progress. They need to lock in the gains made. To prevent backsliding, they must be sure they have institutionalized the new approach to the value chain.

The specific challenge of this phase of becoming boundaryless is restructuring the structure. In order to truly institutionalize seamless collaboration between value chain partners, it is not enough to make the boundaries more permeable, they must also be moved. The points at which the supplier ends and the customer begins must be changed in an ongoing process, a continuing dialogue about shifting boundaries over time.

Companies currently achieving a sustained reformulation of the customer-supplier relationship use the two specific methods listed below.

Two Sustaining Progress Actions
- Integrate information systems.
- Reconfigure roles and responsibilities.

INTEGRATE INFORMATION SYSTEMS

At its core, the relationship between customers and suppliers is held together by information—accurate information. When information is inaccurate, incomplete, or untimely, members of the value chain expend enormous resources compensating for these deficiencies. Many if not most of the problems that occur in value chain relationships can be traced to faulty information flows: for example, billing errors, order filling and shipping problems, stock-outs, and customer inquiry issues. Untold costs are added to value chains in the resolution of these difficulties. Smooth, quick, and accurate information transfer and the subsequent elimination of these costs will therefore represent a quantum leap improvement in competitive advantage for value chain members. Equally important, as customers and suppliers integrate their information flows, they institutionalize their working relationships.

While information can certainly be shared verbally and through the exchange of reports, the most significant benefits accrue when members of the value chain are linked electronically through integration of computer systems. Electronic linkages eliminate transcription errors, misunderstandings, and reams of paperwork. They also speed up cycle time considerably.

Consider the following two cases from GE, which has been a leader in the cross-organizational integration of information systems.

Monogram Retailers Credit Services, Inc. (MRCSI), is a unit of GE Capital that provides credit and credit card services for retailer Montgomery

Ward, with 350 stores in over thirty states. From six locations, the largest of which is in Merriam, Kansas, 2,000 MRCSI associates support over 18 million Montgomery Ward cardholders and process millions of transactions each month.

One of the most critical functions MRCSI performs is the issuance and approval of new credit cards, which not only permit customer credit purchases but provide an ongoing channel for communication between the company and each customer. When a potential customer walks into a Montgomery Ward store, needs credit to buy goods, especially big-ticket items, and is within acceptable risk parameters, the retailer wants to allow that person to buy immediately, without waiting. In 1990, when Stephen P. Joyce first became general manager of MRCSI, there were two ways consumers could apply for credit in-store. The potential customer could pick up an application in the store, complete it, and mail it into Merriam. Upon receipt of the application, MRCSI contacted the appropriate credit bureaus to see if the person fit the proper credit profiles, and if he or she did, the card would be embossed and mailed. Total transaction time for this method was seven to ten days. In the meantime, the customer had to pay cash for transactions or use a bank card (which costs Montgomery Ward more money per transaction). Alternatively, the completed application could be faxed from the store to MRCSI along with a "pending sale" message. If the customer was willing to wait in the store for thirty to forty minutes, MRCSI could process the application immediately, authorize the sale, and send out the new card for use in future purchases.

While thirty-minute new credit authorizations were as fast as anyone in the retail credit industry could provide, they were still too slow for customers and salespeople. It was awkward for customers to wait around, and downright annoying if, after that wait, credit was denied. Moreover, salespeople had to leave the floor to use the fax machines, thus compromising service to other customers. On the basis of focus groups, customer surveys, and other research, Steve Joyce, in collaboration with Montgomery Ward management, determined that the total process needed to be completed in less than five minutes.

To reach the five-minute turnaround goal, Joyce and his team constructed a three-way electronic linkage between Montgomery Ward's point-of-sale system (the cash registers), the MRCSI system, and three major credit bureaus (Equifax, TRW, and Trans Union). With this linkage, a store associate can enter identifying data for the potential customer (for example, a MasterCard or Social Security number) right into the cash register terminal. The information goes immediately to the credit bureau for a rating. That rating is then sent to MRCSI's computers, which check it against a variety of criteria. If the criteria are met, the MRCSI computer sends an approved new credit card number to the store terminal, and the sales associate issues a temporary charge card on the spot—less than three minutes after the customer has made his or her application. Meanwhile, a permanent card is cut and mailed the next day and will arrive at the customer's home within three days.

Since the electronic approval process has started, the volume of new credit card applications at Montgomery Ward stores has increased by 50 percent. Salespeople eagerly encourage people to open accounts, and creditworthy customers are willing to invest two minutes to make an application. Since their first experience with Montgomery Ward is so positive, they are encouraged to come back. At the same time, the electronic system cut overall processing costs for new applications by 25 percent, helping GE Capital realize huge savings in its back office. Equally important, the partner relationship between MRCSI, Montgomery Ward, and the credit bureaus—key members of the value chain—has now become institutionalized.

Another example of information integration concerns GE Lighting and its relationship with a large North American retailer. For many years, GE lightbulbs were sold in this rapidly growing chain. However, the chain also carried competitors' bulbs and often pushed for lower prices by leveraging the suppliers against each other. Such price reductions meant a continually deteriorating profit picture for GE Lighting.

In 1990, in an attempt to change the downward spiral, GE Lighting approached the retailer about establishing a partnership. The goal of the plan was to take significant costs and time out of the order-ship-bill cycle between the two companies and do it in a way that would provide customer-service benefits as well. Called the "21st Century Partnership Plan," the idea worked like this: GE Lighting and the retailer would exchange information on the retailer's warehouse stock, shipments from warehouses to the stores, stock outages, and so on, through an electronic data interchange (EDI) network. GE Lighting would then use the information to automatically determine product needs, create orders, and trigger the shipping process to replenish stock in the customer warehouses. In other words, GE Lighting would not have to wait for someone at the retailer to call in an order, and the retailer would not have to worry about inventory levels. GE Lighting would also use EDI to transmit shipping notices and delivery dates and to send invoices. Both companies would be connected with a bank so that payments also would be electronic (see Figure 7.3 for a diagram of the process).

By early 1991, the retailer had joined with GE Lighting in this partnership, and both companies were reaping benefits. The retailer reduced inventory levels and avoided stock outages. Both companies reduced paperwork and all the associated costs of purchase order processing, invoice preparation, and disputes. Cost savings were passed along to the consumers, who could be confident that the GE bulb they wanted would be available. On the basis of that confidence, the retailer made GE lighting its sole supplier of lightbulbs.

With this success to build upon, GE Lighting and the retailer then expanded the partnership even further, arranging for point-of-sale data to be sent electronically to GE Lighting's computers. In this way, GE knows within minutes which types of bulbs are being sold in which of the customer's hundreds of stores, and it can further refine ordering and shipping patterns, even shipping directly to the stores instead of a warehouse.

The GE Lighting case illustrates how productive value chain partnerships can continue to evolve over time. As the two companies experienced success and built trust in each other, their view of new possibilities for collaboration and mutual benefit widened and deepened.

The ultimate systems integration is with the end-use customer. This integration is coming faster than anyone realizes, Already, thousands of people do their banking by telephone or personal computer. With the advent of interactive cable television systems, such as those being developed by Time Warner, TCI, and US West, consumers will be able to electronically shop, order movies and other forms of entertainment, get financial advice, and more. The potential benefits of such integration are virtually unlimited and will continue to evolve.

One example of how integration with end-users works today is Fidelity Investment's Touch Tone Trader. Through this system, anyone with a Fidelity brokerage account can execute trades without talking to a

Figure 7.3. GE Lighting Stock Replenishment Process.

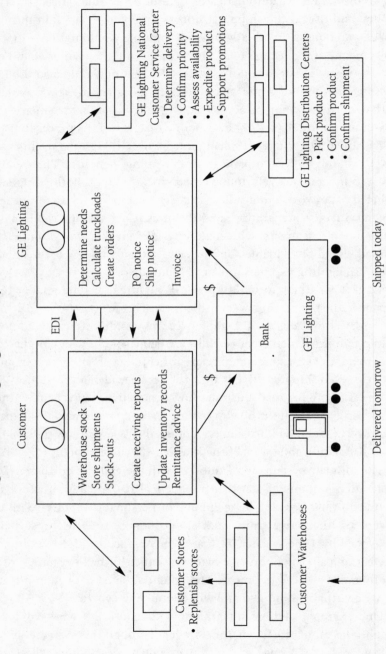

broker or Fidelity representative. The customer merely pushes telephone buttons according to specified "prompts." For consumers, the system lets them place orders twenty-four hours a day, freeing them from having to wait to reach their brokers, especially during peak periods. For Fidelity, the cost of a telephone transaction is far less than the cost of an interactive call with a live representative or a customer's visit to a brokerage office. Thus, the system is a win-win situation for everyone.

Our examples illustrate the power of systems integration in strengthening institutionalized relationships between customers and suppliers. Such integrations, however, are not easy. They must be built on a foundation, first, of understanding and, second, of concrete experiences of success. And they require a great deal of trust and faith on both sides. Installing integrated systems and making them work well requires a real commitment to supplier and customer partners and substantial investments of time and money. It should not be entered into lightly. Once it is begun, however, the potentials for gain are almost unlimited, which makes this a change clearly worth exploring.

RECONFIGURE ROLES AND RESPONSIBILITIES

The ultimate strategy for strengthening a value chain calls for a shift in the roles and responsibilities of the members. The goal is to add value all along the chain at the right times, with the best resources, and at the lowest overall cost. Meeting this goal often means that tasks or activities traditionally done by one member of the value chain must be eliminated altogether or shifted to another place in the chain. The organizations involved must map out the various tasks and processes involved in interaction, assess their value, and determine how best to get them done (if they are needed at all), regardless of which organizational unit has done them in the past.

While such a reconfiguration is clearly a by-product of many actions described earlier in this chapter, here it is an explicit goal. For example, several years ago a group of Pittsburgh Yellow Cab drivers, all of whom owned their own cars, banded together to form a more customer-focused taxi service. Over several dinners at a local restaurant, they thought through the traditional Yellow Cab taxi organization and decided to experiment with some modifications. First, they agreed to continue using the Yellow Cab name, since it was recognized and respected by consumers. This decision also allowed them to continue to obtain reduced automobile insurance rates and group health and life insurance and to take advantage of the Yellow Cab garage for maintenance and repairs. But they would not be employed by Yellow Cab. Basically, they transformed their previous employer into a supplier of maintenance and insurance services.

Second, to make the restructuring work, they changed how they handled information. They replaced the office dispatcher with a rotating driver/dispatcher. They purchased several cellular telephones and drew up a schedule of who would do the dispatching. Customers called in to the driver/dispatcher's cab, and the driver/dispatcher then used the existing radio system to find out who was in the best position to pick up the customer. So a task once done by a central organization was now done by the drivers themselves.

Next, the group decided to create partnerships with local hotels, restaurants, hospitals, universities, and corporations. In exchange for their business, the drivers promised them such benefits as higher levels of service, charge accounts, and clean and smoke-free cabs. The drivers struck the deals themselves, again taking on a former function of the central organization.

Finally, to further streamline the organization, the taxi drivers agreed to eliminate central accounting and profit sharing. They would proceed on the assumption that if they all worked together for the betterment of the group, everyone would do better than under the previous arrangement. Therefore, all fares were kept by the driver who made the run, and each driver operated as an independent business. To cover expenses, such as the cellular phones, each driver contributed a small monthly fee, which was more than made up by additional revenues.

Although clearly different from the transformation of a large corporation, the Yellow Cab case illustrates two kinds of task reconfiguration. The first reconfiguration was the shift of functions that were previously centralized within the supplier organization to the next party in the value chain, the taxi drivers themselves. Moreover, after the drivers shifted the functions, they distributed them more, sharing tasks among themselves. The second reconfiguration was the elimination of central accounting, which the drivers felt did not have enough added value to be done at all.

In the Yellow Cab example, a reconfiguration of tasks led to a new kind of organization, creating more value for everyone in the chain. Reconfigurations of tasks can also move entire organizational units or functions to a new part of the value chain. For example, in December 1991, Continental Bank outsourced the management of its entire information technology (IT) services function to an IBM subsidiary, turning over people, equipment, and responsibilities. This shift resulted from a conscious, ongoing reassessment of core competencies and a decision to focus limited resources on basic bank strengths in banking and customer relations.

Although the bank had already outsourced many of its in-house service departments, ranging from food to legal services, Richard L. Huber, the executive in charge of the IT outsourcing, recalls that there was initial concern that the bank would lose control of its "crown jewels" if it gave up control of systems development. However, by reconfiguring the relationship between the bank's business units, the IBM subsidiary that would run systems, and Ernst & Young (which would supply systems development support), necessary control was maintained, previously "never-ending" projects put to bed, and costs substantially reduced.[9]

In this case, the reconfiguration was based on the notion that different value chain members have different strengths or competencies and that the greatest overall value comes from concentrating on those strengths, not on ancillary functions. Continental decided that it was in the banking business, not the systems business. In contrast, the IBM subsidiary was in the systems business. In other words, the determining factor was not cost alone but rather where in the value chain the most value could be added without sacrificing cost, control, or customer service.

Sometimes, however, cost will be the main factor in determining where tasks should be performed, especially when the value added is virtually the same in the different locations. For example, as part of its ongoing effort to reduce costs, Federated Department Stores has asked apparel suppliers to ship clothes on better hangers, so Federated will not have the expense of changing hangers in order to display the clothes. For Federated's suppliers, of course, this change will make sense only if they consider the overall value chain picture and not just their added costs or if Federated shares the costs of the new hangers.[10]

Similarly, reconfigurations in the value chain can mean changed or diminished roles for distributors. Many manufacturers have traditionally relied on distributors to be their sales outlets to consumers. Because this requires merchandise to be shipped twice, first to the distributor and then to the consumer, some manufacturers are now exploring the possibility of delivering directly to consumers' homes. The distributors would continue to provide a sales showroom and follow-up service, but they would not carry inventory or provide shipping and installation services that can be provided directly by the manufacturer.

The last type of reconfiguration to be considered is the shifting of functions from the selling organization to the end-user; that is, the customer is asked to do things previously done by the retailer. Discount or generic brand supermarkets ask customers to bag their own groceries; salad-bar restaurants ask diners to put together their own dinners. One of the best examples of this trend is the strategy of IKEA, a Swedish furniture retailer. As described by Normann and Ramirez:

> The company offers customers something more than just low prices. It offers a brand new division of labor that looks something like this: if customers agree to take on certain key tasks traditionally done by manufacturers and retailers—the assembly of products and their delivery to customers' homes—then IKEA promises to deliver well-designed products at substantially lower prices. . . . Every aspect of the IKEA business system is carefully designed to make it easy for customers to take on this new role. . . . At the front door, customers are supplied with catalogues, tape measures, pens and notepaper to help customers make choices without the aid of salespeople. . . . After payment, customers place their packages in carts to take them to their cars. If the package won't fit, IKEA will even lend or sell at cost an automobile roof rack. . . . IKEA's goal is not to relieve customers of doing certain tasks but to mobilize them to do easily certain things they have never done before.[11]

Today's shifting boundaries between suppliers and customers are a reality not just for organizations but for individual consumers as well.

In summary, reconfiguring a value chain is a major undertaking that needs the insights, collaboration, and full cooperation of value chain members. It cannot be done unilaterally; nor can it be done without the interests of the entire value chain in mind. Thus, manufacturers such as GE Appliances work closely with dealers and third-party delivery services in formulating home-delivery pilots and also survey customer reactions. Continental Bank has worked closely with internal constituents as well as outside IT suppliers to reconstruct its systems value chain. IKEA has constructed a business system that tries to make it easy for consumers to play their new roles.

Once started, however, the reconfiguration of a value chain and the resulting permeable boundaries between participants can fuel an evergreen evolutionary process of learning, change, and improvement. For example, the relationship mentioned earlier between GE Lighting and its retailer began with a straightforward attempt by GE Lighting, motivated by profit margin concerns, to become a more strategic supplier to its customer. From there, the relationship evolved into a model of information systems integration, first through EDI and then through direct systems access. That integration eventually led to reconfiguration of roles and responsibilities, with GE Lighting taking on more of the inventory management, store replenishment, and other tasks. Through this collaboration, the retailer's innovative management processes became visible to GE management, which expressed an interest in learning about them. Consequently, the retailer's CEO and several senior executives spent a day visiting with the GE Corporate Executive Council (the heads of the GE businesses), and the council members also visited the retailer's headquarters to watch the management process at first hand. This sharing has had a profound influence on GE's management style. In turn, GE has sponsored an introduction to town meeting and process-mapping technologies for the retailer, which now uses these tools in its continuous improvement efforts.

In the boundaryless world, the opportunity for such fruitful learning, change, and growth will be ever present. Management's challenge will be to use those opportunities to best advantage.

Making It Happen: Permeating External Boundaries

In this chapter, we have outlined a number of powerful actions for change that can be used to create more permeable boundaries between customers and suppliers. In the final analysis, however, these actions are merely tools. And, like any set of tools, they require proper use. To use these tools effectively, organizational leaders, CEOs, and other senior executives must first help their organizations assess the current *reality* of relationships with customers and suppliers and then, based on that honest assessment, select actions appropriate to that reality. If this diagnostic step is skipped or skimmed over, it is all too possible for organizations to create unrealistic expectations for their customers or suppliers or to waste money on actions that do not pay off. For example, sustaining actions such as integrated information systems are usually little more than fantasy if a foundation of trust, experience, and success is not already in place among institutional partners. To build such actions on sheer expectation is probably a time-consuming diversion at best.

At the same time, organizational leaders need to resist the temptation to dwell on a point-by-point diagnosis of every relationship with every customer and supplier. Organizations can spend years in such assessment processes without ever starting the next step of doing something together. In fact, in some organizations, people use extended diagnosis as a means of avoiding change—hoping that if they study the situation long enough, the pressure to do anything differently will go away.

A more effective approach is to select a few strategic customer and/or supplier relationships where more permeable boundaries could have a significant impact on organizational success and concentrate your efforts on moving these relationships forward quickly. The learnings from these experiences can then be leveraged with other institutional partners, as it makes sense to do so.

One caution: it is not necessary to have a boundaryless relationship with every customer and supplier in your organizational universe. As is true for all relationships, one size does not fit all. It is likely that you will always have various arrangements, all evolving at different speeds, with your many customers and suppliers. The key to success will not be the number of boundaryless partnerships formed. Rather it will be the development of your organization's capability and competence to advance customer and supplier relationships toward boundarylessness *when it is appropriate to do so.* As conditions change, as they certainly will, value chain configurations also will shift. When that occurs, your organization will need the ability to respond quickly, creating appropriate levels of boundaryless relationships with new or transformed members of the various value chains of which you may be a part.

In Part Three, we have described how organizations can strengthen collaboration across the value chain, lowering external boundaries between customers and suppliers. Organizations that combine these external boundary shifts with more permeable internal boundaries across vertical levels and horizontal functions realize tremendous benefits by becoming faster, more flexible, more integrated, and more innovative.

Increasingly, however, these shifts will need to be applied on a global scale, as organizations operate across geographies, cultures, and continental time zones. Global opportunities add a greater degree of complexity and challenge to organizational life but also an opportunity to reach an entirely new level of achievement and satisfaction. Getting the most from such opportunities is the subject of the next and final section: how to cross global boundaries and operate effectively around the world.

PART 4

Free Global Movement

Crossing Geographic Boundaries

8

Toward the Global Corporation

Like Marco Polo discovering a new world of trade, organizations today are exploring vast new markets throughout the globe. The process is nothing less than a revolution, breaking down once sacrosanct boundaries of space, time, and nationality. Suddenly, Marshall McLuhan's vision of a global village, in which trade, business, and information from all corners of the world are commonly exchanged, is no longer a futurist conception. In today's world, there is no longer a dichotomy between domestic and foreign. Global boundaries between companies, markets, and people have become irrevocably blurred.

It used to be different—simple, one might say. Companies could be easily characterized according to their national origin. One knew General Motors was an American company, headquartered in Detroit, producing American cars with American employees. Perhaps some of its business was exported to other parts of the world, but both literally and symbolically, GM was clearly an American enterprise.

Yet in the 1990's, the process of making cars was far more geographically complex, with only a small percentage of the typical North American car made with North American–made parts. And the process of organizing to produce these cars was equally changed. Thus, for its Ford 2000 project, Ford engaged a team of 170 executives to develop a new global organization. North American and European operations were merged, and Ford centers of excellence and activity can now be found in different places around the globe.

In short, managers must now think in terms of a world soon to be populated with "stateless," "borderless," and "virtual" corporations. Take Unilever for example. Although originally an Anglo-Dutch operation, Unilever now comprises over 500 companies in seventy-five countries, producing goods ranging from personal consumer products to foods to chemicals and oils. In size, it is among the top ten companies in the world. How has it achieved such a global presence? Among the many reasons are its small home markets; its headquarters location in the Netherlands, the crossroads of Europe; and its comfort with multiple languages and cultures. There are five nationalities represented on Unilever's board. Another example is ASEA Brown Boveri (ABB), a worldwide Swiss-Swedish enterprise in which 80 percent of managers regularly use English rather than their native tongues and whose board and senior management are composed of numerous nationalities. Similarly, SmithKline Beecham, the Anglo-American pharmaceutical company, has five nationalities on its board. Such managerial demographics are not in and of themselves measures of global reach, but they are strong indicators that global boundaries have been breached.

For companies such as Unilever, ABB, and SmithKline Beecham, globalization has become a natural part of their business, an integral part of their mission and culture. For most companies, however, the goal to become truly global in mindset, staff, and market seems a stretch. Although the opportunities are tempting, the effort, knowledge, and skill required are much greater than for running a domestic operation, and the risks—once you probe beneath the surface—are equally enormous.

In this chapter, we will present the general picture of what companies need to do to break through global boundaries—the dividing lines of geography, time, and nationality. We first put forward ten reasons why organizations might want to become more global. We then discuss the sizable challenges companies face in making the global leap. And we conclude with a diagnostic tool that assesses your organization's current progress toward global boundary breaking. Many of today's organizations are at the beginning stage (Global Learners), some are at the intermediate stage (Global Launchers), and perhaps a few will find that they are at the advanced stage (Global Leaders). In the next chapter, we suggest ways of moving forward, from Learner to Launcher and from Launcher to Leader.

Why Go Global?

The rationale to go global is perhaps not as evident as are the reasons to break down vertical, horizontal, and external boundaries. While loosening the latter boundaries directly increases the ability of the organization to meet the new success factors of speed, flexibility, integration, and innovation, attacking global boundaries would seem, on the surface, to be only of minor consequence to companies that are successfully satisfying their domestic markets.

However, it is clear to us that penetrating global boundaries will be a necessity for the successful organization of the twenty-first century. Already, global reach is becoming a new business standard. According to the United Nations Conference on Trade and Development, there are more than 24,000 transnational firms originating from the world's fourteen richest countries.[1] Many different opportunities stimulate these firms to cross national boundaries. Some are seeking new markets; some are taking advantage of new cross-border trade agreements; some are exploiting new technology; some are looking for less expensive labor or new sources of capital.

We have identified ten of the most significant causes of the urge to globalize (summarized in the following box).

Top Ten Reasons to Globalize
- Competitive survival
- Cost spreading
- Trailblazing
- Rule of three
- Domino effect
- Evolutionary forces
- Technological revolution
- Search for innovation
- Ripple effect
- Benchmarking against other companies

COMPETITIVE SURVIVAL

Survival in a highly competitive world is perhaps the single most potent reason to globalize. Survival is often an issue of reducing costs and increasing margins. For many companies, this means finding cheaper labor by setting up shop in whatever country offers the least expensive labor pool. This issue is not as clear-cut as it used to be, however. For decades, globalization largely involved North American, European, and Japanese companies seeking cheap labor in South Korea, Taiwan, Malaysia, and Thailand. But in recent years, wages in those countries have begun to rise and an unexpected turnaround is now occurring. Scores of South Korean and Taiwanese firms are setting up plants in Britain, where the growth of wages is expected to be slower than in Korea over the next few years.[2]

Another aspect of competitive survival is the drive to expand markets to achieve better economies of scale. For example, if a manufacturer's breakeven twenty years ago was a million units, its breakeven today may be doubled or tripled to compensate for years of research, design, and new tooling and setup costs. At the same time, standardization in manufacturing can create savings of 20 to 30 percent, as a company operates fewer plants, buys from fewer suppliers, and reduces duplication. Globalization thus gives companies the leverage to reduce costs, achieve breakeven earlier, and increase profits over the widest possible market.

Some companies must service local preferences that cannot be satisfied by standardized or universal products exported or distributed abroad. Competitive survival requires that these companies be in many locations and have the capability to create new product or adapt domestic-designed product to closely match specific customer tastes in each cultural region. While some economies of scale are lost, the benefits of being local are the ability to compete in a market in which a standardized product is not acceptable. For example, the Japanese giant Matsushita set up a microwave division in Europe to be closer to its European customer base. The move allowed Matsushita to discover the distinctions among various European tastes, that "British people like crispy fat on top of meat, so you need a stronger heating element in their ovens. Germans like their potatoes overcooked, but the British like them almost crunchy, so you have to design the cooking controls differently." As a Matsushita marketing specialist observed, "It's hard for product engineers sitting in Japan to understand all that."[3]

COST SPREADING

Practically no industry today escapes the trend toward a mounting number of mergers, alliances, and joint ventures within and between the largest of North American, European, and Japanese firms. One cause of these alliances is the desire to spread or share costs for various capital-intensive investments. For example, the exorbitant cost of R&D in high technology, communication, transportation, pharmaceutical, and medical equipment fields is at the root of many companies' need to join up with other firms around the world. Neither the smallest nor the largest of firms can afford to go it alone in funding the level of research necessary to many new products, much less pay for the large-scale product launches now required.

As GE's Jack Welch wryly points out, GE's medical equipment business has spread its cost and operation "everywhere": "Boundaryless behavior in our company leads a medical business based in Milwaukee . . . to empower a Swedish manager in Asia . . . to use a Japanese associate . . . to make diagnostic equipment with components sourced from India and China . . . for sale in Europe."[4]

TRAILBLAZING

For many companies, expanding into new territory is a trailblazing strategy, an exciting, aggressive stretch that demonstrates their capacity to win new markets and create new products. Like the great explorers and discoverers of history who opened up new trade routes, many companies cannot help but seek new adventure because there is nowhere else to go. In today's world, the most alluring new frontiers for trailblazers are probably China and India, and many companies are aggressively attempting to expand into these potentially huge markets.

Although trailblazing is often founded on the drive of a single executive or management team, its benefits are significant for the entire organization. Leading the pack in its industry increases a company's value and enhances its image. Coke, Nike, Sony, Nestlé, Toyota, and Citibank are recognized throughout the world precisely because they have led their fields. Today, many ambitious small firms are recognizing the merit of crossing boundaries in order to set themselves up as industry leaders. For example, the small Taiwanese firm Teco Electric & Machinery Company established a small plant in England because it "felt it had to enter Europe to reach its plan to be one of the top five in its industry (electric motors) within six years."[5]

The perspective that an organization must maintain when making an aggressive stretch is summed up in the classic anecdote of the two shoe salesmen who travel to a foreign land. The first salesman cables back to headquarters, "No one wears shoes here; coming home soon." The second salesman cables, "No one wears shoes here; send me 100,000 pair ASAP." Trailblazing is a matter of vision. Some companies may be paralyzed by the risks. But those that set their sights on being first in their industry will recognize the value of crossing borders and the opportunities they find on the other side.

RULE OF THREE

Related to trailblazing, the Rule of Three pertains to the truism that three companies will always garner the lion's share of a market in many product areas while those that arrive late receive only crumbs.

Over and over, it seems to work out that an industry has three major players, followed by lots of small, usually niche players. In telephone long-distance services, the major players were AT&T, BT/MCI, and Sprint. In the automotive industry, the three stars were the U.S. big three until Toyota virtually knocked out Chrysler, which downshifted to fourth place, typically a difficult position and usually closer to the laggards than the leaders. As a result, when untapped markets open, the need for market share invigorates companies to compete so they can maintain or ensure their place on the winner's dais. Today, many of the world's more successful companies understand the importance of establishing a major presence in emerging markets if they are to recover the high start-up costs of simply entering a new market in the first place. Coca-Cola and Pepsi, for example, are aggressively fighting local soft drink producers in many developing countries to gain a position in the top three. Similarly, Nike, Adidas, and Reebok are fighting for position in Southeast Asia. The goal is to become a major player in targeted local or regional marketplaces as well as to preserve their worldwide top-tier positions.

DOMINO EFFECT

The domino effect is the sequential benefit that companies gain when they cross one global boundary and realize that succeeding in a new territory makes it easier to enter another—just as toppling the first domino in a chain is the hardest, but the others are ready to tumble once that first move has been successfully made.

The domino effect is especially valid when cultures and customs are similar from country to country, and the challenges overcome in the first new market strongly correlate with the expected challenges in the second. For example, a company that learns how to do business in one Latin American country often has fewer problems setting up business in another Latin American country. But even when markets are dissimilar, some degree of learning from the first will still be transferred to the second and will still be an important enabling factor. To put it another way, the domino effect begins simply by getting one's feet wet.

EVOLUTIONARY FORCES

Globalization is also a natural, evolutionary growth process for certain types of organizations, particularly those that originate in small countries where markets are de facto limited. These organizations often have no international department because they cannot afford to make a distinction between "domestic" and "foreign." They are forced to see their natural market as lying beyond their national boundaries in order to achieve sales and profit. For example, Lila Pause, a German chocolate manufacturer, established its products as a "Eurobrand" right from its start, placing them in ten European countries. Some companies evolve more slowly but reach the same conclusion. Italian pasta maker Barilla SA was well established in its home country as a maker of premium and mass-market products before it decided to expand into other European countries.[6]

The increasing homogenization of the world contributes to such evolutionary growth. Whereas in the past it was considered a truism that people are more separated by their differences than joined by their similarities, today's world is quickly getting smaller and its cultures more similar. Furthermore, companies are also discovering that some local customs and preferences can be changed or modified with the right mix of marketing and product design. For instance, a *Wall Street Journal Europe* survey showed that more than half of Europe's twenty best-selling brands, ranging from detergents to pet foods, are available in all ten European countries. The rise in global homogenization gives companies a substantial motive to take advantage of evolutionary expansion to lower production, advertising, and packaging costs.[7]

The force of evolution also affects companies in maturing markets with waning growth potential. For these companies, globalization is a natural response to stagnating sales and declining profits. Some of the largest worldwide U.S. companies, for example, are now generating more than half their revenues outside the United States. In the second quarter of 1994, Exxon generated 78 percent of its revenues from foreign sales; Motorola, 70 percent; Gillette, 67 percent; Coca-Cola, 67 percent; Digital Equipment, 64 percent; and Cray Research, 62 percent.[8]

TECHNOLOGICAL REVOLUTION

The revolution spawned by technology is an enabling factor in globalization and levels the playing field for smaller companies. Whereas, formerly, only the richest of companies could compete on a worldwide scale due to the cost of overseas travel, today just about any company eager to create an overseas venture or form an alliance with a foreign firm can conduct much of its business relatively inexpensively through phone and fax communication as well as e-mail and videoconferencing. Time differences are minimized when voice mail and e-mail allow fast, extended, and precise communication without the need for both parties to come together in real time.

In short, technology has made borders and time zones essentially meaningless in separating people from other people or from information. Organizations that can maximize communication technology and take advantage of the wealth of information available electronically, regardless of company size or location, are poised to succeed on a global scale.

SEARCH FOR INNOVATION

Another reason why companies aggressively seek to cross global borders is to pursue innovation, perhaps one of the most critical factors for business survival in the modern world. Going global enriches the innovative spirit by putting organizations in closer touch with worldwide trends that may lead to new products or services. The need to innovate is visible in industries. Moreover, as the time and cost of R&D increases, innovation often requires new sources of ideas and financing that can only come from an increasingly large base of operations.

Toshiba is an example of a firm that has profitably used international alliances to supplement its creative efforts and to obtain new technology, either through research or licensing. Toshiba is the oldest and third largest of Japan's electronics giants (after Hitachi and Matsushita), and its more than two dozen global alliances include a joint venture with Motorola that makes it the world's number one producer of large-scale memory chips; a joint venture with IBM to manufacture color liquid crystal displays for portable computers; and a codevelopment deal with

Apple Computer to create CD-ROM multimedia players that can plug into television sets. The view of Fumio Sato, Toshiba's president and chief executive, is that "it is no longer an era in which a single company can dominate any technology or business by itself. The technology has become so advanced, and the markets so complex, that you simply can't expect to be the best at the whole process any longer."[9]

RIPPLE EFFECT

When companies are suppliers to companies that have chosen to go global, they may feel the ripple effect. That is, they must often make the decision whether to follow their customer abroad or risk losing even the domestic contract with that customer. Typically, what happens is that the globalizing company prefers to start its foreign ventures using the same suppliers it uses domestically, which reduces its costs and gets it up and running more quickly with greater consistency of quality. The burden is then on the supplier to follow the customer or lose the business entirely. The ripple effect is visible in the automotive industry when suppliers to the major U.S. carmakers establish plants in Eastern Europe and Asia while suppliers to the Japanese carmakers open up shop in the United States.

BENCHMARKING AGAINST OTHER COMPANIES

Benchmarking, the process by which organizations compare their business practices with those of the best companies of the world to ascertain their own soft spots, is more than simple intelligence gathering. Done properly, it pushes a company to examine its own operations, compare them with others' performance, and set up programs to improve its methods to meet world-class standards.

Widespread benchmarking pushes companies toward globalization in two ways. First, companies often obtain insights into how other companies break through global boundaries, thus gaining confidence about their own global potential. Second, the benchmarking process is easier and yields richer data when the company doing it already has global operations. In other words, going global makes benchmarking a more effective tool. As an article in *International Business* puts it: "Learning about the best practice from foreign companies bedevils large and mid-size [U.S.] companies alike because American culture, in particular, is much more open than most European and Asian cultures, experts say. . . . Of course, any company with foreign operations, or in a joint venture with a foreign partner, has an advantage."[10]

From Intention to Implementation: Challenges for the Globally Minded

Many organizations will recognize at least one of the above reasons as a sufficient rationale for crossing global boundaries, and most will recognize far more than one. The challenge, however, does not usually lie in finding something to drive globalization but in finding the right path to globalization and implementing it in a fashion that suits the organization. As discussed in previous chapters, what managers know they should do (theory) and what they actually do (practice) are often miles—or kilometers—apart. The horror stories of failed cross-border alliances, conflicting cultural values, nationalistic parochialism, and weak global organizational structures are all too common.

Consider, for example, a common method that organizations use to globalize: the joint venture with a foreign or overseas firm. Many companies in the automotive industry have tried this route to internationalize their production and reap the benefits of economies of scale, trailblazing, and the forces of evolution. Chrysler and Fiat (1990), Chrysler and Renault (1990), and Volvo and Renault (1993) were all cases in which high hopes were eventually dashed because of conflicting visions, management disagreements, and powerful cultural differences between the parties. Expectations were high, for example, when the news of an alliance between Swedish-based Volvo and French-based Renault was announced in 1993: "Slowly, with one step back for every two steps forward, a generation of truly European companies is taking shape. Renault/Volvo, announced yesterday, can hope to build on the apparent success achieved by such recent combinations as ASEA Brown Boveri, Reed Elsevier, and GEC Alsthom. It must try to avoid the problems that beset Carnaud Metal Box and, a couple of decades before, the ill-fated merger between Dunlop and Pirelli."[11] Just four months later, what should have been one of the most significant and sensible mergers in Europe was halted: "Volvo and Renault are like two lovers who canceled their wedding on the eve of the ceremony. Now they have to pick up the pieces of their broken relationship and see what can be salvaged. This will not be easy. There are bruised feelings on both sides."[12] This highly visible failure to create a cross-border alliance is just one of many reminders that the path to globalization is strewn with potential problems.

The other side of the story is that a multitude of extremely astute companies and joint ventures have benefited richly from globalization. Some of these companies—Shell, Boeing, IBM, Matsushita, and Unilever for example—are among the world's largest firms and have financial resources and technological capabilities that have certainly helped their international success. However, one of the most noted examples of a profitable globalization effort is ASEA Brown Boveri (ABB), formed from the merger of ASEA, a Swedish engineering group, with Brown Boveri, a Swiss competitor. Their merger created a strong pan-European firm that eventually had the clout to take on another one hundred acquisitions and joint ventures, encompassing over 100,000 employees. In short, the successful management of its globalization process changed ABB from a rather localized engineering organization to a worldwide leader in electric power generation, high-speed trains, automation and robotics, and environmental control systems.[13]

We have investigated the winners and losers of past decades to identify not only the challenges but the factors that sustain success. And it is clear that a wide variety of integrated and consistent shifts are required of the organization that becomes truly global. In our experience, companies seeking to globalize must first struggle with a number of critical challenges, and we will discuss seven of the most daunting (listed in the accompanying box).

Challenges for Breaking Through Global Boundaries

- Challenge 1: establishing a workable global structure
- Challenge 2: hiring global supermanagers
- Challenge 3: managing people for a global environment
- Challenge 4: learning to love cultural differences
- Challenge 5: avoiding parochialism and market arrogance
- Challenge 6: designing unifying mechanisms and a global mindset
- Challenge 7: overcoming complexity

CHALLENGE 1: ESTABLISHING A WORKABLE GLOBAL STRUCTURE

Establishing a workable organizational structure has always been one of the first issues faced by companies seeking to cross geographic boundaries. In the 1970s, many global firms grappled with the same classic centralization, decentralization, and matrix choices that we discussed as horizontal boundary issues. In fact, a landmark study by J. M. Stopford and L. T. Wells showed that many worldwide corporations typically adhered to the following structural progression as they expanded globally:[14]

Early stages: centralized approach.   In the early stages of foreign expansion, when both foreign sales and foreign product diversity are limited, companies typically manage their international operations through export departments and/or international divisions. They maintain control using the managerial skills and technical expertise at the center.

Growth stages: decentralized approach.   Next, as sales abroad expand into new regions, many companies adopt an area (regional) structure. If sales expand via a substantial increase in product diversity, companies may adopt a worldwide product division structure. In either case, the decentralization allows country or product manager initiatives based on local or market needs and often on a manager's own managerial and technical resources.

Peak stages: matrix approach.   In the third growth phase, when both foreign sales and product diversity are high, companies often turn to a global matrix structure—organized by region/product, region/function, or product/function—with dual reporting lines connecting product and geographic management structures.

Globalization in the 1980s, however, reinforced centralized structures for a variety of reasons, summarized by Paul Evans, professor of organizational behavior at INSEAD, a French business school.

> Global clients began to demand worldwide coordination of their needs. Economies of scale in sourcing and purchasing necessitated greater global coordination, as did technology and manufacturing. Duplication of local initiatives in MIS, QM [quality management], and the like had to be avoided, and the transfer of learning from one business or country to another became more important. Greater control was needed to enter and leave the growing number of joint ventures, alliances, sales and acquisitions of operations. Closer relations between local detection of opportunities, central research, regional manufacturing, and local marketing became important to speed up time to market, which in some industries was becoming a major source of competitive advantage.[15]

In the late 1980s, as business globalization was increasing, Christopher Bartlett and Sumantra Ghoshal studied three formal structural approaches that they found were used by nine major international companies.[16]

Multinational.   Multinational companies utilize a decentralized structure and a diversity of strategy that allows them to be sensitive and responsive to local conditions. Essentially, this structure creates a federation of national entities stemming from a single parent. The external organizations have some degree of independence and operating autonomy. Examples are Philips, Unilever, and ITT.

Global.   Global companies are significantly more centralized than multinationals in their structure and strategy. Organized around a strong headquarters, they focus on scale efficiencies. They treat the world market as an integrated whole, with universal consumer demand more dominant than local market demand. Examples are Matsushita, NEC, and Kao.

International.   International companies are structured to adapt and transfer the parent company's knowledge and competencies to foreign markets. The parent maintains substantial influence and power in decision making but less than global companies do. National units may adapt products and ideas disseminating from the parent to suit their localized needs. Examples are GE, Procter & Gamble, and Ericsson.

All the approaches used by globalizing companies throughout the 1970s and 1980s are reminiscent of the classical structural solutions based on either hierarchical or functional approaches. By the late 1980s, however, many analysts began to recognize that the global centralization/decentralization debate was as pointless as the domestic one. Bartlett and Ghoshal, for instance, proposed a new organizational model that would be more responsive to the "forces of global integration, local differentiation, and worldwide innovation." To compete successfully in this environment, "a company has to develop global competitiveness, multinational flexibility, and worldwide learning capability simultaneously. Building these multiple strategic competencies is primarily an *organizational* challenge, which requires companies to break away from their traditional management modes and adopt a new organizational model."[17]

Bartlett and Ghoshal named their new organizational model the "transnational organization" and described it as neither centralized nor decentralized but containing pieces of each strategy. In a transnational structure, the parent organization may centralize certain core processes such as research and development—keeping them either at headquarters or at another site—in order to benefit from shared expertise. However, functions such as marketing, pricing, sales, and distribution are handled locally in order to respond to market demands for speed, innovation, and responsiveness.

The difference between a multinational and transnational was aptly described by Henry Wendt, when he was CEO of SmithKline Beecham.

> The difference in outlook between transnationals and multinationals
> is the difference between a globe and a map. The surface of a globe
> has neither a beginning nor an end, neither a center nor a periphery;

it is a continued integrated whole. A map has a definite center, peripheral places, and remote corners; it is a discontinuous, hierarchical fragment. And for the traditional multinational, the home market and the headquarters stand at the center of the map and send out expeditions to progressively less important provinces. In sum, transnational corporations view the world as one vast, essentially seamless market in which all major decisions are grounded solely in the desire to gain a global competitive advantage.[18]

The structural debate continues today, but in our view, the evolving boundaryless solution, founded on Bartlett and Ghoshal's transnational format, might best be described as *glocal* because it aims to merge a global strategy with a respect for local presence. The glocal structure is like the improvisational jazz ensemble we used earlier as a metaphor for the domestic organization, except that this ensemble is composed of players from around the world. The glocal company utilizes solo players at times (local control), but it also calls for ensemble work at other times (central integration and economies of scale). Above all, the glocal ensemble keeps a constant ear open, listening for whatever song the customer requests, and making changes to accommodate that request.

Ford Motor Company is a prime example of this new type of glocal structure. In its Ford 2000 project, Ford merged its North American and European operations, replacing its multinational structure with five global product divisions. The divisions are split according to basic car design (small front-wheel drive, large front-wheel drive, rear-wheel drive, pickup trucks, and large trucks). Each group is quasi-autonomous in its responsibility to design and develop new models and to handle their manufacture, marketing, and profitability. However, decision making in each group is coordinated and checked by worldwide vice presidents for product development, marketing, and manufacturing who reside at Ford headquarters in Dearborn, Michigan. Many vehicle designs are intended to satisfy global demands, and so integrate R&D efforts and market research across both the U.S. and Europe. At the same time, significant local market differences are factored into other designs (for example, Americans' love of big cars versus Europeans' preference for smaller ones). Furthermore, the global divisions are not isolated from each other. Engineers and executives talk to each other via videoconferencing and computer networks to transfer best practices and learnings. Ford expects to merge its Asian and Latin American operations into this structure within a few years as well. By globalizing in this fashion, Ford estimates it can save over $3 billion a year in development, purchasing, and supply costs.

3M Company is another good example of reorganizing for a glocal environment. *Financial Times* journalist Christopher Lorenz summarizes the shift this way: "First, in the interests of greater cross-border effectiveness and faster decision-making, 3M has shifted most strategic and operational responsibility away from its national subsidiaries (the geographic side of its organization) and centralized it in the hands of 19 product divisions, each with Europe-wide responsibility. Second, the residual geographic responsibilities . . . have been shifted from the smaller countries to several of 10 new European 'regions.' Unlike many other companies which have made such a change, 3M has given the regional heads equal rank to the European Business Center directors."[19]

As this description makes evident, because structure affects decision making, flexibility, competitiveness, and many other critical areas of a global concern, the question of the right structure is highly complex. Many organizations struggle continually to find the right solution for gaining the global synergies and coordination they desire. In our own experience, we have noted a structural paradox worth highlighting. On the one hand, every boundary-crossing company we deal with is constantly examining, reexamining, and redesigning its organizational charts to enhance global coordination. On the other hand, many executives we talk to always stress that the real key to working across borders is less a matter of structure and more a matter of people and processes. The remaining challenges we have identified for globalizing organizations deal precisely with these issues.

CHALLENGE 2: HIRING GLOBAL SUPERMANAGERS

Following structure, the second key challenge most organizations face is finding the right global managers to lead them across borders to new territory. But there is a debate over just who qualifies as a good global manager. To some, a good global manager is no more than an effective manager operating globally. After all, good management is good management, wherever it is practiced. To others, however, the qualities and characteristics of a global manager are different from and go beyond those of a domestic manager because managing a global operation differs from managing a domestic operation.

We agree with the latter view. In the broadest sense, a true global manager is someone with a sizable knowledge of and sincere appreciation for international issues—both geopolitical and cultural—and their impact on business. Some have said that worldwide companies need "supermanagers" who have all the attributes of basic management skills plus advanced linguistic, cultural, and people skills. That is, managers "who not only know how to order in foreign restaurants but are also trilingual and can handle a variety of jobs anywhere in Europe" (or elsewhere).[20]

The challenge, then, is learning how to identify or grow global managers. To date, two factors appear to be significant: country of origin and global management competencies.

Country of Origin

Nationals of small European countries (for example, Sweden, Holland, and Belgium) seem to be more natural global managers than most other individuals. As products of minority cultures in the larger European context, they seem to realize more innately than others that the world neither starts nor stops at their doorstep. In addition, as young people, they often lived and studied outside their home countries. They usually speak one or more foreign languages, often fluently. And they are used to thinking in terms of worldwide markets. Third-country nationals are also good candidates to become global managers. They took the first step toward leaving their home culture when they went to work for a multinational based in another country and thus are more open to work in yet a third country. Another positive demographic factor for global managers is cultural heritage. Individuals whose parents are of different nationalities, or who have lived in several countries when young, are likely to be better candidates. In short, experiences of diverse nationalities through one's parents, schooling, jobs, and postal addresses equate to the breadth of experience and exposure required in a global supermanager; and a promising interview might include an exchange not too different from this imaginary one:

INTERVIEWER: Where are you from?

CANDIDATE: Well, sir, it's a long story. I was born in Italy, my father is French, and my mother is Argentinean. My father worked for a Swiss company, and he was assigned during my high school years to Japan, so I learned Japanese. I went to school in the United States and had my first assignment in Germany. But now I'd like to come back to my birthplace, Italy, for a few years.

When you hear such backgrounds, you still may not truly know where the person is from, but you have more than likely found a global manager. Unfortunately, such natural-born multinational managers are increasingly in demand but of limited supply.

Global Management Competencies

The search for the global supermanager can also be based on developing key competencies, because global managers are not just born. Some can be "grown" through experiences and management training. What competencies are required for managers who are routinely required to operate across geographic borders? A number of studies have been conducted to help companies to select and/or develop more effective global managers. One profile, developed by Stephen Rhinesmith,[21] argues that the global mindset contains six dimensions with a corresponding personal characteristic and competency for each, as shown in the following list.

Global Mindset	Personal Characteristic	Competency
Bigger, broader picture	Knowledge	Managing competition
Balance of contradictions	Conceptualization	Managing complexity
Process	Flexibility	Managing adaptability
Diverse teamwork and play	Sensitivity	Managing teams
Change as opportunity	Judgment	Managing uncertainty
Openness to surprises	Reflection	Managing learning

Another study translated the training in the Jesuit order into an ideal model for the international manager. The model suggests the development of six qualities: an aptitude for searching and combining things in new ways, the ability to communicate ideas and turn them into action, the command of several languages and knowledge and sympathy for several cultures, honesty and integrity, the willingness to take risks and experiment, and faith in the organization and its activities.[22] While the precise characteristics of the global supermanager are still emerging, it does appear that the successful global leader sees the larger worldview, is focused on process, and is willing and able to manage global complexities.

Disney's Search for a Global Manager

A prototypical case exemplifying the challenge of finding a global manager was the effort of the Disney organization a few years back to locate an executive to head up its consumer products group based in Paris. At the time, Disney needed to transform a loose federation of eight European wholly owned subsidiaries, each in a different country, into a more integrated, cross-border business. The firms operated in twenty-six different markets and basically had been running themselves for years in a multinational structure.

With the establishment of their Euro-Disney theme park and several new lines of business in licensing and in videos and other products, Disney believed the time was right to establish a European headquarters in Paris and to hire someone to oversee and coordinate its entire European region. All eight country heads had spent substantial time in their positions as loyal and effective managers. The French manager had been hired by Walt Disney personally and was considered a living legend, credited with having built Disney's European business since World War II. He was also considered the titular head of European operations. However, after forty years in his role and at seventy years of age, he was not considered a candidate for the headquarters job. The country managers from Denmark, Germany, Belgium, Italy, Spain, Portugal, and the U.K. were also not considered candidates.

The task of Disney's new European head would be complex. Disney had established an ambitious growth plan requiring cross-business synergies. A high degree of uncertainty was anticipated. Building a team out of individuals with varied and often conflicting cultural backgrounds would be difficult. In the end, Disney chose Dennis Hightower, an example of the rare breed of global supermanager. Aged forty-five when hired by Disney, he had served eight years as an Army intelligence officer in the Far East, earned a Harvard M.B.A., worked at McKinsey for four years, and been a country manager for GE in Mexico. Next he joined Mattel as vice president of corporate planning involved with their European expansion, and then he worked for a recruiting firm, primarily with international clients. Overall, he had lived in over fifteen countries, spoke six languages, and had worked in many different industries in staff and line roles. He operated with values and a style similar to the Jesuit characteristics described above. In addition, he was an African American, which, he said, was good preparation for being sensitive to different cultures.

Disney's choice of candidate appears to have been astute. Hightower achieved significant growth for Disney in Europe year after year, despite initial difficulties of the Disney park in France. He offered this brief synopsis to us of the challenges of being a Euro-Global manager:

> You must have a large propensity for risk to take a job like this. It requires an "out-of-national" experience. The most important thing is the attitude and mindset; managing in a multinational is a frame of mind. While there are certainly many universals in management practice, you must come to understand that how you execute varies from culture to culture. I understood that I had to listen to people and not have everyone adjust to me. For example, I found that issues took three times as long to discuss and debate in the Italian office. In Germany, [similar issues] took often just a matter of minutes.

Hightower's observations, too, reflect the many special qualities needed in global managers. Organizations must be highly sensitive to this management challenge and strive to find or grow a new breed of leader for the future. Indeed, Hightower himself was ultimately succeeded by a Frenchman who had a wide range of geographic, functional, and global company experience.[23]

CHALLENGE 3: MANAGING PEOPLE FOR A GLOBAL ENVIRONMENT

A natural corollary to the second challenge is the challenge of ensuring the preservation and development of human resources once they are found and hired. However, organizations often are blocked by three obstacles to developing global talent.

The perception of a career block.   The adage "Out of sight, out of mind" often looms large in the heads of bright, sophisticated, qualified personnel who are assigned to foreign sites. Their attitude is often based on the old organizational paradigm in which foreign assignments usually meant a form of exile from the real action at domestic headquarters. The global company operating according to the new organizational paradigm must therefore work hard to redefine overseas assignments and highlight their value to the organization's bottom line and to the manager as a stepping-stone to further career advancement.

The fear of undesirable locations.   As more and more territories throughout the world open up to global business, it is inevitable that some people must be assigned to locations that are inconvenient, distant, lonely, or extremely foreign. For example, Price Waterhouse won a contract to audit a factory outside Shanghai, China; unfortunately, the factory turned out to be located in an extremely remote location more than ten hours by train from Shanghai, and the nearest hotel to the plant was two hours away. Global job assignments such as these appear to offer no solace, so organizations must develop programs to maintain fairness when hardship is an issue.

The disruption to families.   An equally important obstacle is employees' concern over global assignments that split up families or move people to locations that are not family oriented. While managers may accept these assignments, cultural differences and language barriers can have a deleterious effect on a spouse and children, who may not be willing to tolerate the location. Such stressful situations require new incentives and supports to counteract the inevitable feelings of loss and abandonment that many people experience in a globalized company. While people who will accept overseas or foreign assignments are a de facto requirement of such companies, the management of such assignments is a critical challenge.

CHALLENGE 4: LEARNING TO LOVE CULTURAL DIFFERENCES

Cultural differences are an inevitable consequence of geographic and linguistic boundaries. As a result, it is a rare company that does not find itself managing cultural conflict when doing business in global settings. People living in foreign cultures invariably find themselves disturbed by the personal habits, dress, customs, holidays, language, beliefs, and eating and drinking patterns that differ from their own.

Unfortunately, cultural clashes are often vastly misunderstood, leading to a number of disastrous problems. One major problem is what might be termed cultural paralysis. Many companies enter into a global relationship and fail because they come to believe they cannot work with foreigners. In many cases, these failures can be traced to misunderstanding and miscommunication based on cultural stereotypes. For example, a joint venture between a U.S. company we know and a French company was plagued in its fifth year by numerous cultural and operational differences between the groups. When the firm brought in a consultant to help people overcome the clashes, he initially asked each group to describe what they thought of the other group. Both groups produced documents that typify how difficult it is to break down stereotypes and *appreciate* authentic cultural differences. The American description of working with the French is shown in Exhibit 8.1.

To overcome cultural paralysis, companies must learn that many cultural differences are real, reflecting deep-seated values and attitudes that cannot simply be subsumed into the home company's mindset. One study, for example, distinguishes six basic viewpoints or attitudes that can vary greatly from culture to culture.

Universalism versus particularism (behavior based on general versus specific relationships)

Collectivism versus individualism (group-based versus individual behavior)

Neutral versus expressive emotional attitude (open versus closed manner of emoting)

Achievement versus affiliation view of status (personal versus positional power)

Attitude about time, especially the future

Attitude of molding the environment versus going along with it

Given these cultural variations, the study concludes that companies may be viewed as organized around various combinations of these attitudes; this combination is the "company culture." For instance, the study identifies the "family" culture, which centers leadership in an authoritarian father figure who is viewed as knowing more than subor-

Exhibit 8.1. A U.S. Company's Perceptions of Its French Partner.

- French experts can't be objective and [they] hinder objective evaluations. In France, it often seems that anyone can be an expert, and that philosophy spills over into other scientific evaluations. Reports are biased.
- The French don't tell the whole story and tend to take the easiest route (give the easiest explanation). They don't delve into other explanations or don't share that information.
- Reports are done initially in French, then translated to English when they have people on staff who could have written the reports in English from the beginning.
- The French abide by gentleman's agreement—they abide by the spirit and intent of the agreement at the time it is reached, whereas we abide by "if it isn't written then it's subject to interpretation or changes."
- In France, working up to the event is as important as the event itself: pre-meeting dinners, toasts after dinner. They recognize and affirm relationships. Americans have a bottom-line mentality—get to the bottom line—cut the B.S.
- Protocol is important in France; in the U.S. our attitude is, what does it take to get the job done? The French use a lot of body language/facial expressions and these expressions are sometimes interpreted by the U.S. as the French reacting negatively to an issue, and so on.
- Communication: the French are more talkative than Americans. French people are more emotional but Americans are not sensitive to the emotions of the French.
- Each company should have a mutual understanding and sensitivity to the other's needs, such as financial requirements and how research is conducted. But why can't the French do more to meet our needs?

dinates, making delegation difficult and matrix-reporting structures impossible (a culture typical in Japan, India, Belgium, Italy, and Spain); the "Eiffel Tower" culture, which is highly hierarchical, rule driven, and impersonal (typical in France, Germany, and Holland); and the "guided missile" culture, which tends to be more egalitarian and individualistic but also impersonal (typical of U.S. and U.K. companies).[24]

The point is that cultural attitudes affect nearly all aspects of working and living abroad, including people's conceptions of management's role, of performance appraisal and reward systems, and of priorities. Moreover, all these differences in priorities, management style, and attitudes are often subtle and may not be detected until it is too late. Learning how to be a multicultural multinational in which many cultures and ideas coexist is therefore a major challenge.

Companies must also remember that cultural variations occur even at regional and urban levels. For example, a large pharmaceutical company R&D lab located in north London met considerable resistance to its plan to move to south London because its employees resented the difference in life-style, accent, and environment that the new location would have imposed on them. The same can be said about nearly every country where, just as in the U.S., there are major regional differences from north to south and east to west.

CHALLENGE 5: AVOIDING PAROCHIALISM AND MARKET ARROGANCE

Parochialism and arrogance are corollaries of cultural stereotyping. Parochialism is any narrow-minded view that does not accept outside ideas; it frequently stems from ethnocentrism or egocentrism, and it is counterproductive: as *The Economist* once phrased it, "an organization that relies on one culture for ideas and treats foreign subsidiaries as dumb production-colonies might as well hire a subcontractor."[25]

Parochialism is often the reason many global organizations do not hire native managers to run their foreign operations and do not move company headquarters to new countries. It also appears to be a factor in explaining why many organizations refuse to hire foreign nationals as senior managers or to include them on boards of directors. For example, a survey of more than 700 international managers from over a dozen countries indicated that an overwhelming number agreed that their companies did not have "enough foreign nationals at any level" in corporate headquarters, nor were there policies to recruit and promote foreign nationals to top management positions.[26]

North American corporations appear to be particularly xenophobic about asking foreign nationals to join their boards of directors. According to a study by the Accord Group, a global network of executive search firms, fewer than 40 percent of the 50 largest U.S. stock companies have even one foreign board member.[27] A study by Korn/Ferry International showed equally disappointing results: of 348 U.S. companies, less than 14 percent had a non–U.S. director. In contrast, nearly every one of the top 50 stock corporations in France, Germany, Hong Kong, Spain, the United Kingdom, and Sweden had from 3 to 15 percent foreigners on its board.[28]

Arrogance is related to parochialism in that it reflects a closure to outside opinion. The most disastrous arrogance, of course, is failure to understand one's market. An example of such arrogance was McDonald's McPloughman lunch, offered in its British outlets to compete with pubs that offered the traditional British repast of bread, cheese, and pickle. After a brief, disastrous test period, McDonald's backed off and admitted it had neglected to research customers' interest in its fast-food version of the lunch. Not only did British consumers hate the concept, feeling that McDonald's had trivialized a proud English tradition, employees were even embarrassed to offer the meal.

Market arrogance happens frequently and such lack of respect for the real wants and needs of a host market reflects serious flaws in design and marketing processes. While homogenization of tastes is occurring in some areas, the majority of products must still be customized to local preferences and cultural demands. (Apparently, McDonald's learned a lesson from its British experience; it now serves teriyaki burgers in Tokyo and wine in Lyons, France.)

The value of avoiding parochialism and arrogance is clear. Organizations must become adept at recognizing the importance of other cultures and take action to understand, appreciate, and respect them. Narrow vision and misplaced pride cause companies to lose out on the development of a truly multicultural and open environment across whole organizations, a better awareness of overseas trends and markets, and improved communications between headquarters and foreign sites. Combating these forms of myopia requires a commitment to worldwide recruitment and promotions and a strong orientation toward learning.

CHALLENGE 6: DESIGNING UNIFYING MECHANISMS AND A GLOBAL MINDSET

Going from a domestic to a global organization is like moving from a one-room schoolhouse in a small village to the bullpen of an international stock exchange. Whereas the old structure was a small space in which everyone spoke the same language, knew everyone else's business, and was accustomed to cooperating according to a certain set of rules, the new structure may include several languages, be staffed by people with many different values and attitudes, and function without a solid foundation of trust and respect. Furthermore, the new organization must operate over time and distance and handle substantially greater amounts of information and data. The result, of course, is most often a feeling of disintegration and chaos, because the organization does not have the internal mechanisms and mindset to hold itself together.

Global organizations, therefore, require some unifying mechanisms, what Paul Evans calls "glue technology."[29] Glue technology allows the global company to integrate its many functions over time, distance, and culture without resorting to the stifling power of centralization. It consists of a hierarchy of tools that range from simple to complex, inexpensive to sophisticated.

- ◆ Regular face-to-face meetings that help to eliminate stereotypes, break down interpersonal barriers, and develop networks of people who trust each other based on personal relationships
- ◆ Horizontal project groups that learn teamwork and problem solving without an imposed management structure delivered from headquarters
- ◆ Project-oriented training that develops competencies
- ◆ A career and mobility management program that assists people in

developing long-term skills to meet the demands of global management and develop cross-cultural competency

◆ The building of a shared vision and values through the definition of business goals and organizationwide values that mobilize energy and action

◆ The application of the previous tools to human resource development programs so that the integrated organization can become self-perpetuating

These tools create an organic network, with some ties stronger and some weaker, but everyone nevertheless linked and interconnected at many different points throughout the web. The network acts as the nervous system of the organization, keeping it responsive to the outside world. As Evans writes, an organizational nervous system that functions effectively "requires 'loose ties'—knowing someone who knows someone who knows someone. Network theory and research show that a relatively small number of strong ties (strong relationships) among appropriate 'gatekeepers' can provide a vast set of potential linkages. Moreover, the nervous system facilitates responsiveness. The soft signals and information on competitive moves, technological shifts, and the like are transferred through the network, rather like the proverbial grapevine."[30]

A related means of unifying the global company is the development of sophisticated communication and information systems that enable the free exchange of data and ideas and help to bridge operations from office to office. Especially as global companies grow larger and more diversified, they must have compatible computer systems, e-mail, videoconferencing, and other high technology solutions to help them *routinely and naturally* communicate over time and space. Without such routine and natural communication of ideas, organizational members cannot maintain the glue that binds them.

CHALLENGE 7: OVERCOMING COMPLEXITY

Although much of this chapter is predicated on the assumption that the world is becoming a smaller and simpler place, globalizing organizations cannot forget that in many locations, doing business is still subject to the vicissitudes of bureaucracy, politics, and ethical dilemmas. Throughout vast regions of Eastern Europe, Asia, Latin America, and Africa, operational complexity is the rule rather than the exception. What could occur without a hitch in one's home country requires endless hours and money in another culture due to differences in negotiating styles, time perceptions, and financial dealings. When automotive supplier Loranger Manufacturing Corporation, as just one example, established a plant in Hungary, it spent eight months and $8 million to overcome political blocks and fix ancient facilities before it was even allowed to start operations.[31]

Complexity can also be an internal dilemma. Many organizations stumble in developing and implementing the right structure for their global effort and must then backtrack and reconfigure their structure at great expense. Many fail in their attempt to globalize through joint ventures or acquisitions. Still others overcommit themselves, going into too many regions at once, draining their resources and management capabilities. Cultural clashes can also stop a globalizing effort in midtrack when not managed properly.

In short, the complexity challenge can affect all globalizing firms, ranging from those that are just starting to those that have been global leaders for decades. In fact, global leaders often risk running into more complexity barriers than firms that are just starting out, by virtue of being involved in more areas of the world or in more ventures.

Crossing Global Boundaries: How Much Progress Have You Made?

This chapter has identified the rationale behind removing the global boundaries of time, space, and nationality, and outlined key challenges facing global companies. Chapter Nine describes specific tools for crossing global boundaries. We suggest that you pause here to use the diagnostic questionnaire that follows (Questionnaire #5) and to identify how far your organization has progressed toward going global. This will enable you to customize the action ideas that follow.

Questionnaire #5

Stepping Up to the Line: How Far Along the Path to Globalization Is Your Organization?

Instructions: Assess your organization's efforts to remove global boundaries and operate across space, time, and nationality. Use the scale to indicate the extent to which each of the following statements characterizes your organization, circling a number from 1 (not true at all) to 5 (very true).

	Not true at all				Very true
1. Managers in our company have a global outlook.	1	2	3	4	5
2. Managers in our company speak more than one language.	1	2	3	4	5
3. We have managers responsible for global products, services, or customers.	1	2	3	4	5
4. We communicate well across borders.	1	2	3	4	5
5. We respect cultural differences in management styles.	1	2	3	4	5
6. Top management constantly stresses its desire to become a global competitor.	1	2	3	4	5
7. We routinely engage in cross-border task forces on projects.	1	2	3	4	5
8. Top management's calendars (daily schedules) reflect their commitment to globalization.	1	2	3	4	5
9. Training programs include significant exposure to global issues.	1	2	3	4	5
10. Leadership positions in our company include people from culturally diverse backgrounds.	1	2	3	4	5

11. Accepting international assignments is a stepping stone to future success. 1 2 3 4 5

12. Information about global competitors and customers is well known throughout the company. 1 2 3 4 5

13. Travel budgets enable us to take necessary international trips. 1 2 3 4 5

14. Our structure allows us to operate seamlessly across borders. 1 2 3 4 5

15. Our customers recognize our ability to operate across borders. 1 2 3 4 5

16. We operate across borders significantly better than our competitors. 1 2 3 4 5

17. We recruit in places where "globally minded" candidates can be easily found. 1 2 3 4 5

18. We have many examples of culturally diverse teams. 1 2 3 4 5

19. Our culturally diverse teams generally work together in a way that the whole is greater than the sum of the parts. 1 2 3 4 5

20. Other companies have, or could, benchmark our efforts to remove geographic boundaries. 1 2 3 4 5

Questionnaire Scoring

Add all the numbers circled to figure your total score. You can also view your scores in four key areas: human resource practices, organizational structure, organizational processes and systems, and overall global mindset.

Total score: Add scores for all items. ____
Human resource practices: Add scores for items 2, 9, 10, 11, and 17. ____
Organizational structure: Add scores for items, 3, 7, 14, 16, and 18. ____
Organizational processes and systems: Add scores for items 4, 8, 12, 13, and 19. ____
Overall global mindset: Add scores for items 1, 5, 6, 15, and 20. ____

- *Total score: 20 to 55.* Your organization is probably a Global Learner, at the beginning stages of globalization. At this time, many organizational supports are not developed, and resistance must be overcome.
- *Total score: 56 to 75.* Your organization is probably a Global Launcher. It has made considerable progress on the path toward removing global boundaries, but certain areas must be improved.
- *Total score: 76 to 100.* Your organization is likely to be a Global Leader. It has demonstrated a serious commitment to removing global boundaries and is probably in the midst of solidifying and institutionalizing this way of operating.

A comparison of your total scores in the categories of human resource practices, organizational structure, organizational processes and systems, and global mindset will show you which boundary-crossing characteristics are strongest and which are the weakest in your company. This secondary examination can help you determine if barriers to globalization are equally in evidence across all the categories or if your company has conspicuous gaps primarily in one or two categories.

Questionnaire Follow-Up

Ask several colleagues to complete the questions also and then compare responses. For this questionnaire, involving associates from operations outside your domestic base (if you have them) would be especially useful to you.

9

Actions for Global Learners, Launchers, and Leaders

In Chapter Eight, we identified ten reasons why organizations might want to make their geographic boundaries more permeable, and we discussed the challenges of doing so. To overcome these challenges, an organization's goal of loosening geographic boundaries must be matched by its actions. To do this, it must make skillful use of a varied set of digital switches.

Our goal in this chapter is to help people walk their talk with a number of specific geographic boundary–breaking techniques and practices. If well managed, these actions for change can help Global Learners become Global Launchers and Global Launchers become Global Leaders. The first section of this chapter deals with specific actions for moving from learner to launcher, and the second section includes actions that launchers can take to become leaders (refer to Questionnaire #5 in Chapter Eight to identify your organization as a learner, launcher, or leader).

293

The ideas in both sections are divided into three categories:

◆ Human resource practices
◆ Organizational structures
◆ Organizational processes and systems

The remainder of the chapter contains a case study of an organization that has shifted from one stage to the next and some thoughts on pitfalls to avoid as you move across geographic boundaries.

From Global Learner to Global Launcher

A large percentage of today's companies would probably characterize themselves as Global Learners. Whether or not they feel competitively required to go global, they are sincerely interested in developing some level of cross-border contacts or sites to expand their markets and profit from global synergies and international efficiency. Yet they are inexperienced in international business. How can such learners transform themselves into launchers?

No specific sequence of steps can be prescribed for all organizations because the requirements for cross-border relationships and a truly global approach to business depend on many factors, including the industry; the level of international competition; the market opportunities desired versus resources committed; and the legal, social, and cultural hurdles of the desired foreign locale. However, we can describe a wide range of actions (summarized in the following box) that an organization may initiate to take its important first steps into the global arena.

HR PRACTICES: FOCUS ON CULTURAL AWARENESS AND DIVERSITY

The most basic task in any globalization effort must be to sensitize people to the vast landscape beyond their own doors. Perhaps the first step in this sensitization is some degree of foreign language learning.

Human Resource Practices
- Supply language/cultural sensitivity training.
- Standardize forms and procedures.
- Set up an overseas presence via joint venture, modest acquisition, or establishment of a headquarters.
- Engage in extensive cross-border relationship building.

Organizational Structures
- Arrange short-term visits and international assignments.
- Staff for more diversity in management and board of directors.
- Use e-mail and videoconferencing to maintain day-to-day contact.

Organizational Processes and Systems
- Establish worldwide shared values, language, and operating principles.
- Conduct fact-finding missions.
- Design ad hoc transnational teams.
- Hold global town meetings and best-practice exchanges of information.

Although English remains the international business language, most non-English speakers strongly feel that Anglophones should not be immune to language training. At the least, people will have enough commitment and training to speak basic phrases in the language of the locale in which they do business and to listen to and understand light social conversation. Most foreigners greatly appreciate any effort of business people from other countries to speak and understand others' native tongues.

Even more important, however, is cultural awareness training. People doing global business must become familiar with critical cultural differences, business practices, cultural attitudes and values, and socialization customs. The best global companies have developed extensive orientation programs for managers heading for foreign assignments. These programs may include computer simulations of special cultural circumstances, especially ones likely to be perceived as problems, as well as factual information and discussions about cultural differences.

For many managers in U.S. companies especially, cultural awareness training is not a trivial issue. North Americans often have, to put it mildly, a parochial outlook, little international exposure and experience, and a false sense that the world revolves around American habits. This is often due to the distance between the United States and other countries. To see the world in its true diversity of cultural practices and traditions—and to learn to understand, respect, and appreciate these differences—is a challenge that requires commitment and an open frame of mind.

Home-country programs in foreign languages and cultural awareness training are the first step in preparing people to travel to foreign locations and commence dealing with international counterparts. Next, short-term visits are the necessary fuel that ignites the beginnings of any globalization process: fact-finding missions, exploratory discussions, and setting up legal and financial arrangements. A bigger step, when the time is right, is to assign selected staff to live abroad for a year or two, establishing a permanent office or representative site. This longer time frame produces a much better acquaintance with the business methods and cultural values in the host country than do short-term touristic visits. It also enhances opportunities for establishing personal relationships with local customers and suppliers.

An example from Samsung, South Korea's largest company and a Global Leader, indicates how seriously Global Leaders take international assignments and the development of cultural awareness. Samsung recognized that it sorely needed more familiarity with foreign cultures and markets, particularly Japan and North America. It began by taping cards up each day in the company bathrooms to teach a phrase of English or Japanese to employees. Then, managers who were assigned to go overseas were placed in an immersion atmosphere, a month-long boot camp, where they were awakened at 5:30 A.M. for jogging, meditation, and lessons on table manners, dancing, and avoiding sexual harassment. The company also sent about four hundred of its brightest junior employees overseas for a year with a specific mission to "goof-off." Some went to the United States to hang out at the malls, watching American consumers. Others went to Russia to live, eat, and drink with the Russians for a year, study the language, and travel to every republic.

Beyond cultural training, the next most significant HR building block is the establishment of a set of global values and principles that will form the basis of a shared mindset for all members of the organization. This action can range from creating mission statements on corporate globalization goals to writing policy manuals that document standard operating procedures everywhere the company has business. Of course, research has indicated that mission statements are often considered nothing more than pretty words unless they are truly backed up by action and frequent review.[1] Therefore, as ASEA Brown Boveri former CEO Percy Barnevik pointed out, these statements must relate directly to people's behavior:

> Our policy bible, which was produced at the inception of ABB and presented at our Cannes meeting for 250 managers, . . . describes our mission and values, where we want to be several years from now, and gives guidelines for overall behavior. It also describes how we should behave internally. To illustrate, one value is that it is better to be roughly right than exactly right with respect to speed. Then there are rules about minimizing overhead, about integrating newly acquired companies, about rewarding and promoting people. But the most important glue holding our group together is the customer-focus philosophy—how we want to be customer driven in all respects. The values describe how we want to create a global culture, what can be done to understand each other, the benefits of mixed nationality teams, and how to avoid being turf defenders. Our policy bible is not a glossy brochure with trivial and general statements, but practical advice on how we should treat each other and the outside world.[2]

A second aspect of developing a shared mindset is a seemingly small but highly important consideration. As a company moves into global competition, it must be sure that key administrative and corporate procedures are implemented in the same manner throughout the organization.

Such standardization helps ensure a one-firm concept and has four additional beneficial results.

◆ *Efficiency.* People at each location should not be developing their own forms or procedures; this is both time consuming and costly. All forms should be usable worldwide.
◆ *Common metrics.* The global firm will function better when people use common measures that have meaning regardless of geography (for example, cash flow).
◆ *Common strategy and vision.* Standardized procedures reinforce the organization's common goals and vision.
◆ *Consistent image to the marketplace.* A global company benefits from promoting a consistent image regardless of location.

All of the actions just discussed point to many fundamental HR steps that can be taken to prepare an organization for doing business in different geographies. Each clearly reflects the need to expose employees to other cultures and business practices—a prerequisite for avoiding debilitating stereotyping and misunderstandings.

ORGANIZATIONAL STRUCTURES: THE DILEMMA FOR LEARNERS

Most learner companies are initially hesitant to totally overhaul organizational structure when planning their first expansion across borders. A fact-finding task force is therefore a useful way to open the organization to new information and to identify opportunities. The task force can carry out data collection and market research that familiarizes the company with the targeted territory. For example, the French public utility company Électricité de France (EDF) was once primarily a domestic provider of electrical energy and services. However, given the saturation of its domestic market, opportunities to export its technology to other countries, and the trend toward more competition and privatization in the utilities, EDF set out in the early 1990s to expand its export opportunities. To identify such opportunities and better understand the challenges of cross-border business, EDF took a very simple and modest first step: it set up an eight-person task force to study and examine the international arena and to prepare a report for top management. The group served as a change catalyst by making recommendations as well. EDF has since expanded modestly into the international arena as a result of the recommendations of the fact-finding exercise.

Beyond this simple kind of exploration, the Global Learner must opt for some kind of first step that likely will bear upon structure. At a minimum, doing business globally requires that the organization initiate an overseas presence, if not an autonomous headquarters, moving part of itself away from its traditional geographic or corporate base and closer to the new customers. On-site location is a powerful indicator of a firm's intent to participate in a foreign market, and management based on-site rather than in the home country has a constant reminder that it must adapt to a new business climate and culture.

Alternatively, Global Learners can penetrate a geographic boundary using what we call a *soft structure*, meaning a structural change that is reversible and can be limited in length, commitment, and financial investment: a joint venture, for example, or a small acquisition of a foreign company. At this early point in a globalization effort, a soft structure makes sense because it keeps flexibility open while the firm explores markets and develops expertise. Soft-structure arrangements limit organizational risk because they tend to leave the main organizational structure intact. If the firm needs to rethink its plans or if a failure of the soft structure appears imminent, the firm's core foundations are not damaged.

A joint venture is perhaps one of the safest ways to get one's feet wet in an international arena. Its value is to combine expertise and capability from two firms synergistically, forming a more powerful and efficient operation than either firm could mount on its own. In the global context especially, a joint venture using the knowledge and on-site presence of a foreign firm may be one of the best strategies for a monocultural organization that wants to break out of its boundaries.

However, joint ventures do commonly disintegrate over time, as corporate differences emerge after the sparkle of the first meetings. One study by McKinsey & Company showed that fully 70 percent of all joint ventures (not just international ones) break up within three and a half years.[3] Other studies have indicated that even the cooperative ventures that survive do not achieve the expectations of the participants. Of course, joint ventures with overseas companies are even more complex than domestic ones, given the language and cultural barriers to be crossed as well as the potential for substantive differences in operating style and strategy.

As a result, we suggest that companies enter international joint ventures without the expectation of a big direct payback. The most valuable results will be learning experiences: opportunities for developing a greater awareness of the success factors in the new culture, making connections and contacts with industry leaders, obtaining benchmarking information, obtaining new technology to use in your own processes, and exploring new markets that you can ultimately tap independently. And the significance of this learning process is not to be underestimated. Many studies have shown that the joint venture partner who learns the fastest can dominate the relationship and dictate the terms. Yet some studies show that Japanese organizations excel at learning from others, while North Americans and Europeans have more trouble with it,[4] suggesting that this is an area deserving an organization's close attention.

Two additional elements of initiating a successful overseas joint venture are also important. First, choose a partner with whom you feel compatible. A personal relationship based on trust and mutual respect is a critical part of the glue that holds partners together. Personal incompatibility is thought to cause more failures among joint ventures and alliances than any other reason. Second, take time to fully evaluate the venture and its goals. Do not rush headlong into a deal without clearly identifying the market opportunities, potential drawbacks, and long-term gains.

In some cases, the acquisition of a small company abroad can move an organization into the international arena more quickly than a joint venture. In theory, an acquisition also carries less risk. The acquired company comes under your control and the chances of disagreement with that company's management are reduced. Nevertheless, the word "modest" should be emphasized when it comes to a foreign acquisition. Without experience in a culture or market, the Global Learner may wind up throwing resources away on improvements, restaffing, training, or any number of constraints imposed by the foreign government. The keys to a successful acquisition, like the keys to a joint venture, are to ensure that the planning phase has covered every decision point in depth and to keep expectations and investment low. As is also true in joint ventures, an ability to learn from the experience is vital, as is the ability to adapt quickly if it becomes clear that the original plans are failing.

As the company gets more involved in its foreign operation, its domestic structure should include increasingly diverse senior people. The Global Learner should begin to seek the involvement of top managers representing a range of nationalities, experience, and professional backgrounds in accordance with the geographic area of its globalization. We have seen the dynamics of companies change significantly with the arrival of a few foreign members. Managers with diverse experiences often yield different insights into the cultural impact of decisions. Diversity can be difficult to manage initially, but companies need to recognize that a long-term perspective is required when establishing a new global mindset.

In particular, adding foreign directors to the board has been shown to produce many benefits. Knowledgeable foreign leaders can expand company perspective and open doors to new contacts for business. They can often obtain better negotiations in their country of origin. Smaller companies, especially, can gain from the advice and intelligence a foreign director might offer—advice that would cost them much more if they had to buy it from an international consulting firm.

ORGANIZATIONAL PROCESSES AND SYSTEMS: GLOBAL COLLEAGUES AND MEETINGS

More and more, the starting point for crossing borders effectively is getting to know your global colleagues. In many companies in the early stages of globalization, people literally do not know their counterparts from different countries. And even when they do know them, they may still have distancing stereotypes that interfere with normal business processes. An important tuning action here is to give people intense, even if not frequent, opportunities to be together in both social and task situations. Both will socialize them, and a socialization process, says Paul Evans, builds a network of personal contacts throughout a global organization, and that "network becomes the nervous system of the organization. [Moreover] a network does not require everyone to know everyone else." As we quoted Evans saying previously, for a network "to function effectively, it requires 'loose ties'—knowing someone who knows someone who knows someone. Network theory and research show that a relatively small number of strong ties (strong relationships) among appropriate 'gatekeepers' . . . can provide a vast set of potential linkages."[5]

Consider the example of a multibusiness conglomerate with its central headquarters in London but much of its business in Asia. The company annually sent a group of managers to a month-long business school program specially designed to upgrade management capability for the company. The group was made up of carefully selected equal numbers of British managers and Chinese managers. Each year, faculty of the program met with senior management to discuss the training. But training was not the program's sole or perhaps even its primary purpose, as the company chairman made clear when he reputedly instructed the faculty, "I don't really care what you do in the classroom as long as they are getting drunk every night together. That's the best way to break down cultural barriers and create a lasting bond together!" Of course, a drinkfest should not be considered the only technique to accomplish this end, but the intense socializing experiences go a long way toward removing barriers between people and breaking down stereotypes.

Another example of Global Learner was the former Chemical Bank Europe (now Chase Europe), a regional structure dedicated to pan-European coordination and synergies. When Chemical originally merged with Manufacturer's Hanover Trust, its people had to get to know the other company, reaching across not only geographic but also corporate cultures. Despite a cost-cutting climate, the merged bank's European head, Herb Aspbury, decided to convene a three-day off-site workshop in which his top one hundred marketing managers gathered to clarify common goals, work on serving the needs of common clients, and build trust among each other. The workshop combined intense work and intense play. Every meal table, every breakout discussion, every sports activity, and so on was carefully designed to socialize a different group of people. Over the course of three days, each individual had the opportunity to meet virtually all the others. This workshop became an annual event for Chemical Bank Europe after the merger and has been a valuable source of bonding, which supplements many other of the bank's global processes.

The Global Learner must carefully discover the balance of universal versus local needs in designing and developing new products or services. Therefore, another action, or digital switch, for Global Learners is the use of ad hoc transnational teams to develop projects that would benefit from a global perspective. As we have discussed before, modern technology and communications have essentially eliminated many of the barriers of time and distance that once blocked frequent use of transnational teams. Both electronic mail and videoconferencing have many advantages besides speed and cost effectiveness. E-mail documents conversations and can be a face-saving way for people from different cultures and with different language capabilities to communicate without having to cope with pronunciation of the spoken language and the cultural conventions that dictate boundaries of personal power and distance, such as how close people stand to one another and how subordinates agree or disagree with managers. Videoconferencing allows participants to see facial reactions and body language and perhaps gives a better picture of attitudes and behaviors.

Moreover, technology is essential to making managers' offices geographically boundaryless. As Philippe Chevaux, head of an AT&T business located near the French-Italian border, said to one of us about his ability to communicate easily with clients or his home office, "We are a global business, open twenty-four hours a day. My office is anywhere I am." That mentality must be part of the mindset for any global company.

Two final processes recommended for learners are global town meetings and best-practice exchanges. The global town meeting works very much like the domestic town meetings we described earlier. People from related functions among multiple worldwide locations come together for the purpose of identifying common problems or challenges that cross borders. For example, an international bank might conduct a town meeting to resolve conflicts over originating new products, conflicts such as: Should the products be uniform for all markets or tailored to individual locales? Who owns the market intelligence that determines the decision: headquarters or the field? If one country develops products on its own, what mechanism does it use to share those ideas with other countries? As in any town meeting, people must feel able to honestly and openly exchange information and to resolve differences of opinion on the spot or in a timely fashion. They must go back to their home countries knowing that issues raised have been resolved.

The objective of the best-practice exchange, again, is to see whether what works in one territory might work in another. Too often, people in different countries operate by a not-invented-here mindset. They want to reinvent the wheel each time a problem comes up, because then it will be their wheel. Best-practice exchanges need to counter this wasteful mindset. They are ultimately a form of sanctioned plagiarism of good ideas from any and all geographies and locations within the organization, and they should be explicitly encouraged through newsletters, e-mail, and conferences.

THE CLIFFORD CHANCE EXPERIENCE

Clifford Chance, a global law firm with roots in the U.K., is an excellent example of how a Global Learner can become a Global Launcher.[6] It is a prototype for companies that have long-standing reputations for domestic or regional success and now realize that their marketplaces can be, or must be, far more expansive.

With a few exceptions, legal service firms have generally remained strictly local. However, the growth of the Euromarket in the 1970s, followed by the emergence of the global financial marketplace in the 1980s, prompted a few law firms from the advanced economies to consider global opportunities. In recent years, more and more law firms have been restructuring and globalizing, and the international legal services market is expected to be dominated by ten to twenty mega-firms by the turn of the century.

By no stretch of the imagination would the British-based law firms of Clifford Turner and Coward Chance have seemed likely candidates to become global players. But after the two firms merged in 1987 to become Clifford Chance, they worked hard at internationalization. By the mid '90s, Clifford Chance had become the world's second largest law firm, with nineteen offices in eighteen countries and 1,200 lawyers. Its strength—both strategically and organizationally—catapulted it to a position of international renown. It currently serves business clients worldwide in areas of corporate finance, banking, tax, property, and international law.

How did Clifford Chance make its transformation? What actions for change did it use? How did it move from being a Global Learner to a Global Launcher? And what lies ahead as it deepens its attempts to serve other multinational clients?

Some premerger history is relevant. The firm of Coward Chance, founded in 1881, had sixty-one partners in 1987. Its reputation was built on a combination of its technical knowledge and its understanding of the needs of fast-developing financial markets. In 1976, it had been one of the first law firms to enter the Middle East, and it had served the Southeast Asia financial markets from Hong Kong and Singapore offices from the early 1980s. Clifford Turner, founded in 1900, was slightly larger, with eighty-seven partners, and its strength was corporate finance. It served many large British retailers, but it also had established a practice in Japan in the late 1970s. It had several offices in continental Europe and, from 1986, an office in New York to specialize in transatlantic legal matters.

Thus, both firms had been Global Learners, with a presence in several foreign locales, although both still largely operated as U.K.-minded law practices. One critical goal of their merger was to become more international. But the leadership of the new firm quickly discovered that this goal would not happen by itself.

There were many real barriers to further globalization for the newly merged company. Nearly 80 percent of the lawyers were in London, giving the firm a strictly English feel. Its potential global clients and even its young lawyer recruits around the world thought of it as an English firm. Moreover, the older lawyers at the home office cherished their English traditions, personal independence, and lack of bureaucracy in operations. To themselves, they wondered why partners from high-earning offices should invest in less profitable operations in developing countries. As a result, international expansion for the new firm required a combination of changes not only in structure, systems, and processes but also in mindset.

As a first step, Clifford Chance set out to establish a broader presence in several European cities. It could have done this by buying up established law firms. Instead, management opted for a more flexible structure. The firm set up its own offices in each location and slowly hired people according to the evolving client needs that presented themselves. It then opened six new offices—in Barcelona, Frankfurt, Rome, Warsaw, Budapest, and Shanghai—starting very small in each locale.

As the offices developed, management assigned established lawyers from London to temporary postings in these offices. "One of the ways you integrate cultures," said Geoffrey Howe, the senior managing partner, "is by moving around. Increasingly the people who made partner in Paris or Madrid will have spent a year or two in London and vice versa. There is a direct cost, but it is the best way you integrate the people: it is not done by statements or strategies on paper."

But new locations and international assignments were not enough, because people were still *thinking* in the old domestic ways. Many of the lawyers still thought of Clifford Chance as primarily an English law firm with offices in foreign places. As a result, the service to clients was not seamless across borders. One indication of the problem was the use of words and phrases that reinforced the old mindset. Management thus introduced another tuning switch: the "Unwords Campaign," for which the firm newsletter printed a set of linguistic rules—words that had to be removed from everyday parlance and the new words that would replace them:

Unword	*Global Word*
City firm (British equivalent of "Wall Street firm")	Business and financial firm
English firm	International firm
U.K. firm	European-based international firm
Assistant solicitor	Lawyer
Overseas offices	International offices
The [Paris, Madrid, and so on] office	My colleagues in [Paris, Madrid, and so on]
Cross-selling	Integrated service

The technique of teaching employees a new vocabulary to encourage them to think in new ways is not unusual in our experience at all. Clifford Chance simply made it more explicit and more mandatory than many companies.

Finally, to reinforce the global mindset, the firm redesigned its procedures and systems to instill more consistency and standardization across all offices and geographies. It asked secretaries worldwide to use a universal typeface for all documents, right down to the cover sheets for faxes. It increased the use of standard forms, the templates law firms use to draft frequently used commercial documents such as leases, loan agreements, joint venture agreements, or board minutes. The clear signal sent to all employees at every level was, "We are one firm worldwide—with the same image to the marketplace and internally no matter where we are in the world."

The actions just described exemplify some of the steps that have moved Clifford Chance from a Global Learner to a Global Launcher. Given the firm's cultural, strategic, and organizational starting point, its progress has been substantial. Nevertheless, the senior partners still feel they have a long way to go, since their ultimate aspiration is to become, in our term, truly glocal, the hallmark of the Global Leaders. As one law partner in Amsterdam said: "Each office should be a link in the international chain as well as having a focus in its national marketplace. Our strategy is to be recognized not only as part of a major international firm but also as a Dutch law firm in [our] own right."

This difficult global-local balance is still to be achieved. Indeed, one of the ongoing challenges for Clifford Chance is to attract new recruits and compete successfully with established local firms. But even when the firm is successful through new recruits from the local culture, it is sometimes still not clear if these recruits can be adequately trained in the "Clifford Chance way" while retaining their home country expertise (especially in fast-changing developing economies). In other words, Clifford Chance is still trying to learn not to impose a London way of doing things, and to understand and adapt to local cultures. The firm faces as many difficult challenges going forward as it has tackled over the previous six years.

BEWARE OF LEARNER LANDMINES

All globalization efforts carry risks. Experience tells us, however, that the following are the typical landmines lying in wait to block forward progress for Global Learners.

Indecision.   Jumping into the global waters demands a greater under-standing of management, financial, geopolitical, and cultural issues than that required for a domestic operation. Many companies naturally become indecisive when attempting to determine how to dedicate time and resources when many options are available.

Lack of planning.   Planning is an essential element of doing business when different cultures and considerable distances are involved. You must decide certain questions in advance, such as: How far do you want your company to go? How aggressive and ambitious is your global strat-egy? Do you intend to develop a business that will become 20 percent nondomestic, or 50 percent, or 80 percent? The answers to such ques-tions have a direct impact on a firm's willingness to make investments of time and financial resources.

Cultural hypersensitivity.   In developing greater cultural awareness, Global Learners often go overboard and become hypersensitive to dif-ferences in work styles and management philosophies, causing them to excuse problems rather than face them. Recently, a senior manager, about to leave his post in France after two years, told us an anecdote that typifies the hypersensitivity phenomenon. While reflecting on what he learned about doing business abroad, he recalled how he had received extensive cross-cultural sensitivity training at the beginning of his assignment. Although he had originally felt that this made him more understanding when he encountered performance problems, he now believed he had bent over too far to accommodate cultural differences when he should have followed "universal" principles of good manage-ment. For instance, when employees identify a date by which they will complete their work, they should be held accountable, period. In short, Global Learners must balance cultural awareness with basic manage-ment principals, hard-core analysis, and market experience.

Ironically, perhaps the best detection system for many of the land-mines learners face is an early mistake. We often find that organizations hit early by error are able to learn from it and make rather painless adjustments compared to firms that discover a mistake only after a sig-nificant investment of time and financial resources. The more effective way to avoid stepping on landmines, however, is to benchmark other companies that have recently traversed the same territory. For example, an Israeli pharmaceutical company contemplating the acquisition of a privatized Hungarian firm closely studied GE Lighting's experience with Tungsram before making a decision.

Finally, the global learning organization requires a leader with exceptional personal qualities of courage and humility, as well as ambition, to support whatever stumbles happen among first steps. As in any infancy, the leader must encourage celebration of any early accomplishments with pride. Clifford Chance has had such leadership. Along with other decision makers in the firm, managing partner Geoffrey Howe has helped ensure the consistency, courage, and continuity to enable the firm's success. The importance of this leadership task to breaking down global barriers cannot be overestimated.

Global Launchers to Global Leaders

For organizations that have become Global Launchers, moving to the next stage of global leadership entails a new set of challenges. For the most part, a Global Launcher has developed a global strategy and vision. It has some experience under its belt at trying to remove geographic boundaries, and it appreciates how difficult the challenges will be. It also has seen the progress born of some of the steps described in the Global Learner section. What launchers must do next is to deepen commitment to removing geographic boundaries. They must also (as summed up in the following box) recalibrate their human resource practices, their organizational structures, and their systems and processes accordingly.

HR PRACTICES: LIQUEFY HUMAN RESOURCES

Global Launchers need to develop a *liquefied* workforce, so that they can pour it into whatever vessel they must fill. The rationale for resources liquefaction is that, in a completely globalized market, companies need to move people with flexible sets of skills from location to location or task to task to respond to customer needs with speed and

Human Resource Practices
- Seek complete liquidity of human resources: recruit outside the domestic base; place foreign recruits within the domestic base; promote the best people to global assignments; rotate people internationally; use twinning.
- Aim for a glocal structure.
- Map global processes.

Organizational Structures
- Provide continuing global leadership training and regular transnational training to reinforce the global mindset.
- Remove/minimize country managers and replace with global managers and focus on global customers.
- Routinize real-time global communications.

Organizational Processes and Systems
- Use global reward systems.
- Multiply ongoing transnational project teams.
- Work for global integration (for example, total global sourcing, global design, global engineering, and global purchasing).

innovation. For example, ABB routinely moves its managers laterally to positions in other countries to ensure that they develop a wider understanding of local markets. Many professional service firms, such as McKinsey and Arthur Andersen, have also developed systems for routinely assigning professionals to projects around the world for temporary periods of three to six months, as their clients require.

To develop liquefied human resources, the Global Launcher organization must put in place high-quality HR programs that attract the best people and then assign them to top global positions, regardless of their country of origin. Such programs send out a clear message that international assignments are among the company's most valued and critical positions, not career dead ends. As openings arise, HR must fill them with individuals who are recognized to be among the most talented and successful in the company at working globally. Launchers benefit particularly at this stage by making good use of the different educational backgrounds and viewpoints of its personnel, demonstrating that the firm is able to do business from a multicultural perspective, without prejudice or ethnocentrism. In short, launchers moving to leaders must allow the free flow of individuals from country to country, without regard to national origin.

Launchers also progress globally by bringing recruits from operations abroad to work within the domestic base, as Gillette's international trainee program does. Several hundred trainees have passed through the program since its inception in the early 1980s. Begun originally as an internship operation, the program changed when Gillette realized that many interns wanted to return to work in Gillette plants in their home countries. The company then transformed the program into a formal training tool. University graduates from business schools around the world begin the program by working for Gillette plants in their home countries for six months. The best and brightest of these people are then transferred to one of the three Gillette headquarters (in Boston, London, and Singapore) for more intensive work. Successful trainees have the opportunity to be assigned to management positions back in their home countries or in other Gillette facilities. Many eventually become general managers or senior operating managers in their home countries.

Another critical element in liquefying resources is the same kind of regular rotation of people around the world that ABB and McKinsey engage in. Rotations give managers the experience and enlarged perspective to tackle a wide range of problems. International experience allows people to:

◆ See local conditions firsthand and obtain direct exposure to markets and ways of doing business abroad.
◆ Live in others' shoes for a while to learn others' ways of thinking.
◆ Develop loyalties to various regions or segments of a business.

Another value of regular rotations is the development of alternative worldviews that boost the quality of decisions. We hear many U.S. managers with global experience take a healthy contrary point of view in organizational discussions, saying, in effect, "We don't see it the same way as you do in the United States." Living and breathing a different culture has shown them new points of view. It is for this reason that many firms hesitate to have a local person running an important center unless that person has proven himself or herself in another country as well as in a headquarters or central staff role. Ultimately, rotations help all members of the organization learn and grow.

Launchers moving to leaders also benefit from consistent transnational training, such as seminars and management workshops, that continues to develop a global mindset and shared values among all organizational members. Price Waterhouse each year brings newly appointed partners from around the world to a location (a new one each year) where they are educated on the firm's basic values and principles. This serves both purposes of training and international socialization.

Another technique to foster continual training and learning is twinning, the process of assigning one local and one foreign person to the same job for a time. GE Lighting employed twinning at Tungsram so that GE managers would learn about global issues while Tungsram people learned about Western business practices.

Although perhaps more subtle than the actions just described, restructuring reward systems is another important adjustment made by Global Launchers moving to become leaders. The new compensation systems reward a broader view of performance than formerly and encourage managers to use their expertise more flexibly in such areas as improving market penetration worldwide or helping sister companies in other countries. For example, IBM introduced performance measures that rewarded managers for working with international colleagues. Goldman, Sachs & Co. implemented a new compensation and organizational structure that promotes cooperation. In this system, "because compensation is based more on subjective criteria than on transaction count, officers in different departments don't constantly bicker over how much credit they should get for a particular deal. And unlike other firms that are organized by geographical region, Goldman brings in the firm's heaviest hitters . . . to pitch in on a transaction in any region."[7]

ORGANIZATIONAL STRUCTURE: RESOLVING COMPLEXITY

The Global Launcher is likely to have grown according to a multidomestic approach, in which numerous sites or headquarters dot countries around the world. To become a leader, the launcher must establish a structural approach that resolves the complexities of a large transnational management. It must learn how to balance the centralizing that will achieve a pooling of resources and economies of scale at the global level with the decentralizing that will cater to local preferences with speed and precision.

For many firms, the choice boils down to converting to a loose matrix that interlaces management by product, customer, and function with a continuing country or regional structure. This solution offers the advantages found in both centralizing certain kinds of decision making and expertise and maintaining a strong product or local orientation. As the *Economist* summed it up, "In theory, this means that management can make decisions without regard for national borders—but only if they want to."[8]

However, the verdict is still out on the solution that best fits the advanced stages of globalization. The best answer for any one company most likely depends on a number of variables: type of product, number of markets, methods of distribution, and long-term strategy. Nevertheless, the active search for a solution to complexity in the best global companies is significant in that it suggests that these organizations have definitely moved away from a multidomestic structure and are progressing into highly complex arrangements. On the one hand, Sony uses a four-zone global operation—Japan, America, Europe, and the rest of the world—while maintaining product managers as well. IBM reorganized into fourteen worldwide industry groups—such as banking, retailing, and insurance—but also kept its geographic chieftains. The "new" Ford consolidated its efforts in five product groups, but the groups coordinate with international executives headquartered in Dearborn. Unilever uses a regional structure with local managers in the areas of Africa/Middle East, Latin America, and East Asia/Pacific. However, in Europe and North America, where consumers tastes are similar, they use a worldwide products orientation. On the other hand, one Global Leader has dismantled its matrix structures. Dow Chemical returned to an earlier structure, giving lines of responsibility back to geographic managers. Thus, the trend toward complex glocal structures, to use our new term again, does not seem to be a universal prescription.

ORGANIZATIONAL PROCESSES AND SYSTEMS: TECHNOLOGICAL SOLUTIONS TO COMPLEXITY

Successfully managing complexity in processes and systems is a major challenge for launchers who want to become Global Leaders. Launchers typically must deal with extensive R&D, manufacturing, sourcing, purchasing, and distribution networks that cover wide territories and consumer needs. A key action for strengthening and globalizing these systems is process mapping (see Chapter Five). Examples of processes to be mapped include development of a new product from design through delivery to the warehouse and fulfillment of an order from customer request to delivery. Global process mapping reveals the links and kinks in operations and where companies may be able to save time, money, or space.

For example, the global company at the launcher level may have orders coming in from different parts of the world to a central order bank, which then transmits them to manufacturing or distribution centers at other locations. However, if a process map shows that most orders for certain products arrive from one region of the world, the organization might decide to adjust warehousing and distribution patterns to accommodate that regional need.

Launchers who want to become leaders make more use of technology than learners do, and at higher levels, to achieve *real-time* global communications. Dedicated trunk lines, groupware, paging devices, and portable computers with fax and modem cards allow people to communicate at length and instantaneously across time zones, at any hour of the day or night, and with a common language.

Two organizations that emphasize the use of technology are the former Price Waterhouse and SmithKline Beecham. Price Waterhouse, which subsequently merged with Coopers & Lybrand to become the largest professional service firm in the world, increasingly focused its attention on serving multinational clients. To do so, it recognized the need to abandon a long-standing tradition of treating the local office as supreme in favor of a worldwide operating structure and decision-making process that could mobilize human resources, investment advice, and technical information from any office as needed. To accomplish this, it turned to groupware technology that connects everyone through an elaborate electronic system.

A prime example of the use of groupware is the development of a client proposal. Formerly, a local office developing a proposal had to communicate with other members of the firm by phone or by fax across time zones, a process that was time consuming and had a high rate of incomplete contacts. Today, the groupware system allows an office developing a proposal to collect data and information easily from any of the resources throughout the twenty-six worldwide offices. Within a matter of days rather than weeks, the lead partner can then write a draft proposal, send it electronically to others for review, receive feedback quickly, and even enjoin colleagues to help rewrite the proposal.

SmithKline Beecham's groupware process, "R&D Team Connect," allows researchers throughout the company to hook their personal computers or terminals to a common set of databases for information sharing. Team members can also carry on electronic conversations to get comments and feedback about their experiments or clinical results.

In short, launchers becoming leaders recognize that technology contributes extensively to their ability to be global. They routinely follow new technological developments and install the latest equipment for employees if it can save time and contribute to gathering information and making decisions that otherwise would require unwieldy meetings, exorbitant travel costs, or excessive investments of time.

Finally, launchers becoming leaders must identify opportunities for global sourcing and purchasing, global design, and global engineering to reduce costs and maximize economies of scale. An additional common benefit from centralization of these processes is the transfer of learning across the organization.

THE ALCATEL BELL EXPERIENCE

An informative illustration of the move from Global Launcher to Global Leader is Alcatel Bell (AB). A leading supplier of telecommunications equipment, AB is in an industry that has seen intense competition in expanding geographically to take advantage of both emerging markets and the increasingly sophisticated needs of advanced economies. As a result, the challenge for AB has been to globalize as effectively and quickly as possible.

Alcatel's history has had some effect on current activities. AB is a Belgium-based subsidiary of Alcatel Alsthom, an international producer of technologically advanced infrastructure equipment for the communication, energy, and transport sectors. Alcatel Alsthom ranks among the world's leaders in all its areas of activities. Highly aggressive and ambitious, it has dedicated itself to internationalization through growth and almost two hundred acquisitions.

At one time, Alcatel Bell had been a very local business, with long-term secure contracts for serving the Belgian telephone company and a reliable revenue stream from its Belgian world of business. In the 1960s, 70 percent of its business was local. In the 1970s and 1980s, its business widened, becoming 50 percent global but largely through export and licensing agreements. However, in the 1980s and 1990s, it began globalizing substantially, attempting to become a Global Leader. Through joint ventures, start-ups, mergers, and acquisitions, AB sales today are only 30 percent Belgian; most of its attention is focused on the international world. (AB's global evolution is summarized in Table 9.1.)

What switches has AB used to enable the radical retuning of both its business mix and its business mindset? What did it take to transform this rather localized business into a leading world player?

One major action taken was to fill critical senior positions with people (insiders and outsiders) who had extensive international experience and orientation. The new players understood the structures, people, and systems required to build and sustain a global business. They shaped a new strategy and direction of deepening globalization in such places as Russia, China, and Turkey.

The new leaders also filled key appointments in Belgium with people who were comfortable in an international context and who had lived as

Table 9.1. Alcatel Bell's Globalization.

Period	Local Sales (Percent)	Global Sales (Percent)	Strategic Steps
1960s	70	30	Local manufacturing; exporting to international locations; first licensing agreement (Romania)
1970s	50	50	Multiple licensing agreements and turnkey contracts (for example, India, Taiwan, Yugoslavia)
1980s	50	50	Joint ventures in China, Mexico, Russia, Turkey; centralized engineering; exporting to seventy-two countries
1990s	30	70	Starting new companies (for example, in Russia and Colombia); making mergers and acquisitions; managing businesses worldwide

expatriates elsewhere. As joint ventures and acquisitions were made, the leaders relied on a select group of these best and brightest to serve as managers in the resident positions abroad. They also called on a cadre of functional specialists from engineering, finance, and technical operations to service various areas in the world as needed. In short, no functional specialty was excluded from international assignments. Specialists had to be prepared to be sent to any country in which AB operated.

In addition, AB invested heavily in ongoing people development. Managers and employees worldwide continually are sent to Belgium for special training. For example, employees from newly acquired subsidiaries spend three months to two years in Antwerp for technical training. New customers also are trained on equipment in Antwerp, while managers are familiarized with AB management techniques there. On any given day, the number of languages spoken at the training center mirrors the United Nations, even though the training is conducted in English. In addition, in China and Russia, people trained by AB train other people locally, in their local languages.

In these ways, AB has instituted many of the practices summarized at the beginning of this section, namely, HR practices that enable top talent from different parts of the world to work together regularly, processes and systems that integrate key functional areas and expertise, and many ongoing transnational project teams.

To understand the progress of AB, we interviewed one of its key regional managers, Stan Abbeloos, AB general director in Russia. A Belgian by birth, Abbeloos has an engineering degree and speaks English, French, German, and some Russian in addition to his native Flemish. (Every one of the AB general directors speaks two or three additional languages.) In 1994, at forty-two years of age, he was completing his third year in Russia. Prior to that, he had worked for Alcatel in China for four years. In many respects, he is a pioneer as he works to solidify a large business in Russia. A glimpse into a month of his life is telling of the kind of energy and work needed by Global Leaders:

> I started the month traveling to Anadyr, Russia, near Alaska. It took five days to get there because of the weather. But we signed a contract for $4 million by the end of the day. Then we waited two additional days to get the plane back. And you must fly Aeroflot—you have no choice! If you want, you could take the train, but it would take a lot longer to travel, often up to thirty-six hours between cities.
>
> Then I next went to Novosibirsk, in the middle of Siberia, where we have one of our offices. It's actually a joint venture in which we have 75 percent control. I had to negotiate next year's delivery of product.
>
> Then I went to Surgut, also in Siberia, where the temperature was minus twenty-six degrees centigrade, but I got final acceptance to sell a System 12 toll exchange, and they signed a maintenance agreement.
>
> I then went back to St. Petersburg, where for one week I was managing the creation of a space for refurbishing our products. Then I went to Anadyr to finalize a contract, then on to Moscow for a steering committee meeting to coordinate international activities across Alcatel Alsthom, and finally I was sent to France for one week to attend a "High Potential Leaders" training program!

What can we see in this hectic month of activity? First, it is an excellent example of a glocal executive's focus. Although the better part of the month represented intense attention to local matters, the end of the month provided two global links—the corporate task force on global coordination and the leadership training with worldwide representation. Such agenda balancing is crucial if a company is to become a Global Leader.

Second, the example reveals the stress tolerance required of Global Leaders. Operating in this mobile, fluid fashion was not unusual for Abbeloos and the other general directors, especially in emerging marketplaces. It is the grueling stressful life of a pioneer, albeit challenging and gratifying. Abbeloos found that "one of the major limiting factors [of operating this way] is family. You have to have a fluid family or give it up, especially in places like Russia and China." While that principle by no means applies for all aspiring to be Global Leaders, there is no denying that people operating across the world stage must accept a heavy wear-and-tear factor.

Finally, the example reveals how AB created a multiplier effect as it expanded and integrated. It opted to create a roving team of Global Leaders such as Abbeloos, who would be willing to accept the sacrifices and stresses inherent in such assignments. The members of this transnational team could then learn from each other as they came to truly understand the cultural differences required to operate in different parts of the world. For example, owing to cultural differences, marketing in China is done by the local Chinese. AB people are rarely involved. But in Russia, AB people do the marketing because the Russians are not interested in selling. In Russia, then, knowing the language becomes more critical for foreigners doing business there.

The process of becoming a Global Leader is not over for AB. It still must figure out better ways to integrate those who have served in foreign countries back into other assignments in their home countries and ways to hand new assignments to local talent. But Abbeloos is one who is confident that AB has built global leadership: "In terms of operating in Europe, we have all [the] languages and capabilities required. Our real opportunity now is across the world. Here we have the flexibility required. We know that in China, the Chinese must be with the customer. We know that in Russia, expatriates are more effective with the customer. And we have marketing and sales people who can be deployed from throughout AB to be 'door-openers' and a full organization behind them able to serve customers wherever they are."

BEWARE OF LAUNCHER LANDMINES

Beyond the sheer complexity of running an international firm with a slew of variables including diversity of workforce cultures, varying raw material suppliers, currency fluctuations, political swings, and a multitude of other unpredictable factors, several specific landmines lurk buried in the ground Global Launchers must cross to become leaders.

First, global firms seeking to grow from launchers to leaders often find themselves triggering unexpected domino effects. They solve one problem only to see the solution engender another. Some of these firms end up in seemingly no-win situations, such as growing so large they end up competing with themselves. For example, Matsushita now finds that its cost-effective and productive overseas subsidiaries in southeast Asia produce so much and export so much back to Japan at cheaper prices that Matsushita employees back home cannot keep up. The one-time slogan of Matsushita's Malaysian plants, "Let's catch up with Japan," has been quickly outmoded because these plants outperform the Japanese plants in both quality and efficiency. Similarly, Fuji Xerox, the Japanese affiliate of Fuji Film and Xerox, found itself embroiled with its parent company Xerox over sales territory and R&D independence.

A second landmine is sociopolitical and cultural embroilment. As launchers become players in more and more geopolitical regions, they automatically face a greater probability that they will encounter political, social, cultural, and ethical values that differ significantly from their own and lead to turbulence and moral dilemmas. For example, on the one hand, several Global Launchers have been fined for obtaining contracts in certain countries by using a form of bribery that in their view was acceptable if not required in those cultures. On the other hand, companies such as Levi Strauss withdrew their initiatives to open up plants and operations in China because of continuing human rights violations that they viewed as contrary to their corporate values and principals.

Overall, Global Launchers require a perspective that guides them toward grand but realistic ambitions. Many companies look at China, for example, and imagine that if one billion persons each bought a $1 product, they would produce $1 billion in revenues. This is a grand but unrealistic ambition because doing business in China today is far more difficult than the scenario suggests. A grand but realistic ambition in this situation might also recognize the potential market in the large population but at the same time plan to explore deeply the cultural and political differences in the Chinese market and to understand the complex arrangement of structures, processes, and systems that would support success in that market.

Similarly, at the individual level, the perspective required is explained by the familiar adage, "Think global, act local." Managers in Global Launcher and Leader companies must maintain a vision of the world that is complex and sophisticated but also simple from where they sit. It is analogous to playing chess. The players must be able to think strategically and continually about the overall course of the game, but each must also be able to focus on just one move at a time.

The Global Village of Tomorrow

As companies like Matsushita, Sony, IBM, AT&T, Hewlett-Packard, Toyota, Coca-Cola, McDonald's, Alcatel Bell, and many others will testify, becoming a Global Leader is a tough transition. Many tools are available to organizations, and we have described a good number of them here. But senior management must have the skill and foresight to use the right tools in the right way, at the right time, and in the right sequence. There are no magic bullets, no matter where you are in the global learning curve. Each stage requires structures that enable the crossing of boundaries, systems and processes that drive global behavior, and people who can learn to extend their thinking beyond their present outlook. If these goals are consciously set and strongly pursued and achieved, the ultimate reward is an international organization rich in multicultural diversity, a complex and sophisticated management outlook, and successful global products and services.

Conclusion

10

Making It Happen

Leading Toward the Boundaryless Organization

Through much of the twentieth century, management theory and practice emphasized a paradigm for business success that fostered the creation of well-structured, unbending organizational boundaries. These boundaries allowed a relative handful of managers to control vast organizations, harness a variety of specialized skills, and extend the reach of mass-production and mass-service organizations around the world. Today, there are new success factors confronting fast-paced, flexible, and global businesses. These new success factors have made an emphasis on boundaries increasingly dysfunctional in the later part of the twentieth century. We have described specific tools and techniques to increase the permeability of the four most enduring and intractable boundaries in organizations: vertical boundaries between hierarchical levels, horizontal boundaries between functions, external boundaries between customers and suppliers, and geographic boundaries between various parts of the world.

In this concluding chapter, we view the transformation to a boundaryless organization through a different lens—the lens of leadership. In our experience, boundaryless organizations do not come about as an autonomic response to changing economic and social pressures. Rather, they arise from effective changes in structure and process, and they are actively driven by organizational leaders who ignite the sparks of transformation, fan them to keep them alive, and then control the flames to make the transformation productive.

Leadership Change Challenges

Leading the way to the boundaryless organization is one of the most imposing but exhilarating tasks facing senior executives today—largely because it requires executives to overcome at least five different leadership change challenges, listed in the box below, during the course of the transformation. Most executives already have the skills to successfully deal with one or two of these challenges. To manage the remainder, they may want to seek experienced support, either from colleagues or outsiders. The following discussion is meant to provide perspective on these challenges and the kind of support that might be most useful.

Leadership Change Challenges

- Transform for tomorrow while doing business today.
- Manage an uncontrollable change process.
- Lead to an unclear destination.
- Deal with disruption.
- Confront the need for personal change.

TRANSFORM FOR TOMORROW WHILE DOING BUSINESS TODAY

Executives who want to move their companies toward the boundaryless world of the twenty-first century cannot simply stop what they are doing today in order to focus exclusively on the future. Despite the bad rap Western managers often take for their short-term focus, the reality is that most companies need to secure their present in order to have a future. GE Chairman and CEO Jack Welch once made this point when one of us asked whether he worried that his focus on short-term results would compromise his long-term agenda. Welch said: "It's been ten years so far, and my businesses keep delivering the numbers *and* doing the right things for the future. They have to do both. People keep telling me that at some point things will fall apart, that [doing both is] not possible. But I haven't seen it yet."

A challenge for most executives is to create and maintain this dual focus, to be an "ambidextrous" manager, with one hand steering the course of today's business while the other hand manages for tomorrow, all the while facing down resistance from subordinates who say, "Boss, if you want us to make these long-term changes, we'll have to sacrifice some of our profits this year"; or "Boss, if you want us to make these profits, we'll have to delay our long-term changes."

A dual focus on the present and the future requires managers to truly put in place and believe in a "balanced-scorecard" approach to assessing performance; they must look beyond the numbers.[1] After all, in most companies, financials are lagging indicators. They draw a somewhat static picture of past performance. They rarely offer insights about future threats and opportunities or about what to do in either situation. Managers with a balanced scorecard look not only at financial performance but also at series of hard and soft "leading indicators" that are constructed almost like "Star Trek" probes into the future. These indicators include employee satisfaction, customer service levels, speed of new product introductions, key process cycle times, competitor and industry innovations, and more.

When leaders ask about these indicators with the same passion with which they review operating numbers, they signal that the future and the present must both be preserved. But this change requires breaking long-standing habits of focusing only on numbers that require reports to the board and analysts and that make stock prices rise and fall like boats bobbing on the waves. The temptation to stay focused only on the numbers is great; but it is making the numbers while also creating the future that is the real challenge.

MANAGE AN UNCONTROLLABLE CHANGE PROCESS

Books need to be written in sections and chapters. Real organizational life defies such neat categorization. This means that executives working to transform their organizations cannot limit themselves to changing one variable at a time. Inevitably, for example, shifts in hierarchical patterns will influence the ways in which functions work together. Moves to delayer and to give more autonomy to operator teams in manufacturing will almost always result in the teams' seeking greater degrees of cross-functional participation. Often, this leads to greater vendor participation and a greater focus on both internal and external customers. In a global company, teams often seek out peer teams in other plants around the world to share best practices, coordinate material supplies, and so on. In other words, once the boundaryless transformation begins (and no matter which boundary is attacked first), it likely will snowball. This is particularly true when organizational people get turned on, excited by the opportunity to control their own destiny. At this point, leaders need to follow Peter Drucker's often-repeated dictum to effective managers to "get out of the way."

The challenge for senior executives, then, is to live with the ambiguity and uncertainty of an uncontrollable process. Transforming organizational boundaries is probably more akin to genetic reengineering than industrial engineering; the process unleashes tremendous energy and chain reactions with the potential to evolve in ways difficult to predict. For many managers, this kind of uncertainty is unnerving and may lead to a conscious or unconscious avoidance of boundaryless change strategies. For others, it is exhilarating—the essence of creative management.

LEAD TO AN UNCLEAR DESTINATION

Another kind of uncertainty, which may plague traditional senior executives if they let it, is the lack of definable outcomes, or end states. Probably the most productive view of the transformation to a boundaryless organization is similar to the view summed up in the total quality mantra that "quality is not a destination but a journey." Many managers struggle with such concepts, but trying to define the ultimate boundaryless organization is like trying to define infinity. There is no time when the changing is complete and, therefore, no ultimate static state to talk about. There is no "after." While writing this book, we interviewed a number of senior executives who were actively engaged in creating boundaryless organizations. Every one of them asked us the same question: "Can you tell me about an organization that has already done it, that has succeeded in becoming boundaryless?" In other words, the executives that many managers consider models of boundaryless leadership are still searching for their own models because they are unclear about where the process is taking them.

But the indefiniteness of the boundaryless end state is entirely appropriate. After all, the boundaryless corporation is a living entity in the process of evolution. As with the human race, it is impossible to predict how much more potential exists in the life-form.

Although it is possible to look backward and define what the boundaryless organization is not, each new development from that defined state leads to new insights about what else is possible. Companies begin dialogues with their customers, and from these, new possibilities such as shared information and recalibration of roles and responsibilities emerge. Such identification of new possibilities, we suspect, is never ending, limited only by the imagination and creativity of the participants.

The challenge for executives is to get comfortable with the anxiety that an undefined end state can generate. This can be especially difficult for managers who are used to setting attainable goals, strategic plans, and definable objectives, all of which depend on specific measurements and indicators of progress that tell managers when they have arrived. Conversely, when Jack Welch began the GE Work-Out, he described it as a "decade-long quest" and insisted he would not create any new measures to assess Work-Out success. When pressed about how he would assess progress, he said, "If we start to measure it, we'll kill the process. We have to just let it evolve. We have enough measures already to tell us how we're doing. Let's just use those." Later, when many GE managers continued to ask for clarification about the ultimate goal of Work-Out, Welch designed a presentation slide that showed success as the point at which GE was "the most productive company on earth."

If moving toward the boundaryless organization is truly an evolutionary process, then when GE or any other company becomes the most productive company on earth that achievement will only be a starting point for seeking galactic excellence. The process will continue if the anxiety can be mastered and transformed into excitement.

DEAL WITH DISRUPTION

Another cause of anxiety to be overcome is the real or imagined organizational disruption that may be involved in loosening boundaries. The drive toward a boundaryless organization may or may not make companies smaller, but it will definitely make them different, and the shifts spurred by these differences will be difficult for some people, perhaps even personally painful. A common example is the way reducing hierarchical boundaries changes the role of middle managers and supervisors. This shift is an exciting opportunity for managers who can learn new skills and change their roles from controlling and directing to coaching, counseling, setting visions, and deploying resources. But for those who cannot change or change fast enough, there may be no opportunity. Similarly, managers who grew up with the expectation that career advancement would be associated with advances in hierarchical position may or may not be intrigued by the idea of careers as series of lateral moves, each one of which requires new skills.

All the boundary changes we have described require such shifts in roles and career definitions and have enormous implications for the opportunities that people can expect in organizations. A major challenge for executives who want to embark on the boundaryless journey is to deal with their own anxiety about such shifts. It is one thing to plan organizational strategies and drive the organization toward greater speed, flexibility, integration, and innovation. It is another feeling entirely to be responsible for career disruptions, layoffs, and family crises. Most executives, like most everyone else, want to be liked and loved rather than the focus of personal animosities. Unfortunately, there is no easy way out of the dark side of the boundaryless transformation. Avoiding or even delaying the transformation can cause even greater organizational disruptions due to flagging competitiveness and knee-jerk layoffs, as seen all too often in the past decade. Perhaps the only solace is to trust in human resilience and creativity. If people are given the straight story and challenged to change for good reasons that they can understand, then the ball is in their court to make the best of the situation. The challenge for leadership is not to be hard-hearted but to help everyone be realistic about how to succeed in the boundaryless world.

CONFRONT THE NEED FOR PERSONAL CHANGE

While helping others grapple with the new realities of the boundaryless world, senior executives must also confront their own needs for transformation. This is probably the most difficult challenge of all. Most of today's corporate executives grew up with models of leadership that were extremely effective in the 1970s and 1980s. Leaders like ITT's Harold Geneen, GM's Roger Smith, IBM's John Akers, Chase Manhattan's David Rockefeller, Citicorp's Walter Wriston, and many others were tough decision makers who ran their companies with an iron hand, fought hard with unions and governments, and tolerated little dissent. Moreover, they were deal-doers who bought and sold companies, and they were financially astute control people who squeezed money out of every operation.

Having learned at the knee of leaders like these, many of today's senior executives are well-schooled in leadership patterns that worked well in the past decades but have proved less effective in the 1990s and may be disastrous in the twenty-first century. Today, instead of driving decisions, leaders need to drive discussion and create buy-in. Rather than confront unions, governments, suppliers, and customers, leaders need to build partnerships based on mutual respect and trust. Instead of controlling, leaders need to be empowering, coaching, counseling, encouraging, and supporting their people—freeing them to use their talents to the greater good of the corporation.

This does not mean that the old skills are unusable. On the contrary, senior executives today and into the foreseeable future will still need to make tough decisions, understand financial issues, and be prepared to reconfigure their organizations both through buying and selling and through constant restructuring and unstructuring. But there is no doubt that the boundaryless world will be a new world for leadership as well as for the troops. It is unrealistic to think that the loosening of hierarchies, functions, and other boundaries will not require new kinds of personal leadership—both to make it happen and to provide ongoing direction. At the end of this chapter, leaders will have an opportunity to assess their personal shifts toward new styles of boundaryless leadership. The point for now is that the challenge of making a personal transition is one that executives, too, will face. It is always easy to tell others to change. It is much tougher to say the same thing to that familiar face in the mirror.

Learning from Experience: Leadership Leverage Points

There is no simple, straightforward formula or magic strategy for meeting the five change challenges. Each leader will deal with them in his or her own way—probably with lots of hard work, an almost Zen-like tolerance for ambiguity and uncertainty, and a large degree of courage. The shift toward a boundaryless organization requires you not only to fight through your organization's immune system response but also to overcome your own natural inclinations for control, clarity, and certainty. Success at dealing with these challenges will be dependent on your openness to learning and your willingness to change.

Throughout this book, we have cited examples of leaders who have demonstrated openness to learning and change, grappled with the five challenges, and moved their organizations toward a boundaryless paradigm. Their experiences suggest the three major guidelines listed below for executives who are determined to transform their own organizations.

Guidelines for Boundaryless Transformation
- Start with a focus on measurable short-term business results.
- Create an iterative vision, not a grand plan.
- Bust the boundaries in order to bust the boundaries.

START WITH A FOCUS ON MEASURABLE SHORT-TERM BUSINESS RESULTS

Perhaps the most important lesson to be learned from the boundaryless organizations described here is that the initial focus of change must always be measurable business results. Leaders must keep in mind that the ultimate purpose of loosening boundaries is a more effective, competitive organization, capable of achieving whatever results are necessary to ensure its survival.

In our experience, one of the most dangerous mistakes executives can make is to unintentionally reverse figure and ground, that is, to emphasize the new organizational forms and relationships as primary and assume results will automatically follow transformational change. Nothing could be further from the truth.

The recent experience of many corporations with Total Quality Management (TQM) illustrates this point all too painfully. Thousands of organizations rushed into TQM with the honest belief that if they changed enough organizational variables, bottom-line results would emerge like Venus from the sea. They crafted quality-oriented mission statements; trained managers and employees in quality thinking and quality tools; set up quality contests, assessments, and awards; and organized cross-functional steering committees and conferences. The only thing missing in many of these ambitious efforts was a focus on short-term improvements in quality results. In fact, in the orthodoxy of many quality projects, short-term results were anathema, a result of limited thinking. Managers were actually told not to pressure people to achieve results quickly because it would prevent them from really changing their fundamental values and relationships. A number of well-known corporations even proudly published charts showing a sequence for TQM in years: year one was the Year of Understanding; year two was the Year of Training; year three was the Year of Fundamental Change; and year four was to be the Year of Results.

Unfortunately, all too many of these corporations never made it to year four. A host of assessment studies showed, instead, a pattern of disappointment. A McKinsey & Company study of thirty quality programs found that two-thirds had stalled or fallen short of yielding real improvements. An Arthur D. Little survey of five hundred North

American manufacturing and service companies reported that only one-third of them felt that their total quality programs were having a significant impact on their competitiveness. An A.T. Kearney survey of over one hundred British firms produced a similar finding—less than one-fifth believed their TQM programs had achieved tangible results. And an American Electronics Association 1991 membership survey reported that while 73 percent of association members had TQM underway, most had failed to markedly improve quality defects through the effort.

Due to these disappointments, a number of corporations closed up their total quality programs. Others shifted to reengineering or reinventing. But if companies move from one change to another and still fail to focus on results as the fundamental driver of change, they may not fare any better.[2]

Professor Michael Beer and his associates at Harvard have studied dozens of corporations engaged in major change programs, and they, too, have concluded that the successful companies had an unrelenting focus on results while the less successful companies focused on activities that kept people busy but were aimed at changing intermediate variables (such as organizational structure, communication patterns, and job skills) rather than bottom-line results.

Beer and his colleagues pointed out that "while in some companies, wave after wave of programs rolled across the landscape with little positive impact, in others, more successful transformations did take place. They usually started at the periphery of the corporation . . . and they were led by the general managers of [the] units, not by . . . corporate staff people. The general managers did not focus on formal structures and systems; they created ad hoc organizational arrangements to solve concrete business problems. . . . [T]hey focused energy for change on the work itself, not on abstractions such as 'participation' or 'culture.'"[3]

The importance of focusing directly on results as a driver of boundaryless change is also supported by another Harvard researcher, Nitin Nohria. Looking at U.S. industrial trends over the past several decades, Nohria found an inverse correlation between competitive market position and expenditures on organizational change programs. He suggests that companies have actually lost competitive advantage by focusing on the implementation of "organizational fads" instead of on how to get results by using the various change programs. To reverse this trend, he calls for managers to become more "pragmatic," that is, to aim directly at achieving results, using whatever works from the panoply of powerful tools that managers have at their disposal.[4]

In all cases where we have seen leaders succeed at reducing their organizations' boundaries—leaders such as Lawrence Bossidy at Allied-Signal or Robert Galvin at Motorola—never has the change been made for purely ideological or intellectual reasons. The focus was always on how best to achieve business results. If reconfiguring boundaries was a good way to get there, then that is what was tried. There is little doubt that if these managers had not achieved bottom-line business gains, those specific boundaryless configurations would have been scrapped and something else would have been tried. The goal was never to be boundaryless. The goal was to be a successful, effective, competitive organization.

CREATE AN ITERATIVE VISION, NOT A GRAND PLAN

The second lesson that emerges from the cases in the previous chapters is that a major boundaryless transformation does not need a grand master plan and, in fact, should not have one. The move to looser boundaries is (like tuning with digital switches) iterative and empirical, based on constant innovation and experimentation in the context of a flexible vision. Anything more structured would be useless or even counterproductive. The world is changing so rapidly that any fixed master plan is outdated before the ink dries.

For example, who would have imagined just a few short years ago how extensively facsimile technology would permeate organizational life? In the late 1980s, executives who received faxes were unusual, and Federal Express lost millions trying to promote Zap Mail, a type of fax. By 1994, however, fax transmissions accounted for up to 36 percent of some Fortune 500 phone bills,[5] fax modems were becoming standard in personal computers, and the home fax market was booming. Today most organizations cannot imagine life without the fax machine. Moreover, the possibilities of facilitating boundaryless behavior through this technology are enormous. Fax machines have speeded up the pace of business and effectively opened up entirely new channels of communication between cross-functional teams, customers, and suppliers and across geographies. And this is only the effect of one technology! Add to it interactive communications tools, teleconferencing, Internet and the Worldwide Web, voice-recognition computing, global satellite networks, and more—and the possibilities for further organizational transformation become mind boggling. In addition, the world is speeding through vast social, economic, and political changes that are redrawing the maps of commerce and creating whole new markets. In this kind of world, planning predictably is virtually impossible. The executive of a large financial services company told us: "If people ask me where we'll be in a couple of years, I tell them that I don't know. I can make a few guesses, but my guesses probably aren't any better than theirs." Most of the executives we talk to who are engaged in boundaryless transformations make similar statements.

Their attitude—their *reveling* in uncertainty—is contrary to the popular wisdom of strategic planning with its extensive data collection and analyses leading to projections of the future. It is more akin to what McGill University professor Henry Mintzberg calls "strategic thinking." In Mintzberg's view, strategic thinking is what successful companies use to track changing social and economic trends, to assess their implications, to experiment with new ways of doing business, and to build on empirical experience. It is a continuous process, inculcated into the fabric of the organization, rather than a one-time planning exercise that aims to complete a series of forms and concludes with a fancy presentation. It is "about synthesis. It involves intuition and creativity. The outcome of strategic thinking is an integrated perspective of the enterprise, a not-too-precisely articulated vision of direction. . . . Such strategies often cannot be developed on schedule and immaculately conceived. They must be free to appear at any time and at any place in the organization, typically through messy processes of informal learning that must necessarily be carried out by people at various levels who are deeply involved with the specific issues at hand."[6]

The boundaryless companies we have seen are strikingly kaleidoscopic; they keep changing form and feel. Like the transformer toys popular in the late 1980s, they are always changing shape. In fact, during the time we were writing this book, several of the companies we work with completely reorganized several times. Yet none of the reorganizations were laid out well in advance in some sort of strategic plan. Rather, they were the result of constant dialogue between members of the management team, between managers and employees, and between everyone and customers. In the course of this dialogue, managers kept revising their vision of the business, its opportunities, its threats, and its challenges. Then the boundaries, the structure, and the strategies were adjusted to the changing vision, and adjusted again and again.

As organizations navigate through this white-water world, increasingly they must keep a finger on the pulse of the future as well as the present. This means they must develop the capability for identifying emerging trends in politics, society, consumer behavior, technology, and other diverse areas, almost like having sensors that can probe the future. In recent years, a whole consulting industry has sprung up around futuristic projection, and many of the boundaryless companies we have seen incorporate such consultant inputs. They also keep probing into new fields of knowledge, looking for applicable lessons or ideas outside their own industry or technology, and they visit other companies, even when they are not in the same business, just to learn and grow.

No matter the tools used, iterative strategic thinking and visioning must be an ongoing process for any organization engaged in the transformation of its boundaries. Given the pace of environmental change, static strategic planning is much less effective.

BUST THE BOUNDARIES IN ORDER TO BUST THE BOUNDARIES

Although it sounds like a tautology, the third leadership lesson our cases show is that boundaryless mechanisms themselves are pathways to the boundaryless organization. In other words, the best way to design a corporation with more permeable boundaries is not for senior executives to sit at the head office and redraw organization charts but for those same executives to pull together people from different boundary constituencies and let them loose to reshape their own destiny. The process they experience and develop as they work together on a meaningful assignment is what breaks down the boundaries.

Several years ago, two of us invented the concept of "organizational dialogue"[7] as a way of explaining why GE's town meetings were such successful vehicles for organizational change. The essence of this theory is that effective organizations intentionally engage their people in ongoing dialogue across boundaries in order to get things done. In large traditional organizations, where boundaries have solidified, dialogue often is stilted and difficult, constrained by suspicion, fear, and lack of skill. People from different parts of the organization or the value chain do not have a common language and social conventions or the basic ability to listen to each other. As in the process of child development, they need to learn "how to talk." Town meetings are a relatively safe forum in which to begin this learning process, to develop a common language in a sheltered environment with the help of a neutral facilitator.

As people in organizations learn how to talk, they also must experience a second stage of development, which we call "learning how to walk." They learn how to translate the results of dialogue into action. The point is that dialogue by itself is not enough for an organization to be effective. In addition, people must be able to work effectively across boundaries, carry out cross-boundary tasks, implement agreed-upon changes, and perform numerous other essential actions. Town meetings produce only recommendations for action. The follow-up process of carrying out the recommendations is just as critical.

Finally, the continuing health of organizations requires that they learn how to "walk the talk," to institutionalize the cycle of dialogue and action. Thus, town meetings shift from "unnatural acts in unnatural places" to "natural acts in natural places," that is, accepted, ongoing processes for getting work done across permeable boundaries.[8] Ongoing dialogue and action require organizations to change their basic supporting infrastructures to reinforce and encourage cross-boundary collaborations. Organizations make these changes with the various actions we have talked about here, rewards and incentives, communication of information, and so on.

Most of the organizational transformations we have described demonstrate that when leaders put people from different organizational places together and encourage them to begin the process of dialogue, boundaries become more permeable. Retailer Financial Services (RFS), the GE Capital credit card business described in Chapter One, is a good example. Throughout a decade of change at RFS, CEO David Ekedahl constantly created opportunities for people to have dialogue across boundaries and gave them the freedom to act on the insights they generated. The earliest dialogue (which continues to this day) was with customers. Subsequently, he created forums for systems and business people to grapple with the nature of their collaboration. Similarly, the development of self-managing work teams in the business centers was a result of dialogue between managers and associates about how best to improve customer service while reducing costs. Even today, the primary vehicle for fostering innovation in RFS is a cross-boundary team.

Of course, the use of cross-boundary teams in RFS, as in most boundaryless organizations, always serves a specific goal; it is not just an excuse to get people talking. Katzenbach and Smith, in their study of effective teams, have noted that one of the defining characteristics of high-performing teams is their mobilization around a shared goal.[9] In boundaryless organizations, the power of teams comes from their drive to achieve goals. And in the process of achieving those goals, they foster the continuing permeability of the organizational boundaries.

Making It Happen: An Evolutionary Process and an Evolutionary Attitude

By following, either consciously or unconsciously, the three guidelines described above, the leaders we have cited created ongoing engines of change that continue to evolve every day. Managers who want to emulate these leaders must also make the shift from the traditional managerial mindset of controlling and directing to a new paradigm focus on unleashing the powers of the organization, from reducing uncertainty to actually creating ambiguity, and from long-term planning to minute-by-minute experimentation. It is this shift in attitude that is perhaps the most challenging part of the boundaryless journey. It will be especially daunting if you "grew up" in a centralized, hierarchical structure, learning the managerial style that is based on personal control, micromanaging the numbers, running major client relationships, making all major decisions from the "top," and essentially keeping the entire business close to your vest. In this style, you need to know all the details, and your managers need to know them, too, if only to answer your questions.

In the boundaryless organization, you still need to ask questions of your colleagues but of a different nature. Now you need to be concerned with processes, growth, and directional trends. You will want to know whether a potential acquisition is a good fit or how best to use your customers to attract additional customers. In particular, you will want to stimulate your people, at all levels, to keep them thinking, questioning, probing, and looking for new ways to do business. You will encourage experimentation, set up teams to explore new ideas, and regularly pull people off their regular jobs for intensive participation in projects. Under your leadership, the organization will be in constant ferment, ready to reorganize quickly to meet emerging market needs, always talking about new ideas with clients, and always looking for new opportunities.

Most importantly, you will never be satisfied. No matter how much your organization achieves, you will always realize that it can all turn around in a moment, that there is no rest for the winners, only the exhilaration of faster laps around the track. But if you can inspire your colleagues, your customers, your suppliers, and all your constituents to run this never-ending race together, then you will have created the boundaryless capability that can propel you into the future.

In a world where seemingly invincible companies like IBM, Citicorp, Philips, United Airlines, Westinghouse, and others suddenly become vincible, an on-the-brink attitude makes sense. And perhaps that is the final key. No structure in the world, no matter how boundaryless, can ever substitute for the innovative leader, the individual, inspired by vision or even by fear, who can instill a sense of urgency and a demand for change throughout an organization. That is the ultimate boundary to be crossed—the boundary in your mind and soul. Effective, competitive, and boundaryless organizations are possible only when leaders cross their own invisible, self-limiting walls and believe that nothing is impossible, that motivated people can achieve the highest heights, and that organizations in the twenty-first century will have no constraints other than those they impose on themselves. Technology alone will not make it happen; strategy will not be enough; luck will come and go. But leaders that push, inspire, motivate, and demand, that bring out the creativity in their people, can move mountains. And when mountains move, there are no boundaries.

◆ ◆ ◆

The last diagnostic instrument (Questionnaire #6) gives you the opportunity to assess your progress toward boundaryless leadership on five dimensions. Because different organizations and situations require different degrees of boundarylessness, the questionnaire is constructed as a gap analysis. That is, it defines the distance between where you are currently on each dimension and where you want to be. You measure yourself against your own needs, not against some abstract standard.

Questionnaire #6

Stepping Up to the Line: Are You a Boundaryless Leader?

Instructions: On each 1 to 10 scale, place an O where you think you need to be, or want to be, to move your organization forward into the twenty-first century. Then place an X where you think you currently are on the scale. The difference between the two scores (O - X) is your gap score.

Gap Score
(O-X)

1. Leadership to break down vertical boundaries

You and your senior management team make most decisions.

1 2 3 4 5 6 7 8 9 10   Most decisions are made close to the action.   _____

You hold information close to the vest—and promote a need-to-know approach to information sharing.

1 2 3 4 5 6 7 8 9 10   You share information about overall performance and business strategy with as broad a base of constituents as possible.   _____

Your recognition and reward system is based solely on individual contributions.

1 2 3 4 5 6 7 8 9 10   Your recognition and reward system is primarily team based.   _____

2. Leadership to break down horizontal boundaries

Your people have narrowly defined roles, responsibilities, and skills.

1 2 3 4 5 6 7 8 9 10   You encourage people to develop multiple skills—so everyone feels ready to do what it takes to get the job done.   _____

You have clear functional agendas that determine the way things get done and the pace of implementation.   1 2 3 4 5 6 7 8 9 10   You ensure everyone is focused on shared goals, across functions.

You have put in place strong controls—with multiple hand-offs and sign-offs—to get work done effectively.   1 2 3 4 5 6 7 8 9 10   You push for integrated end-to-end processes with a single point of accountability to get work done—streamlined, efficient, and value-added every step of the way.

3. Leadership to break down internal boundaries

You and your senior management team focus most of your attention on your own company's current performance.   1 2 3 4 5 6 7 8 9 10   You are focused primarily on maximizing value to the end-user.

You encourage a tough negotiating approach to interacting with customers and suppliers.   1 2 3 4 5 6 7 8 9 10   You actively seek partnership and relationships of trust with customers and suppliers.

You spend a significant portion of your time in internal meetings and in running in-house committees.   1 2 3 4 5 6 7 8 9 10   You spend most of your time with customers, suppliers, and other outside constituents.

You look for new business opportunities solely on the basis of your company's capabilities.   1 2 3 4 5 6 7 8 9 10   You formulate new business in partnership with your customers—based on their needs and changes in their markets.

4. Leadership to break down geographic boundaries

You promote a look-alike culture— 1 2 3 4 5 6 7 8 9 10 You seek diversity in the people
hiring and promoting people who   you hire and promote.
look like you.

To get a shot at the top positions, 1 2 3 4 5 6 7 8 9 10 Significant international experience
executives need to "punch their   is a prerequisite for top positions.
ticket" in a series of domestic
positions.

You try to apply the domestic 1 2 3 4 5 6 7 8 9 10 You always start from the local
model for doing business to each   market conditions and build your
international market you are   business practices around these—
involved in.   taking very little for granted.

5. Overall leadership to make it happen

You are preoccupied with task 1 2 3 4 5 6 7 8 9 10 You are focused on results—
management—constantly trying   you clarify expectations about the
to explain to your subordinates   desired end results and let your
the steps they need to take.   people figure out how to get
                                                            there.

You exercise a command and control model of leadership.

1 2 3 4 5 6 7 8 9 10

You lead through articulating clear goals, then coaching, counselling, and cheerleading people to achieve them.

You prefer to wait for all the analyses, reports, and studies to come in before staking a position about the issues facing the organization.

1 2 3 4 5 6 7 8 9 10

You are comfortable sketching out a rough-and-ready vision of where the organization needs to go and using actions as a way to test and refine the vision and the overall direction.

You are constantly worried about giving people more than they can handle—considering everything else on their plate.

1 2 3 4 5 6 7 8 9 10

You are comfortable putting out exceptional challenges to people— even if you have no clue how people will deliver on them.

You promote a keep-your-head-down policy—one mistake can derail a career.

1 2 3 4 5 6 7 8 9 10

You create an environment in which coming up with and exploring new ideas is encouraged and rewarded.

Questionnaire Scoring and Follow-Up

Add your eighteen individual gap scores to find your overall score. Interpret the results as follows:

- *Gap of 25 or less.* Either your expectations are very low, or you have already achieved an exceptional level of boundaryless leadership. How far to the right-hand side of the scales are your *O* scores, your vision of the leadership needed in your organization for the twenty-first century? If most of your *O* scores are 7 or lower, you might ask colleagues, customers, board members, or subordinates where they would place the *O*'s on the 18 scales. Do they share your views about the kind of leadership needed for the future? Be sure you are not simply extrapolating your current situation into the future rather than imagining possible new markets, technologies, competitive threats, and customer demands.

  If your *O* scores are already over on the right-hand side, congratulations! You may be a model of the leadership needed in the next century. You may want to ask some of your leadership colleagues to assess themselves or even to assess you. Consider the value of having a dialogue with colleagues to confirm your sense of the leadership needed and where you and they are on the continuum from traditional to boundaryless leadership. If you are already a boundaryless leader, this dialogue is probably ongoing in your organization, and perhaps the questionnaire can add talking points to that dialogue.

- *Gap of 26 to 75.* You've begun the journey and made progress, but there is still a long way to go. A middle-range score probably means key boundary areas need your attention. Look through the questionnaire to see if any categories stand out as having larger gaps than others. For example, companies often make progress on breaking down internal barriers before they see progress on external barriers. If some gaps are indeed bigger than others, you might consider targeting them, selecting from the preceding chapters strategies that apply specifically to closing the largest gaps.

  Also, consider whether the larger gaps are reflections of your own leadership challenges. Most executives, at all levels, have a range of skill sets and comfort levels. For example, you may be very effective in producing cross-functional team collaborations but still uncomfortable allowing your teams to "just do it" without checking in with you. Or perhaps you are successful at the hard work of developing successful partnerships with customers but much less clear about how to provide global leadership. If one of these situations or a similar diagnosis rings true for you, you might ask some colleagues or close friends, people who can give you candid feedback, to discuss your findings with you. Remember that your own ability to break through self-imposed boundaries is one of the critical determinants of your company's ultimate success.

- *Gap of 76 or more.* You are just getting started, and there are lots of opportunities to pursue. If your gap score is above 75, then the fun is just beginning. It is probably time for you to pull together your management team, review the strategies we have discussed (particularly those keyed to getting started), and have some concentrated work sessions. Remember, of course, that you cannot change everything at once. Pick your targets, create some successes, and get the process going. Return to this questionnaire and the previous questionnaires periodically and take stock of your progress. As long as you keep learning along the way and building your learning back into your organization, you will make progress toward the boundaryless organization of the twenty-first century.

NOTES

CHAPTER ONE

1. The Sears example is based in part on D. R. Katz, *The Big Store: Inside the Crisis and Revolution at Sears* (New York: Viking Press, 1987).
2. "Letter to Shareholders," *GE Annual Report,* 1993.

CHAPTER TWO

1. Exodus 18:17–26.
2. H.F.J. Porter, "The Realization of Ideals in Industrial Engineering," *Transactions* (ASME), 1905, 27, 352–353.
3. W. F. Muhs, "Worker Participation in the Progressive Era: An Assessment by Harrington Emerson," *Academy of Management Review,* 1982, 7(1), 99–102.
4. S. Haber, *Efficiency and Uplift* (Chicago: University of Chicago Press, 1964), p. 124.
5. See F. J. Roethlisberger and W. J. Dickson, *Management and the Worker* (Cambridge, Mass.: Harvard University Press, 1939), for a full report of the Western Electric research.
6. D. M. McGregor, "The Human Side of Enterprise," *The Management Review,* Nov. 1957, p. 9.
7. W. Bennis, "Organization of the Future," *Personnel Administration,* Sept./Oct. 1967.
8. J. Huey, "The New Post-Heroic Leadership," *Fortune,* Feb. 21, 1994, p. 44.
9. D. Smith and R. Alexander, *Fumbling the Future: How Xerox Invented, Then Ignored, the First Personal Computer* (New York: Morrow, 1988).

10. We are indebted to professor Edward E. Lawler III and his associates at the University of Southern California who first suggested the importance of these four dimensions. For further information, we suggest reading Lawler, Edward E., III, *High-Involvement Management: Participative Strategies for Improving Organizational Performance,* San Francisco: Jossey-Bass, 1986.

11. L. Dyer and D. Blancero, "Workplace 2000: A Delphi Study Working Paper" (Center for Advanced HR Studies, School of Industrial & Labor Relations, Cornell University, 1992).

12. Compare J. H. Shea and R. C. Ochsner, "Top Executive Compensation: Science or Witchcraft?" *Compensation & Benefits Management,* Autumn 1984, *1*(1), 59–65.

13. D. Ulrich and D. Lake, *Organizational Capability: Competing from the Inside/Out* (New York: Wiley, 1990).

CHAPTER THREE

1. See R. Ashkenas, "Beyond the Fads: How Managers Drive Change with Results," in C. E. Schneier (ed.), *Managing Cultural and Strategic Change* (New York: Human Resource Planning Society, 1995), pp. 33–53. Also see R. G. Eckels and N. Nohria with J. D. Berkley, *Beyond the Hype: Rediscovering the Essence of Management* (Boston: Harvard Business School Press, 1992).

2. The concept of organizational capabilities is drawn from Ulrich and Lake, 1990.

3. See G. Will, *Men at Work: The Craft of Baseball* (New York: Macmillan, 1990).

4. R. W. Stevenson, "Watch Out Macy's, Here Comes Nordstrom," *New York Times Magazine,* Aug. 27, 1989.

5. S. J. Frangos with J. Bennett, *Team Zebra: How 1500 Partners Revitalized Eastman Kodak's Black & White Film-Making Flow* (Essex Junction, Conn.: Oliver Wright, 1992).

6. Tony Rucci is now senior vice president of administration at Sears.

7. D. Ulrich, "OASIS: An Empirical Study of Strategy, Organization, and Human Resource Management," presentation at the Academy of Management, 1986.

8. R. Eichinger and M. Lombardo, *Twenty-Two Ways to Develop Leadership in Staff Managers,* Report #144 (Greensboro, N.C.: Center for Creative Leadership, 1990); M. W. McCall, Jr., M. Lombardo, and A. Morrison, *The Lessons of Experience: How Successful Executives Develop on the Job* (Lexington, Mass.: Lexington Books, 1988).

9. W. Tornow (ed.), *Human Resource Management Journal,* 1993, *32*(2–3) (special issue on 360-degree feedback).

CHAPTER FOUR

1. Adam Smith, *The Wealth of Nations* (New York: Viking/Penguin, 1986; originally published 1776).

2. Personal communication from Bruce Phillips, April 1994.
3. R. L. Ackoff, *The Democratic Corporation* (New York: Oxford University Press, 1994), p. 95.
4. R. J. Kramer, *Organizing for Global Competitiveness: The Matrix Design,* Report #1088–94-RR (New York: The Conference Board, 1994), p. 39.
5. J. Galbraith, *Competing with Flexible Lateral Organizations* (Reading, Mass.: Addison-Wesley, 1994).
6. See J. Kochanski and P. Randall, "Rearchitecting the Human Resources Function at Northern Telecom," *Human Resources Management,* 1994, 33(2), 299–315.

CHAPTER FIVE

1. An excellent source for accounts of these tools and how to use them is M. Brassard, *The Memory Jogger Plus* (Methuen, Mass.: Goal/QPC, 1989).
2. J. Katzenbach and D. Smith, "The Discipline of Teams," *Harvard Business Review,* Mar./Apr. 1993, pp. 111–120.
3. J. D. Thompson, *Organizations in Action* (New York: McGraw-Hill, 1976).
4. T. Teal, "Service Comes First: An Interview with USAA's Robert S. McDermott," *Harvard Business Review,* Sept./Oct. 1991, pp. 116–127.
5. Frangos, 1992.
6. Much of the material in this section is based on "Shared Services: From Vogue to Value," an unpublished paper by Dave Ulrich, 1994. Robert Gunn also supplied us with information based on his consulting work, as reported in R. W. Gunn, D. P. Carberry, R. Frigo, and S. Behrens, "Shared Services," *Management Accounting,* Nov. 1993, pp. 22–28.
7. R. L. Huber, "How Continental Bank Outsourced Its 'Crown Jewels,'" *Harvard Business Review,* Jan./Feb. 1993, pp. 121–129.
8. Many of the ideas in this section are drawn from D. Ulrich, M. A. VonGlinow, and T. Jick, "High Impact Learning: Building and Diffusing Learning Capability," *Organizational Dynamics,* Winter 1993, pp. 52–66.
9. C. Argyris, "Teaching Smart People How to Learn," *Harvard Business Review,* May/June 1991, pp. 99–109; C. Argyris, *Reasoning, Learning, and Action: Individual and Organizational* (San Francisco: Jossey-Bass, 1982); C. Argyris, *Overcoming Organizational Defenses—Facilitating Organizational Learning* (Boston: Allyn & Bacon, 1990); C. Argyris and D. A. Schön, *Organizational Learning: A Theory of Action Perspective* (Reading, Mass.: Addison-Wesley, 1978).
10. For more information about Motorola's OEP, see J. Miraglia, "OEP: Motorola's Renewal Process," *Tapping the Network Journal,* Spring 1990, pp. 2–6. Also see the Harvard Business School case study written by T. Jick, "Bob Galvin and Motorola, Inc." (Boston: Harvard Business School, 1987).
11. D. Ulrich, M. A. VonGlinow, and T. Jick, 1993. For a short summary of the report, see "Briefing from the Editor," *Harvard Business Review,* Mar./Apr. 1995, p. 10.

CHAPTER SIX

1. J. Womack, D. Jones, and D. Roos, *The Machine That Changed the World* (New York: HarperCollins, 1990), pp. 138–139.
2. J. A. Carlisle and R. C. Parker, *Beyond Negotiation* (New York: Wiley, 1989), p. 5.
3. R. P. Lynch, *Business Alliances Guide* (New York: Wiley, 1993), p. 7.
4. Lynch, 1993, p. 18.
5. For a brief history of strategic alliances, see Lynch, 1993, pp. 8–15.
6. P. Drucker, "The Shape of Industry to Come," *Industry Week*, Jan. 11, 1982, p. 55.
7. R. Normann and R. Ramirez, "From Value Chain to Value Constellation: Designing Interactive Strategy," *Harvard Business Review*, July/Aug. 1993, pp. 65–66.
8. M. Best, *The New Competition* (Cambridge, Mass.: Harvard University Press, 1990), p. 20.
9. Womack, Jones, and Roos, 1990, p. 194.
10. Best, 1990, p. 274.
11. P. Senge, *The Fifth Discipline* (New York: Doubleday, 1990).
12. S. Strom, "K-Mart Shifting Cost Burden to Toy Makers," *New York Times*, July 29, 1993, p. D5.
13. Carlisle and Parker, 1989, p. 5.
14. *Work-Out Roundtable Gazette* (an internal publication of GE Appliances), July 7, 1993, p. 4.
15. See D. Ulrich, "Tie the Corporate Knot: Gaining Complete Customer Commitment," *Sloan Management Review*, 1989, *30*(4), 22.
16. L. Thurow (ed.), *The Management Challenge: Japanese View* (Cambridge, Mass.: MIT Press, 1985).
17. S. K. Yoder and G. P. Zachary, "Vague New World: Digital Media Business Takes Form as a Battle of Complex Alliances," *The Wall Street Journal*, July 14, 1993, p. A4.
18. Yoder and Zachary, 1993.
19. Lynch, 1993, pp. 174–175.
20. Drucker, 1982, p. 57.
21. Lynch, 1993, p. 23.
22. Dr. Seuss, *One Fish, Two Fish, Red Fish, Blue Fish* (New York: Random House, 1960).
23. Yoder and Zachary, 1993.

CHAPTER SEVEN

1. See, for example, Lynch, 1993.
2. T. Jick, "Customer-Supplier Partnerships: Human Resources Bridge Builders," *Human Resource Management*, 1990, *29*(4), 440–441.
3. Jick, 1990, p. 442.

4. See R. H. Schaffer, *The Breakthrough Strategy: Using Short-Term Successes to Build the High Performance Organization* (New York: Harper Business, 1988), pp. 187–188.
5. Ulrich, 1989, p. 24.
6. See Ulrich, 1989, for more on these and other examples.
7. Normann and Ramirez, 1993, p. 67.
8. Schaffer, 1988, pp. 189–190.
9. Huber, 1993.
10. C. Duff, "Nation's Retailers Ask Vendors to Help Share Expenses," *The Wall Street Journal,* Aug. 4, 1993, p. B4.
11. Normann and Ramirez, 1993, pp. 66–67.

CHAPTER EIGHT

1. "The Discreet Charm of the Multicultural Multinational," *The Economist,* July 30, 1994, pp. 57–58.
2. D. Milbank, "Asian Tigers Are on the Prowl in Europe," *The Wall Street Journal,* Oct. 26, 1994, p. A16.
3. B. R. Schlender, "Matsushita Shows How to Go Global," *Fortune,* July 11, 1994, pp. 159–163.
4. J. Welch, "Productivity: Lessons from General Electric," *Boardroom Reports,* Nov. 15, 1994, p. 8.
5. The Teco Electric & Machinery Company example is related in Milbank, 1994.
6. The Lila Pause and Barilla examples are related in C. Rohwedder, "Eurobrands Take Hold Across Borders," *The Wall Street Journal,* Apr. 28, 1993.
7. Rohwedder, 1993.
8. B. Belton, "Profits Pedal Economic Growth Cycle," *USA Today,* Oct. 31, 1994, pp. B1–B2.
9. B. R. Schlender, "How Toshiba Makes Alliances Work," *Fortune,* Oct. 4, 1993, pp. 116–119.
10. C. Crystal, "Do You Measure Up?" *International Business,* Nov. 1992, pp. 60–62.
11. "Building a Eurocompany," *Financial Times,* Sept. 7, 1993, p. 19.
12. "The Volvo and Renault Combination Has Dissolved," *Financial Times,* Dec. 6, 1993, p. 13.
13. Background information about ABB is drawn from M.F.R. Kets de Vries, "Making a Giant Dance," *Across the Board,* Oct. 1994, pp. 27–32.
14. J. M. Stopford and L. T. Wells, *Managing the Multinational Enterprise* (New York: Basic Books, 1972), cited in C. Bartlett and S. Ghoshal, *Managing Across Borders* (Boston: Harvard Business School Press, 1989).
15. P. Evans, "Management Development as Glue Technology," *Human Resource Planning,* 1992, *15*(1), 85–105.
16. Bartlett and Ghoshal, 1989.
17. Bartlett and Ghoshal, 1989.
18. H. Wendt, *Global Embrace* (New York: Harper Business, 1993), p. 40.
19. C. Lorenz, "Here, There, and Everywhere," *Financial Times,* Nov. 10, 1993, p. 12.

20. "The Elusive Euro-Manager," *The Economist*, Nov. 7, 1992, p. 83.
21. S. H. Rhinesmith, *A Manager's Guide to Globalization* (Homewood, Ill.: Business One Irwin, 1993).
22. G. Hedlund, "The Hypermodern MNC—A Heterarchy," *Human Resource Management*, 1986, *25*, 9–35.
23. Dennis Hightower has since become the head of Disney Television.
24. Cultural study is discussed in C. Lorenz, "Learning to Live with a Cultural Mix," *Financial Times*, Apr. 23, 1993, p. 11, an article based on F. Trompenaars, *Riding the Waves of Culture* (London: Economist Books, 1993).
25. "The Discreet Charm of the Multicultural Multinational," 1994.
26. Johnson & Associates, *How International Are You and Your Company?* (Brussels: Management Centre Europe, 1994).
27. P. Carey, "Foreigners on the Board," *International Business*, Oct. 1994, pp. 24–26.
28. Carey, 1994.
29. Evans, 1992.
30. Evans, 1992.
31. D. Milbank, "It's Not Easy Being the Little Guy Overseas," *The Wall Street Journal*, Sept. 15, 1994, p. A11.

CHAPTER NINE

1. R. Donkin, "Cultural Restraints on Missionary Zeal," *Financial Times*, Sept. 30, 1994, p. 12.
2. Kets de Vries, 1994.
3. D. Savona, "When Companies Divorce," *International Business*, Nov. 1992, p. 6.
4. J. Main, "Making Global Alliances Work," *Fortune*, Dec. 17, 1990, pp. 121–126.
5. Evans, 1992, pp. 85–105.
6. F. Gee, T. Jick, and S. Paine, *Clifford Chance: The Merger (A) and Clifford Chance: International Expansion (B)*, case study (Fontainebleau, France: INCITE, 1993).
7. P. L. Zweig, "Sachs' Spectacular Road Trip," *Business Week*, Nov. 8, 1993, pp. 56B-E.
8. "The Discreet Charm of the Multicultural Multinational," 1994.

CHAPTER TEN

1. See R. S. Kaplan and D. P. Norton, "Putting the Balanced Scorecard to Work," *Harvard Business Review*, Sept./Oct. 1993, pp. 134–147.
2. For more on this subject, see Ashkenas, 1995. Another perspective is provided by R. Schaffer and H. Thomson, "Successful Change Programs Begin with Results," *Harvard Business Review*, Jan./Feb. 1992, pp. 80–89.
3. M. Beer, R. Eisenstat, and B. Spector, "Why Change Programs Don't Produce Change," *Harvard Business Review*, Nov./Dec. 1990, p. 159.

4. N. Nohria and J. D. Berkley, "Whatever Happened to the Take Charge Manager?" *Harvard Business Review,* Jan./Feb. 1994, pp. 129–137.
5. J. Lawlor, "Faxes Taxing Office Life," *USA Today,* Apr. 20, 1994, p. 1.
6. H. Mintzberg, "The Fall and Rise of Strategic Planning," *Harvard Business Review,* Jan./Feb. 1994, pp. 107–114.
7. R. Ashkenas and T. Jick, "From Dialogue to Action in GE Work-Out," *Research in Organizational Change and Development,* 1992, *6,* 267–287.
8. S. Kerr, "Toward Natural Acts in Natural Places," in *Launching and Leading the Boundary-less Organization: Work-Out Best Practices,* an unpublished collection of GE Company working papers, July 1990.
9. J. R. Katzenbach and D. K. Smith, 1993.

INDEX